DREAM KITCHENS

OVER 40 STEP-BY-STEP PRODUCTS

JAMES E. RUSSELL

CREATIVE HOMEOWNER PRESS®

COPYRIGHT © 1990, 1981 CREATIVE
HOMEOWNER PRESS™
A DIVISION OF FEDERAL MARKETING CORP.
UPPER SADDLE RIVER, NJ

Manufactured in United States of America

Current Printing (last digit)
10 9 8 7 6 5 4 3 2 1

Editor: Shirley M. Horowitz
Assistant Editors: Marilyn M. Auer
    and Gail Kummings
Art Director: Léone Lewensohn
Designers: Léone Lewensohn, Paul Sochacki
Additional illustrations: Norman Nuding

Cover photograph by Cookie Samuels

We wish to extend our thanks to the many
designers, companies, and other contributors
who allowed us to use their materials and gave
us advice. Their names, addresses, and individual identifications of their contributions can be
found on *page 159*.

LC: 90-80295
ISBN: 0-932944-92-2 (paper)

CREATIVE HOMEOWNER PRESS®
BOOK SERIES

A DIVISION OF FEDERAL
MARKETING CORPORATION
24 PARK WAY,
UPPER SADDLE RIVER, NJ 07458

FOREWORD

What is your idea of a "dream kitchen?" It can mean many things to many people. As intended by the author and editors of this book, it can mean a modern, traditional, country or European style, but with functionality, convenience and arrangement of food preparation areas so that the homeowner/cook gets the most storage and the best layout for her (or his) needs. You will find both large and small kitchens in this book, some featuring clean, sleek, contemporary designs, others with pots and pans hanging from ceiling beams to create a homey look.

"Dream Kitchens" begins with a discussion (Chapter 1) of good kitchen design and basic floor plans, so that you will know what you are working toward. The projects that follow Chapter 1 are broken down according to their purposes and locations in the kitchen. They range from the very simple to the complex. Simple projects will aid the cook who desires only a rearrangement or additional storage; the more difficult projects will guide the homeowner who is willing to undertake major carpentry.

CONTENTS

1
GOOD KITCHEN DESIGN

Any good kitchen design revolves around family activities and the needs of the cook(s) in the household. Such needs usually break down into these minimum categories: general storage, the three basic work centers for food preparation, cooking and clean-up, and specialized work centers for such tasks as baking, canning, and freezing or drying of food. These needs must be included in planning the layout of the kitchen, although certain available products and manufactured items will aid you in realizing the most desirable plan. In this chapter we will concentrate on design ideas and alternatives, as well as the necessary components that go into a kitchen, and their individual space requirements.

THE FOUR BASIC FLOOR PLANS
Creating a "Work Triangle"
The four most common floor plans are all based on and centered around the "Work Triangle." This triangle is formed by linking the positions of the stove, sink and refrigerator. The triangle plan should include adequate work space on both sides of these elements.

Desirable Dimensions for the Work Triangle
The "ideal" work triangle dimensions for the average-sized kitchen give a total of seventeen feet. The suggested distance are: from sink to refrigerator, four to seven feet; from refrigerator to stove, four to nine feet; from stove to sink, four to six feet. These figures allow a minimum of twelve feet of counter space, and they provide a maximum of twenty-two feet. Keep in mind that these are guidelines, not laws. Each design is unique — and requires individual consideration.

An L-shaped kitchen runs along two adjoining walls. This layout is popular because of its versatility in design.

The Corridor Kitchen
This type of kitchen also is referred to as the galley or Pullman kitchen. It consists of two facing walls, with all equipment and appliances arranged as close to a desirable work triangle as possible. This type of kitchen usually is narrow, and this could create traffic problems if more than one person were working in the kitchen.

Space requirements. Built-in base cabinets should be placed with a minimum of four feet of space between facing units so that the doors can be opened easily. The cabinets are most commonly two feet deep. Because doors of facing cabinets are often open at the same time, the aisle should be eight feet wide. Try not to place the oven and refrigerator opposite each other; they both have large doors. You may not be able to open both doors at the same time.

The One-Wall Kitchen
Although this type of kitchen may be the only possibility in extremely small houses, it has certain inevitable problems. The distances between the three basic appliances may be too great for convenience. If the room opens into another room, the cook may be forced to turn her

A one-wall kitchen may be the only answer in a small house even with its inevitable work space dilemma.

A three-sided, U-shaped kitchen offers lots of space for food preparation and lends itself to the ideal work triangle.

(or his) back to guests while cooking. We suggest a divider or screen in this situation.

L- and U-Shaped Kitchens

L-shaped and U-shaped kitchen layouts are the most popular due to their greater versatility and flexibility of arrangements. L-shaped kitchens run along two adjoining walls; U-shaped kitchens run along three adjoining walls. In some larger kitchens, a peninsula counter or island is added. These floor plans lend themselves to triangulation more easily than do one-wall or corridor kitchens. The sink usually is centered in an exterior wall under a window.

Door Locations

Always consider the effect of an open door when planning your kitchen and cabinetry arrangements. Try to avoid placing any cabinet or appliance at the end of a corridor where its open doors will block an entryway or where any open door would be a hazard to someone who walked into the room. Consider using folding doors between rooms where a swing-out door would be cumbersome and awkward.

SINK PLACEMENT
Physical Limitations

Where you place your sink will depend upon the locations of other appliances and features in your kitchen, as well as the size of the room. It is best to keep the sink within a few feet of its original location, if you must move it, or near the location of plumbing lines serving the same functions. This will minimize costly plumbing work involving the vent stack and water supply lines. There are two essential requirements for a practical and useful food preparation center at the sink: adequate counter space and adequate light. When estimating needed counter space, remember that the counter space on one side of the sink will be used for draining water from washed dishes and pots. If space is restricted, however, it is possible to use dish drainers that fit over or into the sink basins.

Sink Centered under Window

To aid in achieving the required light level — as well as for the aesthetic and morale-improving effects of the outside view — sinks are often placed under windows in exterior walls. In these cases, care must be taken to center the sink under the window to avoid creating a lopsided look to the room or the run of the counter. The window-centered location automatically provides the necessary headroom required for comfortable use of the sink.

Sinks in Windowless Walls

If you place the sink under a continuous expanse of wall cabinets, the missing ingredient in the arrangement will be headroom. There are several means of providing the needed clearance, and none requires costly or particularly difficult procedures.

Since the standard wall cabinet is 12½ inches deep, shallower cabinets (such as 6-inch deep) may be substituted for the 12-inch ones. By the same principle, shorter cabinets can be used above the sink area. Some cooks have chosen to eliminate the cabinets above the sink entirely, preferring open shelving instead. This offers quick access to often-used items, although such items must be selected carefully (see "Open Shelves" below).

Sinks Placed in Corners

There are advantages and disadvantages to corner placement of a sink. A corner sink usually will free up counter space and can allow better placement of the stove and refrigerator in the work triangle. However, in such circumstances it is more difficult to place the sink underneath a window. Also, the area left behind it is triangular, requiring an innovative use of this unusually shaped space.

Behind the sink. Small shelves can be made to fit the space behind the sink. The area may be used as a display area for plants or jars.

The unusual, elliptical-shaped cabinets blend nicely with the window design.

Kitchens adapted for wheelchair-bound people need to consider turning area, knee space and reach limitations.

Below the sink. Since the space below a corner sink may be deeper than the area underneath a sink placed on a long wall, it is a good choice for storage of large or bulky items. Several manufacturers produce base cabinets that can be put in the corner and have access all the way back to the point where the walls meet.

Above the sink. The preferred design would call for a window at the corner, with one or both walls overlooking the sink. Another possibility is to design a shelf to fit into the corner space; the shelf may be open or closed. It can follow the corner angle or run on the diagonal to present a continuous line across the corner. Some homeowners have created raised, artificially lit plant niches above the faucets.

Installation guidelines. The space required for placement of a corner sink can be deceptive. The angles and dimensions must be carefully measured so that you do not buy a sink that turns out to be too large for the available area. You can find double-bowl sinks with the bowls at right angles to each other; other sinks may be

These two islands, one for daily use, the other when entertaining, flank a cozy banquette.

The hand-crafted stucco hood and flora mural above the double ovens set a country theme.

curved to fit a particular configuration. However, a standard double-bowl sink can be installed on the diagonal of the corner, which is the arrangement most commonly used for single-bowl sinks.

STOVE AND REFRIGERATOR LOCATIONS
Cooking Appliances

Cooktops and built-in ovens. The advantage of a cooktop, as opposed to a standard oven with a range above it, is that the space below it can be used as additional storage room. The oven then can be built into the wall, at a height that is more convenient than the usual, lower level found in combination ovens and ranges. One suggestion is to locate the oven so that the bottom of the door is level with the countertop.

If you are placing a cooktop into a tiled countertop, try to buy a unit with dimensions that are multiples of the size of the tile.

Double wall ovens. The height of the double wall oven unit can and should be adjusted to suit the convenience of the primary user. The guideline given above —

When building a double oven into a wall, plan to place storage units above and below, or cover openings with cabinet style panels.

A built-in refrigerator requires special cabinet work, and this must be planned at the time of construction or during a major remodeling.

A popular kitchen design is the double-bowl, corner sink. Some are suitable for both corner and standard countertop installation.

the door opening at countertop level — will probably have to be changed so that the bottom oven will not be inconveniently low.

Corner cooktops and stoves. A drop-in cooktop takes up little counter space and still provides good storage space below. The area behind the cooktop, however, must be counted as lost space. It is dangerous to reach across a hot surface. Usually, the space is too small to be considered much of a loss. The same limitation applies to stoves placed in corners.

Microwave ovens. For many years the microwave oven inevitably took up a certain amount of counter space. However, devices now available enable the homeowner to install the oven above a counter — underneath a wall cabinet. Another solution is the microwave that comes built into and above a stove unit. These microwave units usually do not have as much wattage and, therefore, offer less power than the separate microwaves, but they do give considerable savings in cooking time and have all the other desirable features associated with microwave cooking.

Standard oven ranges. These usually come in heights that will match the height of your countertop. For a listing of common sizes and options, see the "Appliance Dimensions Chart" in this chapter. If you wish the top of the range to be higher

or lower than the rest of the countertop, separate the cooking center from the rest of the counter surfaces. In this way, the height difference will be less noticeable. One solution is to build the cooktop or drop-in range into an island. However, be sure to arrange for a minimum of 12 inches of heatproof countertop on one side of the island oven, with a total of at least 24 inches of counter space.

Refrigerators and Freezers
Standard refrigerators. A refrigerator should not be placed right next to an

oven. Try, if at all possible, to locate your refrigerator so that the opening edge of the door is to the inside of your work triangle. Allow a small amount of space behind and above the refrigerator so that air can circulate in these areas.

Built-ins. Refrigerators are hard to disguise because they stick up and out. However, built-in units can be installed flush with cabinetry and hidden by a panel that matches the rest of the cabinets. Built-ins usually must be planned at the time of the original construction of the kitchen or during a major remodeling, unless you are willing to undertake the structural modifications necessary to permit built-in installation.

Freezers. Because these take up a great deal of space, they often are found in the basement, pantry, or some room other than the kitchen. Although a freezer located in the kitchen is convenient for storage and food preparation activities, it will tend to dominate a kitchen and disturb an otherwise attractive plan. If you feel it is imperative to have the freezer in the kitchen, consider an under-the-counter model, or a large refrigerator/freezer unit that is divided vertically.

DESIRABLE FEATURES
Islands and Peninsulas

Islands and peninsulas are desirable as long as the kitchen is sufficiently large that there is enough space for easy passage on both sides of the unit.

Benefits. An island makes the work triangle more compact, since either the food preparation or cooking (depending upon whether the island has a sink or a stove) can be carried out there. In some open kitchen plans, the peninsula divides the working area of the kitchen from the eating area. Often, one side of an island peninsula becomes a counter for breakfast or snack serving. Also the large interior of an island cabinet lends itself to storage of large items. Of course, both islands and peninsulas increase counter working space. To be useful, an island sink must have at least the same amount of available counter space as provided for sinks in regular runs of cabinetry (see below).

Tops of islands and peninsulas can be of a different material than the rest of the countertops in the kitchen, and also may be of a different height. This is particularly true if you want to turn the spot into a baking center (or some other specialized food preparation area).

Above-island spaces are popular locations for pot racks, which add visual interest and convenience to the layout.

An island can become the decorative focus for a room by hanging plants or pots above it. However, we feel the best utilization of ceiling space over an island is installation of task lighting of either recessed, track or hanging fixtures.

Cooktop counter space needs. If a stove or cooktop is incorporated into an island, there should be at least 18 inches of counter area on each side of the unit, and it is better to have 24 inches on the side toward the center of the work triangle. A heatproof surface should be adjacent to the cooktop.

Sinks in islands. If you will have a sink in a work island, plumbing lines become a prime consideration. They must be moved out from the side walls into the more central portion of the room. This can be costly and is rarely easy. The correct venting will be required by plumbing codes, and this venting requires pipes that run vertically from floor to ceiling. Unless you have had considerable plumbing experience, we would recommend subcontracting with a plumber for this part of the job.

Dishwashers

The usual position for a dishwasher is immediately adjacent to the sink so it can be

Large kitchens, such as the ones shown above and below, are the ideal place for an island with food preparation capabilities. With ample space on all sides, the island helps reduce the walking distance required between the work triangle elements.

Use of one large, recessed central source of illumination above the work island can be supplemented easily by installation of task lighting at the perimeter of the room.

Decorated tile can be used for countertops as well as on walls and for backsplashes. The track lighting serves both general and task illumination.

hooked up to the existing plumbing quickly and easily. However, there are many portable dishwashers available. If you are not sure of the position that will be most efficient for you, you can purchase a portable unit that can be permanently installed at a later date. You may also find that if you need the dishwasher only when you are entertaining or having a large holiday dinner, a portable that can be stored in a closet or back entry area until needed may be the best choice.

A counter built into a dividing wall between kitchen and dining areas provides a location for both food preparation and serving.

Bars and Hospitality Centers

Bars often resemble islands in outward appearance. They can be built to specifications from scratch or created by adapting manufactured cabinet units. Suggested materials for bar tops include laminate, stainless steel, ceramic tile, snythetic or cultured marble, and glass. These materi-

A special drink preparation area should include enough space to store ingredients and accessories and have an accessible outlet.

It is usually best to have one architectural feature serve more than one purpose. This island has a cooktop, sink, eating area, storage and serving space.

als will not be damaged by spills or scratches. We do not recommend real marble because it becomes marred easily. Butcher block, which is porous when unsealed, also is not a preferred surface material.

A bar should have at least one interior shelf in order to store all the bottles, glasses, and accessories involved in drink preparation. The bar should be placed so that it has space around it for not only the host or hostess, but also several guests. A pass-through in the kitchen wall between the kitchen and the dining area is sometimes a desirable location. Another popular place for the bar is between an otherwise unseparated kitchen and an eating area. If the bar is positioned at a distance from the kitchen sink or refrigerator, it may be advisable to install a compact bar sink and a small refrigerator. These can be built into the bar. If hot water is needed, consider installing a flash heater or another type of instant hot-water unit. These units provided hot water on demand and heat only what is needed. Other useful devices for a bar include ice crushers and blenders.

Serving Carts
Small, wheeled tables are helpful when serving and clearing away. Such carts can be bought or built especially to fit in a closet or under a counter. The closet-stored version need be little more than several shelves supported by a frame that is set on casters. The front of the under-counter model should be finished to match the other cabinets. A panel that simulates the drawer and door arrangement in the rest of the cabinets can be used as a false

front; the handle of the drawer will serve as the push/pull fingerhold.

COUNTERTOP PLANNING
As indicated in the earlier discussion of the work triangle, 12 to 22 feet is the usual range of counter space offered in most kitchens. This can be supplemented with island work areas and flip-down or pull-out surfaces. As long as the number of steps between the three appliances in the triangle is kept to a convenient amount, most cooks believe that the more counter space there is, the better the kitchen.

Space Requirements for Appliances and Cabinets
The accompanying chart summarizes the number of inches required on either or both sides of sinks, cooktops, ranges and refrigerators. Sinks, particularly, require at least 54 inches of unobstructed counter space (24 inches on one side and 30 inches on the other) for adequate working space.

In general, standard spacing between the base cabinet countertop and the bottom of the wall cabinets is 18 to 20 inches. If the wall cabinets are placed lower than that, the cook will not be able to see the back inch or two of the countertop. If the cook in the family is tall, taller than the average 5 feet 3 inches, you may want to install the wall cabinets higher than the norm. For example, a cook who is 5 feet 7 inches tall may feel more comfortable with the wall cabinets located 24 inches above the countertop to ensure a clear view of the entire surface.

Counters usually are 24 inches deep, but if your kitchen is small, you may need

cabinets with a depth of 20 or 22 inches instead. However, be careful to coordinate this dimension with the kitchen appliances since most of them come 24 inches deep.

Facilities for the handicapped. For people in wheelchairs or on crutches, adjustments to the standard cabinet requirements must be made. The counter top will be higher — at least 34 inches — and an additional, 8-inch deep wall shelf is suggested at 12 inches above the counter. The counter should be open at the front for wheelchair users; therefore, for safety, any exposed plumbing should be insulated and well padded. Control knobs on stoves must be on the front face of the appliance — never on the top or back.

Angles and Curves
Angles can be used to emphasize placement of a sink or other kitchen feature. The "work niches" can add a pleasing, dynamic focus to an area. However, these areas must be carefully designed to avoid disruption of traffic flow and work-triangle convenience. Angled counters are more suited to large kitchens, where they can provide a more personalized effect without creating problems. Countertops that project at an angle from the straight run of cabinets can offer bonus space without interrupting the layout of the kitchen.

Ideas for Additional Counter Space
In order to gain effective additional counter space, you need not necessarily build counters longer or wider than standard. You can free otherwise unusable areas of clutter by installing small appli-

STANDARDS FOR KITCHEN CABINETS AND APPLIANCES

Cabinets	Minimum	Preferred Dimensions, Inches	
		Standard	Maximum
Base cabinet			
height	30	36	37½
depth	24	25 with counter-overlay	
width	12		72
Corner carousels (diameter)	33	36	39
Countertop			
thickness		1½	
depth		25	
Open sink fronts	18	24	30
Shelves	12	24	
Soffit	6	12	18
Space between counter and wall cabinet	12	14-18	24
Toe Space	3	4½	8
height	26	30	32-34
depth	8-10	12	14
height from floor (mid-point)	66	68	74

Appliances			
Dishwashers			
width	18	24	
depth		24-25	
height		36	
Refrigerators/ Freezers			
width	28	32	35¾
height	58	68	72
Sinks			
width	18	32	43
depth (front to back)		21	
Stoves			
height		34	
width	15	30	46
depth	21	22	24
Washers/Dryers			
height		36	
width	24	30	32
depth		27	30

SUGGESTED ADJACENT COUNTER SPACE, INCHES

Appliances	Minimum	Ideal
Refrigerator on open side	12	18-24
Sink, on each side	24	30
Stove, on each side	12	24

ances into walls or setting them on a small shelf placed above the counter and below the wall cabinet for this purpose. You can build small, shallow boxes to fill this entire area and still take up less than three inches of counter area that often goes unused. Cup hooks will hold objects under the wall cabinets, or you can fit spice racks into this space, which will then be attractive as well as useful. Certain accessories also can be installed in the wall or base cabinets themselves. Spring-loaded shelves that swing or lift into position for use may hold food processors, meat slicers, blenders, or mixers. Sheet-metal-lined bread boxes have been built into kitchen drawers for many years.

Flip-down and slide-out counters are popular solutions to the problem of limited counter space. When not in use, these units slide into recesses or fit into other carefully designed niches that disguise or hide the shelf. Depending upon the material, these bonus surfaces can be suitable for food cutting or pastry rolling.

The serving carts mentioned above also can be tailored to serve as work areas that supplement limited countertop space. If the unit is built with a top of laminate, marble or butcher block, you will have a storage cart rather than a serving cart in which you can keep specialized items and on which you can chop vegetables, assemble ingredients, or roll out pastry.

The angles in this countertop arrangement form a work niche on one side and create an eating bar on the other side.

A countertop need not always be built in a perfectly straight line; angled countertops require careful planning but follow the same principles used when constructing a straight run.

If you use certain accessories frequently, such as food processors, or mixers, electrical outlets can be built into the countertop to provide power where units are used.

If the area above the cabinets is left open, it can be used for decorative display. Built-in refrigerators often require a ventilating through the space above the unit.

The green tile on countertops and backsplash is accented by the chandelier. Tile won't scorch, stain or scratch and is easy to clean.

Tile is an excellent choice above a cooking area because it resists heat and cleans easily. Use colored grout, rather than white.

Materials for Countertops

Although the two most commonly found countertop materials are ceramic tile and plastic laminate, other options are available. We will begin with these two favorites, and then present less traditional alternatives.

Ceramic tile. The recommended tile for countertop installation is a glazed, individual unit, although mosaic sheets also are feasible. Pregrouted sheets of full-size tiles should not be used on countertops or anywhere else to be used as a food-preparation area. The fungus-inhibitor used in the sheets makes it very desirable for use in the bathroom but unsuitable for the kitchen. Nor should unglazed tile be selected; it is too porous for kitchen counter use.

There are several advantages to a tile countertop and backsplash: tile is heat-proof; it wipes clean easily; individual tiles can be replaced — rather than an entire countertop — if an area is damaged; tile is extremely durable; it is available in a number of attractive textures and colors.

Tile does have two frequently cited drawbacks: (1) it has a hard surface — if you drop a glass or ceramic dish on the tile, the object may break; (2) it is more expensive to have tile professionally installed than to have laminate installed. However, if the homeowner is doing the installation, tile may be the less expensive option and offer the easier installation.

Tile installation requires fewer tools and less working room than plastic laminate installation. Decorative tile can personalize any kitchen. It can be used to create borders or be interspersed with plain tile to form individualized patterns. Costs can rise, however, if specially shaped trim pieces rather than square field tiles comprise the majority of a construction or remodeling order.

Plastic laminate. The best-known names in this market are Formica and Micarta, but many other fabricators produce the same type of material under other trade names. In addition to the commonly seen pastel colors, many shades and visual textures have been introduced. These include wood grain, marbleized effects, simulated brick or slate, and geometric designs.

Although it will withstand high temperatures, plastic laminate is not totally heat resistant. A hot pot or a cigarette

Decorative tiles can be interspersed with plain units. The tile can be installed to extend up a wall as well as on the backsplash, tying together the room design.

Decorative tiles can be used to create borders and to highlight a cooking alcove to produce a unique decor.

This tiled countertop is angled at the corner then continues to form an overhang on one side. Add stools and it can serve as an eating area.

Note the placement of the wine rack and storage cabinets in this U-shaped kitchen. A black-and-white decor lends easily to colorful accents.

can cause burn damage. Plastic laminate should not be used as a cutting surface because it will be scratched and marred as the knife cuts through.

Marble. The color range of marble is more limited than the two materials discussed above. However, easy-to-obtain shades include grey tones, black, white with veining, green, brown and pink. Marble counters need to be waxed and polished to prevent damage. They scratch easily and can be cracked; repairs are difficult, if not impossible. However, marble counters never burn. Because of its fine, smooth finish, marble is considered the best surface for rolling pastry. We suggest using a marble insert in a baking center rather than installing marble countertops throughout your kitchen.

Synthetic marble. This looks a lot like marble. The material comes in thicknesses of ¼, ½, and ¾ inches and can be cut with a power saw and shaped with a router. It is said to withstand heat, stains, cracks and moisture better than marble. But it still will scratch easily. Unlike marble, however, the scratches can be erased by sanding and/or buffing.

Cultured marble. This new material resembles marble in color and texture. It resists etching and stains, and is less likely to crack than marble. However, it is hard to repair and is not often used for countertops.

Stainless steel. Ideal as a backsplash or a stove surround, stainless steel needs to be kept clean and dry to avoid a ''spotted'' look. Stainless steel is not desirable as a cutting surface because it will be scratched each time a knife meets the surface, and because it will dull each knife that cuts into it. It will also cause arm fatigue; the surface is unresilient. It is important to use stainless steel over a solid wood base to insulate against sound.

Copper. This metal has a truly beautiful surface when polished. However, copper requires frequent maintenance to prevent oxidation to a dull green. Copper is not affected adversely by heat, although a wood base should be placed underneath the metal to cut down on sound transmission.

Granite and slate. These materials come in natural earth tones that range from blacks and grays to pinks and reds (and sometimes greens and blues). If you want countertops of either of these materials, you will have to find a stonemason to cut

Wood countertops require coats of urethane varnish to ensure a waterproof surface and to prevent scratches — but the extra work is worth it!

and install the counters. Each section must be of one, seamless piece, which means the countertops will be extremely heavy. Your base cabinets will have to be constructed with enough bracing and structural integrity to support the weight. This may mean that your base cupboard and drawer sections will be quite narrow because the run will be interrupted every foot or so by front-to-back dividers that support the countertop.

Granite is more expensive than slate, but it will withstand heat, moisture, stains and scratches better. It also can take a high polish; slate cannot. We do not recommend use of the boxed slate rectangles; a large, single slab will be stronger and last longer.

Butcher block. This term refers to a slab created by pressure-laminating sections of end-grain hardwood. Butcher block is porous; if it is sealed, then it is no longer real butcher block. Although the unsealed surface is hard to keep clean and scratches easily, it can be sanded many times — each time a new finish is desired. Countertop installations should be of thick butcher block, which means the counters will weigh a great deal. It is probably more logical to insert a section of block adjacent to the sink or stove. Butcher block is the most desirable choice for a chopping or cutting surface because the surface is resilient enough to prevent stress on the wrist and because wood will not dull knives.

Wood. These require heavy applications of sealants such as gloss or matte urethane varnish. The wood then will resist moisture, but it still will not stand up to heat. Scratches can be repaired more easily than other countertop surfaces. Although not a widespread choice, wood countertops offer very pleasing visual and textural effects.

Ceramic glass (Pyroceram). Because of its heat resistance, this often is placed next to the stove top as a resting pad for pots. It also serves as a good pastry-rolling surface.

FOOD-PROCESSING

There are several items that will be useful no matter what type of food preparation is involved. These items will aid you in setting up and processing food in an orderly, production-line manner.

You should have several large plastic trays. These should be sturdy and heatproof. Trays will help you organize the preparation process. You can use a tray to hold a bowl and vegetables so that you can sit down while preparing the vegetables.

Find a table with casters to help you move large, heavy loads with little effort. A cart can be bought or easily built. Of course, include large baskets, bowls and pans, which always are needed.

Baking Work Center

A baking center may range from a setup as simple as a portable marble or glass slab used for rolling out pastry to a separately designed and constructed area that contains everything needed for all types of baking. If designated as a specialized work area, the baking center can be placed outside the work triangle as a separate run of counter. The height of the counter may vary from the standard; you should test several levels to find the most comfortable

Specialized cooking areas can be designed to satisfy unusual cooking interests or needs. Wok cooking, for example, is made more convenient if sufficient counterspace is at hand.

Hinged, folding doors hide the mixer when not in use. The corner storage area at the junction of two runs of cabinets provides a permanent and accessible location for the appliance.

A shallow tilting drawer serves as a catch-all to hold the many small cleaning items that so commonly clutter the counter.

height for you before installing the baking center.

Some cabinet manufacturers produce cabinets designed for baking centers. These often include shelves designed to hold mixers permanently. Usually built as the upper shelf of the base cabinet, these shelves pull out and then rise and snap into position even with the countertop. To store the mixer, you merely release the catch, push down and then push the shelf back into the base cabinet. It is possible for a homeowner to adapt a cabinet or build a cabinet with this feature.

Other baking tools should be kept within or next to your baking center. These include: rolling pin, measuring spoons and cups, mixing bowls, flour sifter, tins — for cakes, pies, muffins, and bread — and cheesecloth. It is also desirable to have storage for flour, sugar, baking soda and powder, vanilla, spices, baking chocolate, nuts, raisins, candied fruit, or anything else that you use in baking.

One creative baking-center arrangement is an island with interior shelves and a marble top. A portable cabinet on casters, which can be stored in a closet when not in use, is another possibility. In both cases, all the items needed for baking can be kept in one convenient location.

Canning Work Centers

Cooks who undertake canning projects need lots of counter space, plus storage room for the tools involved and for the resulting canned goods. The canned foods can be stored in any cool, dry place. Many people like to put them on view because they are colorful and attractive, but in order to retain optimal flavor, they should be placed behind closed cupboard or closet doors. Avoid storage on high shelves; since heat rises, these shelves may become too hot.

Shallow shelves, with decreasing height gradations between shelves to allow for many different sizes of cans or jars, will hold the most in the least amount of space. We suggest that the smallest cans be placed at the top, and the largest cans at the bottom. If you cannot fit this type of shelving into your kitchen, other likely locations include fruit cellars, basements, back or side entries, or back hallways.

Glass jar containers. Not just any glass jar will do to hold canned foods. The jar must be tempered to withstand the high temperatures and must be formed to ensure a tight seal. You can buy lids that seal

A wood panel disguises a pull-out cabinet. Its narrow depth allows quick visual assessment of the goods stored inside.

A counter used as a food preparation surface also can become a snack counter. Toe space must be provided on both sides, and there must be enough overhang to provide knee space for diners.

during the canning process itself; as the contents cook, a vacuum forms and holds the lid in an airtight seal. The jars can be reused, but new lids are required each time. All jars must be checked before use; do not use any jars that are cracked or chipped.

Canning equipment and tools. A list of the basic canning equipment includes: pressure cooker, water bath canner, canning jar lifter, wide-mouthed funnel, ladle, mixing spoons, wire strainer or colander, small weighing scale, timer, measuring spoons and cups, sharp knives, food mill, blender, chopper or processor, and tongs. One good system for organizing these accessories, so they will be close at hand when needed, is to use a drawer divider into which you can fit various canning aids. Another desirable arrangement would be a pegboard installation with hooks to hold the utensils. A tall stool will add to your comfort.

Preparing Frozen Food

We have already discussed the most essential ingredient for freezing large quantities of meat, game, fruit or vegetables — the freezer itself. If you will be installing the freezer in the kitchen, look for an upright model; this type of freezer takes up less floor space than a long, low design. It is always handy to have the sink nearby, with storage space for necessary accessories. However, a chest-type freezer usually is less expensive, and can be located in a basement or in a large rear hallway.

Containers and wrappings. You will need an assortment of wrapping materials — aluminum foil, treated paper, and plastic wrap are the wraps most frequently used. Buy only those marked "for freezing" on the box. In addition, you will need a variety of containers with tight-fitting lids. Rectangular containers fit into the freezer more efficiently than round ones. Glass jars may also be used for freezing. Square jars will fit into the freezer space with little waste of space, and you may be able to get partially thawed food out of a square jar with less difficulty than out of a round jar, but this will depend to some extent upon the size of the jar mouth and the shape of the shoulders.

Bags, of course, are another "tool of the trade", particularly if you are freezing irregularly shaped or odd-sized foods. Often, bagged foods are then fit into the rectangular cartons for extra protection and for easier storage. If you are freezing soups or creamed foods, it is possible to line a rectangular container with a bag, pour in the food, freeze and then remove the contents so that the rectangular container can be used to hold another item.

Your freezing accessories should include labels that will adhere to a frozen package, freezer tape and a marker. If you own a hot-seal bag sealer, plan to install it in the specialized work area you are designing. A bag sealer may sit on the counter or you may install it on the wall. As with baking centers, the counter and work space can, if necessary, be outside the work triangle. The stove and sink will be used in the freezing process, so it is advisable that the canning center be as close as possible to them.

Blanching equipment. You will need storage space for at least one large, two or three gallon pot (a water-bath canner or a stockpot are good pots), a blanching basket or large wire colander to raise and lower the vegetables in the pot, containers that will go from freezer to oven or microwave, and tongs.

Storage. Because you cannot see all your freezer contents at a glance, and it is frustrating to have to pull out all the packages in order to find the one you want, we suggest that you divide your freezer into compartments in which you will place only a particular type of food. One section would then house only vegetables, another only fruits or fish. Color-coded labels aid quick identification also. If you have enough persistence, you can keep an inventory notebook. This demands a conscientious listing of everything that goes into the freezer and, preferably, a notation as to where it is to be found. The date the item was put into the freezer should be written on both the label and on inventory list. It you keep such a list, however, be sure to cross out each item as it is used or you will find yourself planning meals around nonexistent food.

Dehydrated Foods

This popular method of preserving food requires no more than a lot of sunshine if you live in the Southwest. The only equipment called for in this case consists of several large trays, cheesecloth, and storage containers such as plastic bags, jars with screw tops, or other closed containers. The aim is to keep the dehydrated food from picking up moisture from the air.

However, if you do not live in the sun-filled Southwest, you probably will need a temperature-controlled oven or dehydrator. There are dehydrators available that will fit into cabinets. Others need a cabinet all their own, or are large enough to command considerable counter space or even placement outside the work triangle or the kitchen. The amount of space taken up will depend upon the size of the dehydrator, which in turn depends on the size of the food loads you will be processing. These devices include forced-air circulation to speed evaporation. Timers and temperature controls are a must.

STORAGE OPTIONS
Open Shelves

There are economic, functional and visual advantages to open shelves. They require fewer materials and so cost less to buy or build. They can be fabricated faster and installed more easily than full cabinets.

Open shelves give quick access to frequently used items. If the items to be displaced are colorful, they can become a part of the room's color scheme.

What should you store (or not store) on open shelves? There are several types of foods and items that should not be stored on open shelves: herbs, because they lose their flavor if exposed to light and heat (they can be kept on open shelves if placed in opaque containers) and canned foods (unless the open shelves are in a cool, dark area such as a basement). The same restrictions apply to storage of wine.

Open shelves are easier and cheaper to build than standard cabinets. Vary heights between shelves according to size of items stored.

This open shelving arrangement combines wall racks for larger pots with cup hooks and an end-wall shelf for smaller, uniform pieces.

Good choices for storage on open shelves are items that are used frequently and thus washed frequently. Anything stored on an open shelf in a kitchen will collect grease and dust. Daily washing will keep the items in usable condition. Other possible items for open shelf storage are baskets, vases, and decorative pieces not used in cooking and displayed because of the decorative qualities. Such items often are displayed above the wall cabinet, in what would otherwise be the soffit area, or on wall or ceiling racks. This takes care of many large and awkwardly shaped pieces that are hard to store in cabinets.

Shelf spacing. One of the advantages of open shelving is that the spacing between the shelves can be adjusted to suit the sizes of the items being stored there. One logical arrangement is to have the height of the spacing between shelves increase as you move upward on the wall. The lower shelves would house small items and the upper shelves would hold tall (but light) goods. It is not a good idea to store large, heavy items above your head. You can work in reverse as you progress up the shelves, from large to small, if all your large objects are heavy. The spacing between the shelves may be permanent or adjustable. The choice will depend upon the type of shelving you have chosen. If you use pilasters and shelf dividers in your walls, the shelves can be adjusted up or down as needed.

Open shelves need not be as deep as cabinet shelves either — 6 inches deep will be sufficient for most grocery items. By keeping the groceries only one row deep, you can see exactly what you have at all times; one item will not be hidden behind another.

"Open" shelves need not always be out in the open. They are particularly suited to large cabinets or closets where they can be installed on the interior face of the door. These shelves have to be shallow, either built to fit or prefabricated vinyl-covered metal wire units.

Wall and ceiling racks. Gleaming pots and pans, baskets or other attractive utensils can be hung from racks attached to the walls or ceilings. The wall-mounted units usually are no more than strips of metal; the ceiling-hung racks come in several configurations. Choices include semicircular, rectangular and straight. In all cases, use sufficient fasteners to support the weight of the utensils that will hang from the rack. Position the racks so that they are within easy reach of the sink and stove.

Built-in Dispensers

Between-stud installations of stainless steel dispensers that hold bread boxes, paper towels and other specialized items without occupying any portion of your countertop are very useful. These in-wall dispensers are particularly well-suited to kitchen designs with clean, modern lines.

Pantries

Traditionally, the word "pantry" has referred to a separate room that was filled with floor-to-ceiling shelves or cupboards. More recently, it has come to include walk-in closets that offer the same comprehensive storage facilities.

Recessed-shelf Storage

Interior walls can provide extra storage space between the studs. Exterior walls usually cannot, because they will be (or should) filled with insulation. The wallboard is cut away between the studs and then shelves are placed on cleats nailed to the studs. You can choose between a series of niches, a floor-to-ceiling recess, or even lighted display shelves. Line the opening with plastic laminate or hardboard, and frame with molding to match or complement the room decor. Doors may be added if desired. The shelves provide an unexpected amount of storage space, but they offer a depth of only 3½ to 3⅜ inches, the same as the dimension of the broad face of the stud. However, these between-the-studs shelves cannot be located at any point where wiring or plumbing lines run through the wall.

Eating Areas

Benches and built-in tables. By attaching one side of a table to a cabinet or a wall, the amount of space it will take up is reduced. Most kitchens will call for a rectangular-shaped table, but free-form or half-circle tables are usable also. Another advantage of this type of table arrangement is that fewer support legs are required than on a regular table. Tables can be cut to wrap around the end of a cabinet run for a built-in table/peninsula.

Cantilevered benches are another solution to minimal space for an eating area. However, it is easier to build benches with at least one leg for support, and preferably

The food preparation/cleanup functions and actual cooking area were divided between two islands in this kitchen.

EATING AREA SPACE REQUIREMENTS

For One Adult of Average Height

Distance from table edge to wall	3 feet
Leg room when seated on chair	20 inches
Leg room when seated on stool	14 inches
Minimum serving or clearing space behind each chair	1 foot

Capacity	Square Table
One adult	12 to 15 inches
Two adults	24 to 30 inches
Family of four	49 to 60 inches

Capacity	Round Table
Four people	3-foot diameter
Six people	6-foot diameter

Elbow room for adults	1 foot either side
Table space depth	15 inches for snacks
	24 inches for dining

Island or peninsula counter	height: 36 inches
	knee space: 12 to 24 inches
Snack bar	height: 30 inches

two. Box benches, built solid to the floor with notched heel spaces, require very little space. These can be cushioned, or have tops that can be raised for access to items stored in the base.

Counters, snack bars, peninsulas. Islands that serve as extra surfaces for food preparation sometimes extend on the other side to provide an eating counter. Such counters can stand at the usual 36-inch counter height if you allow sufficient leg room and use a 24-inch high stool or chair instead of one of the normal height, 18 inches. Base cabinets then could not be used under the counter at which people are to sit unless the eating counter were a fold-out flap.

If you design a peninsula or island that utilizes one side as an eating space and devotes the other to a sink or stove, you will need to separate them in some manner. This can be done by raising or lowering the dining side of the unit, or by building a low divider, perhaps a foot high, between the two. If the snack bar is lowered to table height, ordinary chairs will suffice. It is is raised, 24-inch or 27-inch bar chairs or stools are suggested.

Whatever type or height of dining counter is constructed, allow about two feet for each seated person, giving consideration to leg room. Counters that are not deep or long enough for eating can have hinged drop-leaves added to them; the same is true for islands or peninsulas. If a long section is added, supports will be necessary underneath.

One negative aspect of a snack bar is that, with few exceptions, everyone is seated facing in the same direction. Dining at a bar may be fine for pick-up meals and for breakfast, when people feel less sociable, but it is not a desirable choice for evening meals. We also suggest that you try to position the eating counter so that the diners are facing a window or other open area, not a wall.

Standard Cabinets

Most stock and custom-ordered cabinets come in sizes based on 3-inch and 6-inch increments. For example, sizes can range from 24 to 36 inches wide (in 3-inch increments) from one company, while ranging from 54 to 72 inches (in 6-inch increments) from another company.

Base cabinets. The standard height for base cabinets is 36 inches. This consists of: 4 inches for toe space and base, 30½ inches for the cabinet itself, 1½ inches for the countertop. Some cooks complain that this height is too low. It can be adjusted upward by increasing the cabinet base or adding another layer to the countertop base material (usually plywood). For many cooks over 5 feet 4 inches, 37½ inches is a better height. Cabinet depth usually is 12 or 13 inches.

Wall cabinets. The eye level for a person 5 feet 4 inches tall usually is 4 feet 11 inches. A person of this height can easily reach up to 68 inches, and can place an object on and lift it from shelves up to 71 inches high. If you are taller or shorter than this, adjust the cabinets upward or downward depending on your height. You should have a sturdy step stool available to reach any high shelves. Wall units are not as deep as base cabinets; they are usually 12 or 13 inches deep.

Any continuous run of countertop should be the same height from end to end. If you wish to have a section of counter set at a higher or lower level, separate this section from the main run.

Corner cabinets. If two base cabinets of equal depth abut each other in a corner,

A ceiling-high copper hood and cable-suspended light bridge define the kitchen area.

Two marble-topped islands, one with a triple sink, add to the room's functionality. A walk-in pantry is concealed behind doors to the right of the refrigerator.

The open, airy feeling of the kitchen carries into the eating area and is highlighted by windows, sky-lights and track lighting.

The 5-foot-tall cook demanded that the stove/range be dropped to a height of 30 inches for easier food preparation.

Small appliances can be hidden away in a pantry. If electrical outlets are installed, they can also be operated in the same location.

access to one of them will be partially blocked. This is called a ''blind'' base cabinet. As alternatives, several types of corner cabinets are offered by manufacturers. One design mounts two identical quarter round shelves in the cabinet, one on the cabinet door and the other on the stile. This allows either door to swing out. The second design places several pie-cut circular shelves on the cabinet door. The third is the ''lazy susan'', which is a larger base cabinet that takes up 36 inches of wall space on each side of the corner. A carousel in the interior rotates so that any section of the shelves can be brought to the front. These types of cabinets also can be hung on walls.

European-style Cabinets

European designs are noted for their clean lines and their attention to detail. Every possible inch of space is utilized, so that the result is a collection of specially sized and arranged cabinets that handled the homeowner's particular storage needs. For example, within the base cabinets allowances often will be made for vertical slats to hold trays, or compartments for

Two sliding doors, a clerestory and a window over the sink let in lots of natural light.

tiny items. Ceiling-hung units are another popular feature.

The two most well-known producers of these custom-designed cabinets are All-milmo and Poggenpohl. They import and install the units — however, the price is quite high. We would like to point out that although this type of cabinetry is not easy to build, it is possible. A set of plans, worked out by a Wisconsin architect, is offered later for the experienced carpenter.

Dimensions. The sizes of European styles differ slightly from those of standard cabinets. For example, the depth of the wall cabinets may vary from the 12 to 13 inches of the standard units.

LIGHTING NEEDS
Windows and Skylights

Picture windows. This type of window is highly desirable when it opens onto a lovely view. Another benefit is the great quantity of natural light that streams in. If the window faces south, it can also help store heat in a room that has a tile, brick or concrete floor.

The drawbacks, however, are wide ranging. Many homeowners complain of lack of privacy and of less-than-inspiring sights. Unless it is well caulked and weatherstripped, a picture window can lose valuable heat in winter and cool air in summer. Since it has fixed panes of glass, it cannot be opened for ventilation. We suggest additional, smaller windows that can be opened alongside or nearby in order to provide air circulation.

Bay or bow windows. A ''bay'' window is an angular extension from the exterior house wall; it has sizable windows on all sides. If the projection is curved, it often is called a ''bow'' window. Both of these window styles can be purchased as kits in a variety of sizes. The advantages and disadvantages of these windows are similar to those of picture windows. However, there are quite a few desirable and unusual design ideas that are possible with bay windows, such as installation of window seats and plant displays.

Clerestories. A clerestory is a window placed above eye level. Such a window can be movable, for ventilation, as well as serving as an excellent source of light. Because it is so high, it eliminates the privacy problems that occur with picture and bay windows. Another advantage is that if the windows are placed high enough (above wall cabinets), there will be more space for cabinets and, thus, more storage room. A series of clerestories can increase the usability and attractiveness of most kitchens at a reasonable cost.

Planning window sizes and locations. In theory, you can add a window wherever

A row of windows can highlight a good kitchen view if the space is not needed for storage cabinets.

you please, of whatever size you desire, as long as you are willing to support the wall if studs need to be cut. The most convenient size is 32 inches, which means that it will fit between two existing studs, requiring that only one center stud be cut.

If the window is to provide light for a work area, the lower sill of the window should be 4 to 6 inches above the work area. Lower placement will result in spatters and dirt on the glass or curtain. Higher placement will cut down on the amount of light reaching the countertop. The top of the window should, if possible, align with the tops of other windows in the kitchen, or at least with any on that wall.

If there is shading (shrubs or awnings) outside your south-facing walls, this exposure is a good choice for a window addition. Light through an east-facing window also is desirable, since it gives morning light but not a lot of heat. Western expo-

A bay window over the sink offers abundant light and a place to grow house plants.

Sufficient light and an open plan result in an airy, sleek design for this kitchen, despite use of dark colors and materials.

sures often result in a hot room late in the day; if this is the only possible location for an additional window, be sure to add overhangs, outdoor plantings, shutters or blinds. North-facing windows provide even light, but sometimes allow entry of cool air during cold seasons.

Skylights. Skylights solve the privacy problems presented by bay or picture windows in close-set houses. The natural light can add to the brightness of a room, espe-cially if the kitchen does not have a window on an exterior wall. Skylights range in installation complexity, and come in many shapes and sizes. For ventilation purposes, some can be opened; these should be fitted with a screen. The glazing may be single, double or triple. Sometimes the glass is treated to reduce glare and heat. We suggest that safety glass or acrylic be used rather than regular window glass.

Types of Artificial Lighting and Fixtures

Meeting lighting requirements. There are two light levels needed in a kitchen: general, overall lighting and localized task lighting for specific preparation areas. The latter is preferred above the sink and coun-tertop work areas, and sometimes at the range. If an eating area is within the kitchen, try to include local lighting there also. The minimum light levels suggested are: 50 lumens at the range; 70 lumens at the sink and 50 lumens at the countertop, with higher countertop requirements for food-chopping centers.

The higher a lighting fixture is placed, the wider the area it can illuminate. If a directed light is desired, the addition of a valance or other baffle will help focus the light. To gain the highest amount of illumination per dollar, choose one large bulb rather than several smaller ones. One 150-watt bulb gives off more illumination than two 75-watt bulbs used together.

General lighting. Although the most commonly found situation is one hanging ceiling fixture, this — by itself — usually will not provide enough light to work by. Alternatives include multiple recessed fixtures, indirect lighting, or a suspended ceiling of transluscent panels. These arrangements, however, will use more electricity, be more costly to install, and require more complicated wiring setups than use of just one fixture.

GENERAL LIGHTING REQUIREMENTS

Area	Type of Light	Watts
50 square feet	Fluorescent	60 to 80
50 square feet	Incandescent	175 to 200

Advantages and disadvantages of incandescent lighting. Fixtures for incandescent bulbs come in a greater variety of shapes, sizes and styles than those for fluorescent tubes. Their light is flattering to food and to people, and it can be directed easily toward a specific location, which is why incandescent fixtures are popular for task lighting. However, incandescent lighting adds heat to a room and costs more to operate than fluorescent lighting.

Benefits and drawbacks of fluorescent lighting. The most frequently cited reason for using fluorescents is their low cost of operation relative to incandescents. They take less energy to give an equivalent amount of light. Another plus is that fluorescents do not generate heat, and can be used safely to light areas with plants or to brighten a warm room without adding the heat level. The light is also glare-free and evenly diffused.

The primary criticism of fluorescent lighting has been that it gives off light in an unflattering color, which makes both food and skin tones unattractive. Fluorescent light also tends to be given off with a flicker; this flickering is annoying to peo-

This country-French kitchen and adjoining family room feature more than 20 styles of imported, hand-painted tile. Aged barnwood was used for the ceiling beams.

ple who are working in areas of fluorescent light for long periods of time. A third drawback, but not as serious, is the limited number of shapes and styles of the bulbs and fixtures.

The problems of color tone can be overcome by buying the warm white tubes, which give off light in a color spectrum very close to that of incandescent bulbs. This fluorescent tube, however, costs more than the standard blue-green fluorescent.

Local (task) lighting. Above the sink, we suggest either one double 30- to 40-watt fluorescent fixture or two 75-watt incandescent units recessed into the ceiling, cabinet bottom, or into an extended soffit. Reflector bulbs, which throw light in the desired direction, are another excellent choice. Since the light is concentrated at the specific location, bulbs of lower wattage can provide the same level of intensity as higher-wattage nonreflector bulbs. Your simplest option, of course, will be incandescent or fluorescent bulbs hung on both sides of the sink.

Many range hoods come with provision for a concealed light source. They offer better lighting than bulbs built into the range itself. You can cut a small opening for a recessed incandescent bulb into the

floor of a cabinet built above a range or countertop burners. You may also hang a single fixture under the cabinet.

Some cooks place a strip of incandescent bulbs under the wall cabinet. However, these cannot be left uncovered, because the lights will become coated with grease. The plastic covers that fit over these strips will discolor and distort the light over a period of time. If you want a fixture in this location, try replacing the plastic with a transparent or translucent glass pane.

Countertops below wall cabinets often do not receive adequate amounts of light. Placing the wall units higher will eliminate some of the shadow, but the best solution is to light this area with a strip of lights under the cabinet. If a valance is added to disguise the strip, it will illuminate a narrower area than if left open. If no cabinet is above the countertop work area, recessed ceiling spotlights, track lighting, or reflectors can be used to pinpoint the desired locations.

Track lighting. Track lights are available in two basic models. Tracks with open channels permit you to plug lamps in at any spot you want. Tracks with closed channels are designed for specific locations. "Open" tracks offer more versatil-

Track lighting provides illumination that may be adjusted to light different areas as needed. Well planned designs keep units unobstrusive.

ity, but "closed" tracks are a better choice for the kitchen because the lights will not collect grease.

Track systems focus the light where you want it. If the track is a long one, the light can be aimed at several food preparation areas rather than just one. Light from the track should hit the wall or work surface at a 35° or 40° angle for the best illumination. The location of the track on the ceil-ing is governed by the angle necessary for the light. Adapters can be purchased to provide the system with the wider range of application.

2
COUNTERTOP PROJECTS

This chapter offers modifications to existing countertops and instructions on adding new countertops. Although the two major materials covered are plastic laminate and tile, we would like to point out another attractive alternative shown on this page: wood. The wood countertop pictured here was refinished by homeowners who were taking great care in restoring their kitchen. The intention was to maintain the original material and style, and the result was a countertop of great beauty and durability.

This wood countertop was treated with seven coats of marine spar varnish, with gentle sanding between each coat, to provide a surface that would resist water and indentation. This project took time, but resulted in a unique and lovely countertop.

TILING A COUNTERTOP

Ceramic tile countertops are popular for good reason. They are easy to clean, good-looking, and impervious to heat, cold and dampness. You can lay ceramic tile over most of the materials usually found on a countertop, including old ceramic tile, plastic laminate and, of course, the plywood support in a new countertop installation.

PLANNING AND MATERIALS
Before you begin to tile, you must make several decisions that affect the kinds and amounts of materials you need.

Tile Type
The most common choice for a countertop is glazed ceramic tile, either in single tiles or in sheets of small tiles that are held together with a string or plastic webbing on the back. Do not use pregrouted sheets of tile. These contain a mildewcide that is not FDA-approved for food-preparation areas.

Edge Trim Tile
Ceramic tile comes with several edge trim options. In areas of meal preparation, a curved edge of bullnose trim enables you to scrape chopped vegetables or batter mixtures into a mixing bowl. For the sink area, you may want to install sink cap tiles, which have a raised edge to prevent water from dripping on the floor. In some installations, wood furring strips are used to frame the tile surface.

Methods of Sink Installation
There are three ways to install the sink. In the first, the sink is installed before the tile. The sink rim rests on the existing countertop surface. Then the tile is laid and quarter round trim tile used to cover the sink rim. In the second, the tile is laid first. Tiles are cut to fit around the sink opening. The sink rests on top of the cut tiles to cover the cut edges. This method looks very professional.

Finally, the sink can be supported by a metal edge trim. You must use this method if the sink rim is not made to support the sink. The sink rests either on the countertop or on the trim, tile is laid up to the opening, and the trim covers the seam between the tile and

A tiled countertop often utilizes grout that matches the tile color. However, a dark contrasting grout (as featured here) will hide dirt and aid design.

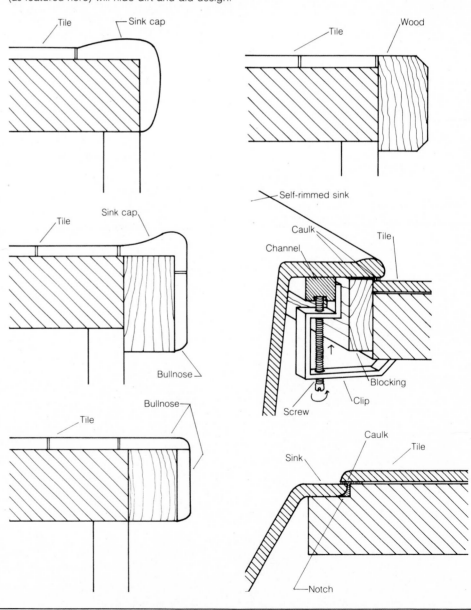

the sink. The biggest disadvantage of metal sink trim is that it creates two seams that are difficult to keep clean.

Backsplash Area
The backsplash area can be handled in several ways. You can stand a row of bullnose tiles between the last row of countertop and the wall. More common is a row of cove tile, which creates a gently curved seam between the wall and the countertop. An alternative that gives a great deal of protection and design continuity is a backsplash that extends up to the bottom of the overhanging cabinets.

INSTALLING TILE ON A NEW PLYWOOD COUNTERTOP
Step 1: Attaching the Underlayment
When you install a new countertop, select an underlayment of ¾ inch Exterior plywood (minimum B-D). To support the top, install cross braces of either 1x2s or 2x4s laid flat. Do not place the braces more than three feet apart. Drill two pilot holes, evenly spaced, into each of the braces. Then, working from below, screw each brace to the top with 2½ inch No. 8 wood screws. To hold an apron or other drip edge trim, nail a 2x2 furring strip to the front edge of the top. This also will be covered with tile.

If you want a straight line up the side of the countertop, cut the underlayment ½ inch shorter than the length of the top. The tile will follow the cut edge

of the plywood to create a flush edge so that you can store an appliance such as a dishwasher next to the counter. The other alternative is to extend the countertop over the appliance, if possible.

Fasten the underlayment with countersunk wood screws. Check that there

are no other protrusions. Fill any holes and defects with spackling compound and sand smooth.

Step 2: Dry Tile Layout
First, lay out the tiles on the top to arrange them for the least number of cut pieces. Work from the front to the back

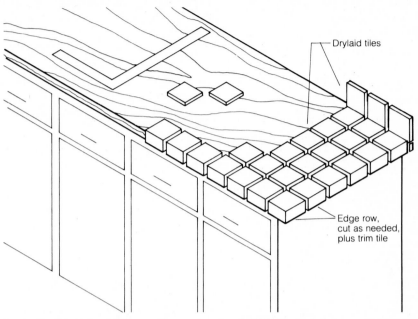

Drylaid tiles

Edge row, cut as needed, plus trim tile

Dry-laying tiles shows how many tiles you need and which tiles must be cut to fit. The row that falls between the edge trim tile and the last full row of field tile is cut to fit.

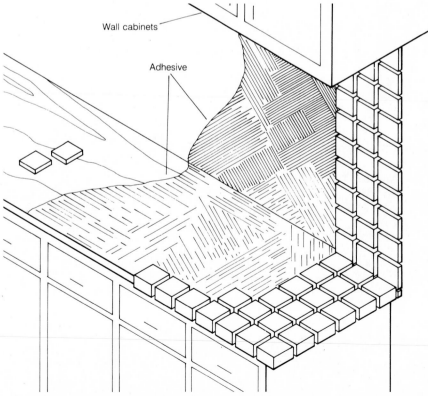

Wall cabinets

Adhesive

A 4-inch backsplash is conventional, but it can extend to the wall cabinets. Adhesive is applied to countertop and wall surfaces; tiles are "buttered" before being placed.

1x2 Cleats nailed inside framing
Optional method: 2x4s flat, toenailed inside frame

24"

1x2s On edge

2x4s Spaced about 3'

Reinforcement for heavy countertop
Because tile is heavy, the countertop should be reinforced with added braces, either 1x2s on edge or flat, toenailed 2x4s.

Project continued on next page

of the countertop so that any cut tiles will fall at the back rather than at the front of the top.

Countertop without a sink. Measuring from end to end, find the center of the countertop and draw a centerline. Lay out the tile along it and down the front edge of the top. Allow for grout lines if your tile has no self-spacers. Use a carpenter's square to check that the courses are straight. Once the tile has been laid to the edges of the countertop, you can see the types of cuts you must make. If any tiles must be cut to less than half their width, go back and shift the original lines to avoid this situation.

Sink set parallel to the wall. In this case, work from the center of the sink toward the ends of the top.

Countertop with a corner sink. An L-shaped countertop with a corner sink must be handled differently than the other settings. Since there is no way to avoid very odd cuts of tile around the sink, work from the ends of each leg of the top toward the sink opening.

Step 3: Placing the Trim Tile
Keep the dry-laid tiles in place while you adhere the edge trim along the front of the lip. Use the countertop tiles to maintain the spacing upon which you have decided. With a notched trowel, apply adhesive along the front edge of the furring strip. Then cover ("butter") the backs of the tiles with adhesive and lay them in line with the rows of tiles on the countertop. With the edge complete, install any special trim tiles for sink openings or corners.

Step 4: Tiling the Countertop Deck
Lift some of the dry-laid tiles, and apply adhesive with the notched trowel. Press firmly so that only beads of adhesive from the notches in the trowel are evident on the plywood deck's surface. Spread no more adhesive than you can cover readily before it starts to harden. Set each tile firmly in place with a slight wiggling motion to ensure a good bond. Lay all the full tiles and leave spaces for the cut tiles.

Cutting tiles. To cut a straight line on a tile, use a rented tile cutter. This scores a line on the tile. Then press the tile over a coat hanger wire to snap the tile. To cut irregular or curved lines, use a tile nipper. Take very small nibbles until the tile is the shape you need.

Setting the tile. To prevent wobbly grout lines, use your carpenter's square to make sure that the rows are straight and square. Use a block of wood covered with carpet to set the tiles into the adhesive. Move the plywood block over the surface of the tile while tapping the block gently.

Step 5: The Backsplash
Apply a coat of adhesive to the area. Then butter the backs of the tiles. Set the tiles in place. Break the circuit that feeds any light switch or fixture before you set tiles around it. If desired, finish off the backsplash top edge with a trim piece.

Step 6: Apply Grout
Run a wide strip of masking tape along the underside of the front trim tiles. This will keep the grout from dripping out from between the tiles before it has a chance to set up. Also mask any surrounding wood surfaces to protect them from grout stains. Then mix the grout and apply it with a rubber squeegee used at an angle to the grout lines. Once the grout has set, clean the surface with a damp sponge to remove excess grout. Caulk the seams between the tile and the sink.

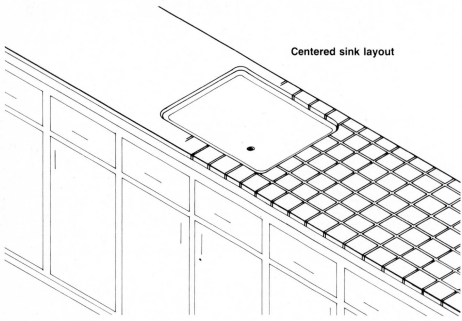

Centered sink layout

This tile was laid after first locating the center of the sink. Start at the centerline and work toward the counter ends. Note the tiles around the sink that had to be cut.

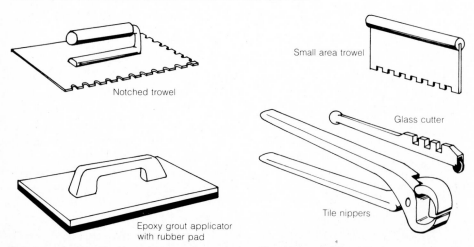

Notched trowel

Small area trowel

Glass cutter

Tile nippers

Epoxy grout applicator with rubber pad

Shown are the hand tools most commonly used when tiling. Very specialized devices, such as a tile cutter, can usually be borrowed from your dealer, with a refundable deposit.

___ PLANTER INSERTS IN TILE COUNTERTOPS ___

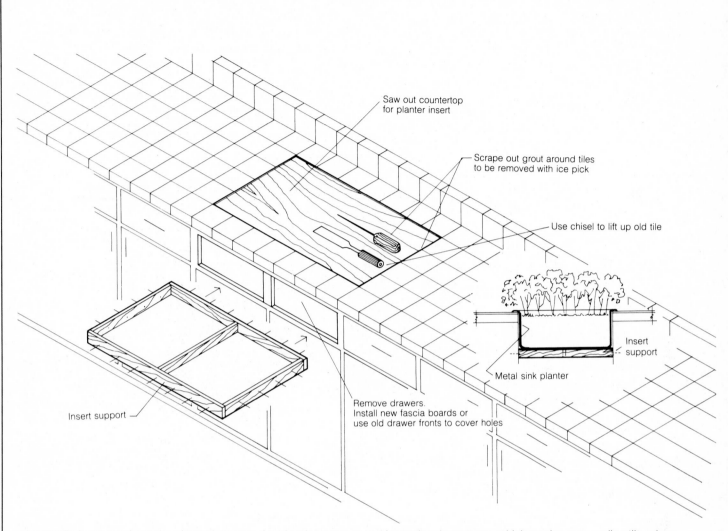

Saw out countertop
for planter insert

Scrape out grout around tiles
to be removed with ice pick

Use chisel to lift up old tile

Insert
support

Metal sink planter

Remove drawers.
Install new fascia boards or
use old drawer fronts to cover holes

Insert support

After the tile is removed, cut the plywood counter. Add framing support and insert the planter trays, which overlap surrounding tile edges.

Metal trays are used for planters in a tiled countertop in this example. The example, shown on page 5, considers planters inserted in an existing countertop. If you were doing the tiled countertop and planter insert from scratch, the installation would be very similar to installing a metal sink.

The most difficult part of this project is removing the old tile. Try to select a tray that will fit into an even number of tiles, so you can avoid cutting tile. Remove the tile by scraping out the grout along the tile to be removed. Use a pointed metal tool like an ice pick or nail. Use a hammer and chisel, lightly tapping the chisel under the tile. You need safety goggles for jobs like this.

When you have the old tile out, provide a counter cutout for regular sink installation.

The metal planter tray will need support framing underneath. The framing is not complicated. Use framing members about the same size as you see around your base cabinet doors: ½ inch by 2 or 3 inches will do. The framing will not be seen, so appearance is not important. But be generous with the framing; place it under the planter as shown. Screw it to the base cabinet sides and/or back.

You will not be able to use the existing drawers because they will run into the tray. Glue the drawer fronts in place or secure them from behind with wood screws.

INSTALLING A SINK

STEP 1: POSITIONING THE SINK

First, inspect your countertop. Note the type of surface (laminate, tile, etc.) and whether or not the countertop is post-formed with the backsplash an integral part, or whether the corners are square. (Illustration 1 shows a typical manufactured base cabinet and post-formed countertop.) Open the cabinet doors and examine the underside of the countertop. Countertops are usually about 1½ inches thick at the supports and are typically 25 inches deep. Since the base cabinets are typically 24 inches deep, the countertop overhangs the cabinets 1 inch at the front.

To locate the sink position on the countertop, first mark the center of the sink at the sink edges (see Illustration 2). Marking the edges where the centerline occurs will help you line the sink up with the desired position on the countertop.

Lay the sink (assume a self-rimmed sink, for the moment) upside down on the counter, approximately where you want the sink to be installed. A sink will typically be over a sink cabinet, with two doors underneath and a dummy drawer that matches the other, adjoining doors. When this is the case, you usually want the sink centered over the sink cabinet. So, locate the center of the sink cabinet in front, transfer the mark to the front edge of the countertop, and extend it all the way across the top of the countertop to the backsplash. The line you mark will help you line up the sink cutout hole (refer again to Illustration 2). Place the sink so that the centerlines match and draw the outline of the sink on the countertop, using the sink as a template.

If you are installing a steel-rimmed sink, center the rim on the countertop (but keep the rim upright) and draw the outline of the rim, using the rim as a template. Either type of sink can be put nearly anywhere you want it, as long as it is at least 2 inches from the front and at least 1 inch from the backsplash.

STEP 2: DRAWING THE OUTLINE

For a self-rimmed sink, mark points approximately ¼ inch *inside* the outline of your sink. Ask your supplier for *exact* cutout dimensions. The ¼-inch suggested here is typical and sufficient for most sinks to rest on, and for most hardware fittings for such sinks, but you need the exact dimensions for your particular sink brand. For rectangular sinks, make one mark at each corner. For round or oval sinks, make 4 or more marks around the circumference. Drill ¼-inch holes through the countertop where the marks are.

Draw the inside outline carefully, using the holes as a guide. The outline made by the inside line is the area you will cut out for the sink. If you wish to doublecheck, you can create a paper pattern and then fit it over both the outline and the sink outline for an exact match.

STEP 3: PROVIDING SUPPORT

Before you begin to cut, look underneath the cabinet top, inside the base cabinet, to see where the holes are. If they penetrated a countertop support, that support should be replaced just far enough from the sink so that it does not interfere with the installation of the sink or its hardware. The supports are screwed to the countertop from the bottom. Simply duplicate the way your supports were installed when you in-

Self-rimming sinks not only look good, but often can be fitted over edges of existing sink openings so that no additional counter cutting is required.

The steel around the sink gives a neat look and hides any ragged laminate edges around the opening. However, the rim joint can be hard to keep clean.

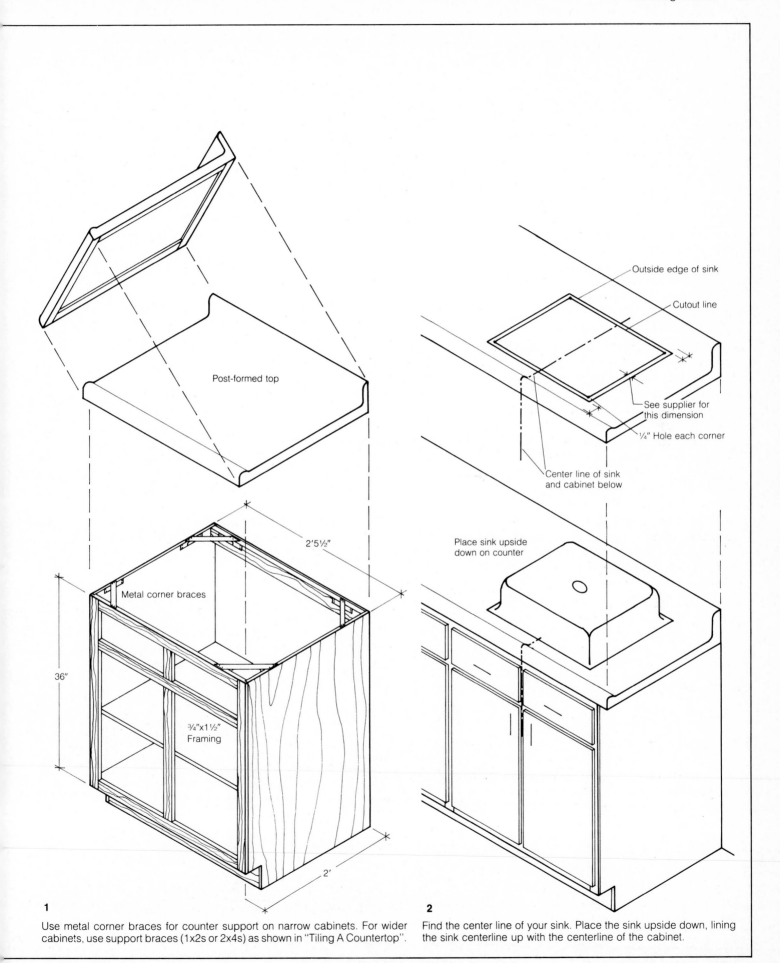

Post-formed top

2'5½"

Metal corner braces

36"

¾"x1½"
Framing

2'

Outside edge of sink

Cutout line

See supplier for
this dimension

¼" Hole each corner

Center line of sink
and cabinet below

Place sink upside
down on counter

1

Use metal corner braces for counter support on narrow cabinets. For wider cabinets, use support braces (1x2s or 2x4s) as shown in "Tiling A Countertop".

2

Find the center line of your sink. Place the sink upside down, lining the sink centerline up with the centerline of the cabinet.

Project continued on next page

stall the replacement support. The old support, the one you drilled through, will have to be removed if it interferes with your sink clips or other hardware. If it does not interfere with the placement of the sink or hardware, you can cut through it when you make the cutout and leave the remainder in place.

STEP 4: CUTTING THE OPENING

Now you are ready for the cutout. Use a sabre saw to cut the appropriate pattern, starting from any of the ¼-inch holes that is convenient to you.

Variation: Steel-Rimmed Sink

The above instructions are for a self-rimmed sink. The procedure for a steel-rimmed sink is the same, except that you make the cutout along the outline formed by the steel rim. Keep the rim right-side up when you draw its pattern on the countertop.

STEP 5: HANGING THE SINK
Self-rimmed Sinks

Self-rimmed sinks are secured with metal clips that fit into channels on the underside of the sink (Illustration 3). All the hardware should come with the sink you buy. However, you need an absolute minimum of 2 clips on each side of the sink (or the equivalent, if the sink is round). The more clips you use, the better, because the forces holding the sink in place will be more uniform.

When you are ready to hang the sink, install a ¼-inch bead of plumbers' putty around the top edge of the countertop opening. The putty should be placed so that it uniformly seals the

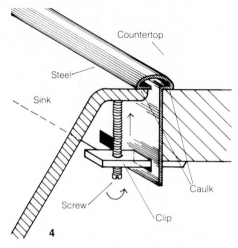

area where the sink is pressed to the counter. Lower the sink into the opening.

Tighten each clip screw all around the sink snugly but not all the way. Check the fit of the sink all around. Some clips may need to be slightly tighter than others to bring the sink and counter together without gaps. Continue tightening the clip screws, gradually, until they are just tight enough to hold the sink firmly to the counter; how tight is a matter of judgment, but do not tighten the clip screws too tight or you may damage the sink. Clean up any excess putty that squeezes out.

Stainless-steel-rimmed Sinks

Steel-rimmed sinks, like the name implies, have a steel rim that fits around the sink. This rim performs about the same function as the channel on self-rimmed sinks and the clip-screw hard-

ware of both types of sinks is similar.

You need a helper to install a steel-rimmed sink because there is no lip over the counter for the sink to rest on while you tighten it down (see Illustration 4). If you do not have help, hold the sink in place with two lengths of 2x4 and wire or rope, as shown in Illustration 5.

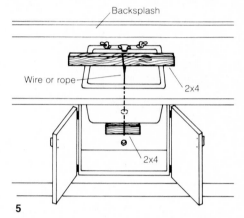

5
You can hold a steel-rimmed sink in place with a pair of 2x4s and some wire or rope. Twist the top 2x4 to raise the one on the bottom.

Before you place the sink and rim through the counter, install a ¼-inch bead of plumbers' putty around the edge of the hole. Put the sink in place and tighten the clip screws all around. Place another putty bead between the sink edge and the metal rim before you draw the sink up tight. Tighten the clip screws all around, gradually, until the sink and the counter fit tightly together. As with the self-rimmed sink, do not tighten the sink too much or you may damage it. Clean up excess putty.

This sink boasts one extra-large basin, a small disposal area, and a space that doubles as a drainboard and — when the drainer is removed — as a chopping board.

BUTCHER BLOCK INSERTS AND HEAT PADS

A glass pad often is placed next to an oven so pots can be set on it.

Butcher block inserts next to the sink (or anywhere else) or glass heat pads near ovens, are desirable additions to any countertop.

STEP 1: CREATING THE OPENING

The procedure for the opening depends on the kind of countertop you have. For a tiled countertop, remove the grout with a nail pushed through cardboard (for safety and ease of handling). Plan the opening to be a full multiple of the tile size.

For plastic laminate, cut as for a sink opening, as described under "Installing A Sink."

If you have an acrylic plastic counter, cutouts for inserts may be made with a sabre or reciprocating saw. When cutting acrylic plastic marble, wear goggles and a respirator and keep the room ventilated during the cutting and when the dust may be in the air. (Goggles and mask are suggested when cutting laminate, too.) For straight cuts, clamp a 2x4 to the acrylic plastic with "C" clamps; the 2x4 acts as a straight-edge for the saw. Set the blade to cut about a quarter inch thicker than the sheets. Use sawhorses with two 2x4s laid across them at each end to support the acrylic while you cut it.

STEP 2: PREPARING THE OPENING

For a butcher block insert, add new framing supports to match existing supports, as shown. Position them so that the top of the new insert will sit flush with the existing counter.

With a glass heat pad, a kit is provided. This includes a steel rim that holds the pad, so that no additional support is needed.

STEP 3: INSTALLING THE INSERT

A butcher block insert may be secured to the base cabinet with metal angles and screws, or glued to the cabinets. Glue is not the preferred method, because glue makes the countertop inserts harder to remove should you decide to modify the countertop and remove the inserts.

The heat pad utilizes a metal sink rim and caulk; follow manufacturer's instructions.

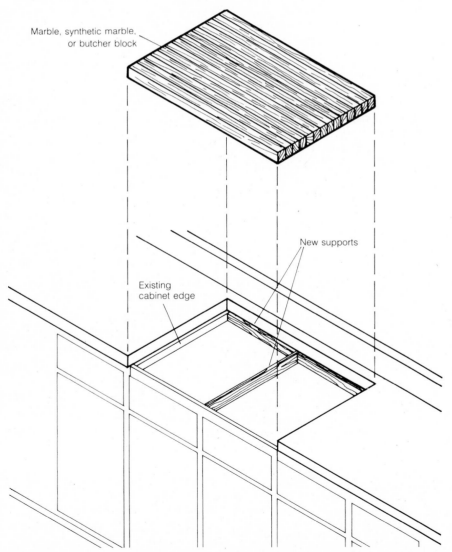

Marble, synthetic marble, or butcher block

New supports

Existing cabinet edge

Outline the area you wish to remove. Drill starter holes at corners and use a sabre saw to cut countertop. Sand or rout the edges smooth before adding framing support.

HOW TO BUILD A LAMINATED COUNTERTOP FROM SCRATCH

A laminated countertop is made by gluing a plastic-laminated material over particleboard, plywood, or a similar material. For the homeowner, plywood is probably the simplest and most durable structure for a laminated countertop, and that is what we will discuss here. The assumption here is that you are discarding the old countertop. The tools and steps for removal can be found in the following project "How to Laminate an Existing Countertop in Place".

Tools and materials. Two pieces ¾ inch exterior plywood, laminate contact adhesive, slip sheets (paper), smooth cut file, laminate scriber or razor knife, power router (if available), brace and bit assortment or power drill and drill assortment, keyhole saw, power jigsaw (if available), tape measure, square, rubber mallet or wood buffer, screws, 1x3 lumber.

STEP 1: CREATING THE CORE

Use two sheets of ¾-inch exterior plywood. Cut the counter to overhang the cabinets by 1½ inches. Glue the two together to form a 1½-inch core. Clamp until dry.

If you want added thickness at the overhang, nail on 1x3-inch strips of solid wood. You can make the top look as thick as you want, by adding 1x3s in a stack. Nail down through the plywood into the 1x3s. Prefit the top and make any adjustment cuts at this time.

Clean the wood and countersink any nail heads so the top surface is absolutely smooth. Sand any rough spots you find, and clean away the sanding residue.

STEP 2: CUTTING THE LAMINATE

Place the plywood on a pair of sawhorses. Draw the countertop outline on the laminate, making the outline about ¼-inch wider than the countertop. This will give you a little extra laminate to work with, in case of error.

If using a laminate scriber, mark the outline on the finish side of the laminate. Then, using both hands, pull up on the laminate; the laminate will snap like glass. It is a good idea to practice cutting the laminate with scraps until you get the hang of it; it is not difficult.

When you cut the laminate, cut the shorter ends first, then the long sides.

If using a razor knife, draw the outline on the back and cut the laminate from the back. The knife will score the material so it can be crimped and snapped off. You will need a straight-edge over which you will "fold" the cut, so the laminate will snap clean and will not crack.

An easier alternative is to use a fine-tooth blade in a power jigsaw. If you have lots of cutting to do, buy or rent this tool. Before you make any "final" cuts, test the blade on a scrap piece of laminate. The blade should not splinter the laminate. If it does, buy a different blade. Special blades are made for cutting laminate.

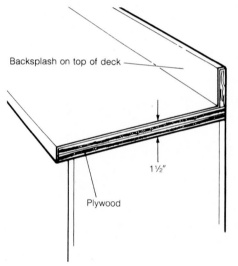

Backsplash on top of deck

1½"

Plywood

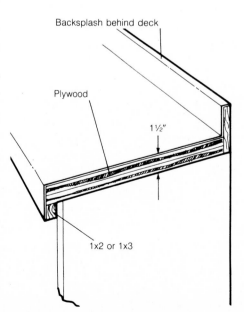

Backsplash behind deck

Plywood

1½"

1x2 or 1x3

Cut the edge strips for the top. Then cut the strips for the backsplash. Again, leave a ¼-inch lip, which will be used later for trimming purposes.

STEP 3: APPLYING THE LAMINATE EDGES

Prefit all the laminate pieces. Begin the laminating with the edges. Apply the suppliers' recommended adhesive to the edge to be laminated and to the laminate. Use a brush to apply the adhesive, then allow it to dry 30 minutes (or as long as directed by manufacturer) before you join the edge to the plywood.

After the adhesive has dried, apply the laminate to the plywood edge, holding the laminate between the thumb and index fingers. You must position the laminate right the first time, because you will not be able to move it once the two surfaces come in contact. Tap the laminate with a rubber mallet or buffered block of wood, working evenly along the surface for best contact.

When all the edges are done, and the laminate adhesive thoroughly set, trim the excess laminate off flush with the top of the plywood. Use a router so that the top surface can overlap the edges. The top levels will be beveled (as discussed later). The bottom

For countertop dimensions, measurements should include any desired overhang. Dishwasher (Chap.8) can be in same counter run.

edges of the countertop should be trimmed, then beveled.

STEP 4: LAMINATING THE DECK

Now apply the top laminate. Spread the adhesive to both sides and let it dry, as you did for the edge pieces. You need a helper to lay the top laminate in place. Adhesive-covered laminate is not adjustable if misplaced. With one person holding the laminate at each end, hold the laminate over the top of the plywood. This requires that one person be the "leader", telling the helper which way to move the laminate and when to lower it onto the adhesive.

Place the laminate and press it down. Tap the top surface with a rubber mallet or a wood block to insure a tight, even contact.

When the adhesive has had time to thoroughly set, trim the top laminate flush with the sides, as described previously for the edges. Check the sides frequently as you work, to be sure the router is not scratching or scorching the edge of the laminate. To insure against scorching, apply a lubricant along the edges — Vaseline or a similar lubricant will work.

The edges of the top laminate should be beveled to avoid cuts and to prevent the laminate from chipping. The router may be used for beveling (there is a bit specifically for this purpose) or you can do it by hand with a file. The file may be easier for amateurs.

Cutting a Sink Opening

To make an insert or sink cutout hole, first cover the area to be cut out with laminate. Draw an exact outline of the cutout. Drill ¼-inch starter holes at the corners, working from the underside. Saw through the laminated plywood with a sabre saw.

STEP 5: ADDING THE BACKSPLASH

Mount plastic laminate onto the backsplash core in exactly the same way as for countertops. Construct the backsplash separately from the countertop core. Make it of the same materials as the core and to the measurements you prefer — it may be as low as three inches or it can reach all the way up to the wall cabinets. For a low backsplash, a 1x4 may be substituted for the plywood. If you do not use a backsplash, apply caulking between the back edge of the counter and the wall to prevent seepage.

First, laminate the edges as described above. Then laminate the front surface and bevel the laminate.

Use a roller to spread adhesive on the top of the core. (Particleboard shown is one alternative.)

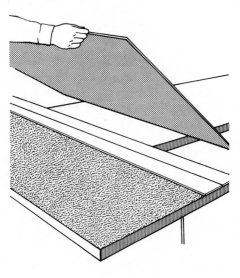

Slats may be used to keep the laminate away from the core until correctly positioned.

Attaching the Backsplash

Predrill screw holes for the backsplash by drilling through the bottom of the countertop where the backsplash will set. Place the backsplash on the countertop where it will be, but do not secure it yet. Run the drill through the countertop again, and into the backsplash about ¾ inch.

Lay a bead of adhesive, such as silicone seal, on the countertop where the backsplash meets the countertop. With a helper, place the backsplash over the sealant and secure the backsplash with 2½-inch long, ⅛-inch diameter flathead wood screws, driven up through the bottom of the countertop at approximately 8 inches on center. There also should be a screw at each end, an inch or so from the end. Use caulk to seal the joint where the top of the backsplash meets the wall.

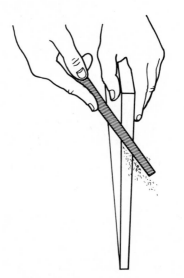

Hold file at angle shown to smooth laminate edges adhered to the base material.

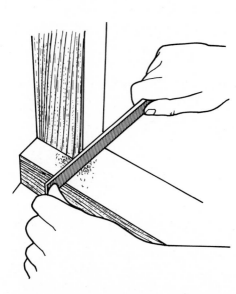

File edges of laminated cabinet; a router doesn't give an exactly square corner.

HOW TO LAMINATE AN EXISTING COUNTERTOP IN PLACE

Although it is more convenient to laminate a countertop by taking it off the base cabinet and laying it over a pair of sawhorses, you can laminate the countertop in place. If possible, first remove the old laminate.

Before resurfacing any existing countertops, inspect the countertop and its supports. Existing countertops should be made even and stable. This is usually accomplished by substituting new supports for any that have been damaged.

NEW LAMINATE OVER OLD

It is recommended that you remove old laminate before installing new laminate. If this is not possible, you can apply new laminate over the old.

If the old laminate has pulled up from the backing, break up the rises and remove the laminate chips. Sand the edges of the broken-out portions and be sure they are secure to the backing. Any loose portions of old laminate will be reflected by the new laminate. It is assumed that the broken-out portions are small (no more than half-dollar-sized) and that there are not too many of them. Otherwise, the old surface would be too uneven to support the new laminate properly. If the old laminate is in bad shape, it is better to remove it.

Apply the new laminate as described earlier in the project "Building a Laminated Countertop from Scratch".

OVER A BARE DECK
Removing the Old Laminate
Here are the tools, materials, and basic steps for removing the old countertop.

Tools and materials for removal. Hammer, baby sledge hammer, cold chisel, butt chisel, rubber hammer, thick-bladed putty knife, coarse, medium, and fine grit abrasive, sanding block, pull scraper.

Tools and materials for new laminate. Adhesive spreader or paintbrush, water putty, screwdriver, mineral spirits, level, square, tape measure, high pressure laminate, contact adhesive, smooth-cut file or router with a laminate blade, building adhesive,

caulking gun shell, keyhole saw or jigsaw with laminate-cutting blade, 1x4 for backsplash, tile and tub caulking.

Step one: lifting the old laminate. With a screwdriver, remove any metal trim from the countertop and backsplash. Also remove any metal cove molding between the backsplash and countertop. Take out the sink.

Find a loose spot in the old laminate and insert a cold chisel, thick-bladed putty knife, or the claws of a hammer under the spot. Pry up. This will break loose a chunk of the laminate so that you can pry, chisel, and chip at it until all of the old material is off the countertop surface. As you work, keep the counter clear of debris.

Step two: smoothing the counter deck. Once the old laminate is off, remove any dried adhesive with a pull scraper. With sandpaper — from coarse to fine — smooth the countertop and backsplash. Fill any holes, cracks, dents, or splits with wood putty and sand the patch smooth and level with the top.

For appearance, you may want to increase the "thickness" of the old countertop by nailing a piece of 1x3 along the edge of the top. This edge will be covered with new plastic laminate.

Step three: applying the laminate. When you are satisfied that the top is smooth, free of old adhesive, patched with nailheads countersunk, you are ready to apply the laminate, which should be precut and fitted to the top.

Test the new laminate to make sure all measurements are correct. Time spent on a "dry run" now can save you plenty of grief later. Mark the pieces for lay-down order.

First, place strips of laminate on the edges. They should extend about ¼-inch above the deck. Apply the adhesive to the back of the laminate. Then apply the adhesive to the surface of the top. Let the adhesive set according to the manufacturer's instructions on the adhesive container, and then press the laminate in position.

Step four: adding the backsplash. Follow the same laminating procedures for the backsplash. If the old backsplash was of rubber molding, you will have to fabricate a new backsplash. For a backsplash 4 inches high, use a length of 1x4. Prelaminate the 1x4 and stick it to the wall with building adhesive. The bottom of the backsplash must butt against the top of the countertop after the countertop has been recovered. Fill this crack with tub and tile caulking to seal the joint.

With a regular hammer, or rubber hammer if you have one, tap across the surface of the top. Use a wooden buffer block to protect the new laminate and to help spread the blows of the hammer along the surface. The tapping helps the glue bond between the top and the laminate.

With a smooth-cut file, trim the joints of the laminate — or use a router with a laminate bit for this job.

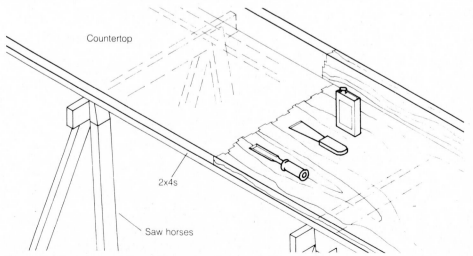

Remove laminate from existing countertops with a wood chisel, a stiff putty knife, and laquer thinner. If possible, tilt the countertop to let the thinner run under the laminate.

CREATING AN ANGLED COUNTERTOP

FOR AN EXISTING ANGLE
Producing the Angle

The only difference between building an angled countertop and a straight countertop is working with the angle. If you have an existing angled countertop, and want to substitute new counter material, make a pattern from the old counter. Place a sheet of tracing paper over the countertop angle. Trace the line of the angle and the edges of the countertop on the tracing paper. Then transfer the angle to the new plywood countertop material.

Laminating and Fastening

Cut and laminate the straight portion of the countertop as described in the previous project. Leave the laminate off the end that will join the angled portion of the countertop. Do the same with the angled piece. Rout the laminate flush where the two countertop sections join. Apply adhesive before you butt the two sections of countertop together. Fasten the counter from underside with wood screws.

FOR A NEW ANGLE
Producing the Angle

If you are building an angled countertop where none existed before, follow the same procedure with the pattern as described above, but spread the tracing paper on the floor and draw the countertop on it, to scale. You may wish to use graph paper instead of tracing paper. Then take the pattern and spread it over your new plywood countertop material and transfer the outline of the counter (as shown in the illustration).

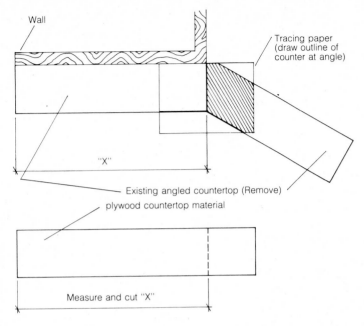

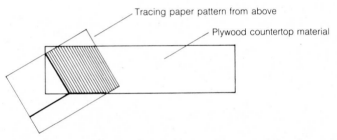

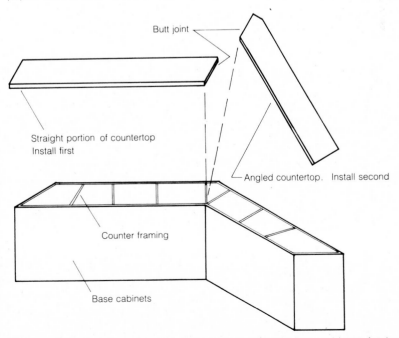

Before cutting laminate for an angle, draw an exact, scaled outline on tracing or, preferably, graph paper. Cut this out and use it as a template.

The angled countertop involves the same procedures as given on pg. 42-44, with the angle worked out before cutting begins.

First secure the straight portion of an angled countertop to the base cabinets. Apply silicone sealant along the ends of the countertops where the butt joint will be.

FOLD-OUT COUNTERTOP

The flip-down countertop in this example folds back to present a lower countertop level when required for specialized tasks, then folds down again to the regular countertop level.

STEP 1: PREPARING THE COUNTER

First, cut out the size desired (approximately 2 feet wide or less). Remove the framing at the front of the base cabinet.

Add all necessary replacement framing due to framing cuts, matching the size of the existing framing. The new framing around the perimeter must support the lowered counter surface. New framing also is needed for the small recessed side walls and the bottom of the recess. Then add a ¾-inch plywood sheet for the bottom. The bottom (¾ inch plywood) can be supported with metal angles.

Laminate the countertop and recessed area — sides bottom, etc., or add preformed laminate sections. For laminating instructions, refer to pages 42-44.

The space between the back of the

Materials List

Plywood: as needed for size of individual project ¾ inch for fold-up surface, lower level counter, sides (if required), and backsplash support.
½ inch for drawer space filler and ledger strips to support perimeter of fold-up surface

Plastic Laminate: to match or harmonize with existing countertop
1 sheet to cover all exposed surfaces and edges

Hardware
3 piano hinges for back, center, and front of fold-up surface
16 to 20 metal angle to support lower shelf
100-125 No. 5 1½ inch wood screws

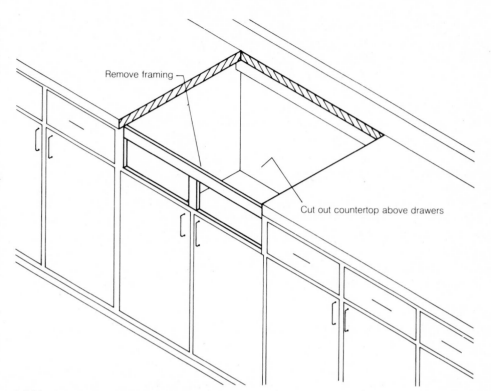

A fold-out countertop can be installed using the space occupied by drawers. First, cut out the required countertop space, then remove the framing at the front of the base cabinet.

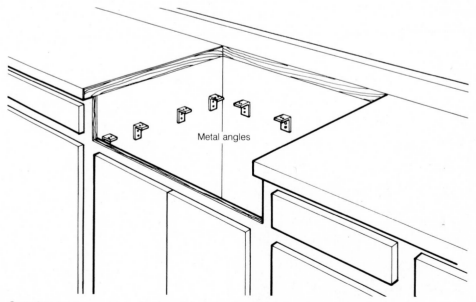

Once framing is removed, attach metal angles (or wood cleats) to support a plywood shelf.

folding top and the backsplash is your choice. But you must have blocking to which to secure the piano hinges.

STEP 2: PREPARING THE LEDGER

Next build the ½ inch ledger. Do not install it yet. This ledger can be laminated if you wish, but it is not necessary. As an alternative, consider using a stained wood, such as mahogany.

STEP 3: BUILDING THE TOP

In our example, the very front portion of the folding top folds down to the position where the drawer fronts were before they were removed. The back portion of the folding top is recessed to allow the short front section to fit flush within it, so the folding top is no thicker than necessary when in the "up" position.

Laminate the folding top before connecting it with the piano hinges.

STEP 4: ATTACHING THE TOP

Assemble the folding top but do not secure it at the backsplash yet. Instead, hold it in place level with the countertop. Have a helper locate the bottom edge of the folding top on the inside of the recess with a pencil. Install the ledgers at the pencil marks for a precisely level fit. Secure them with brass flathead wood screws. Finally, attach the piano hinge at the backsplash.

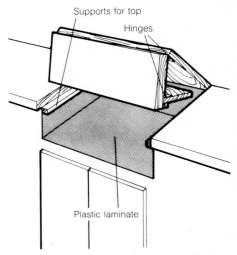

The fold-out counter pushes back against the backsplash to allow access to the lower surface below. Butcher block may also be used.

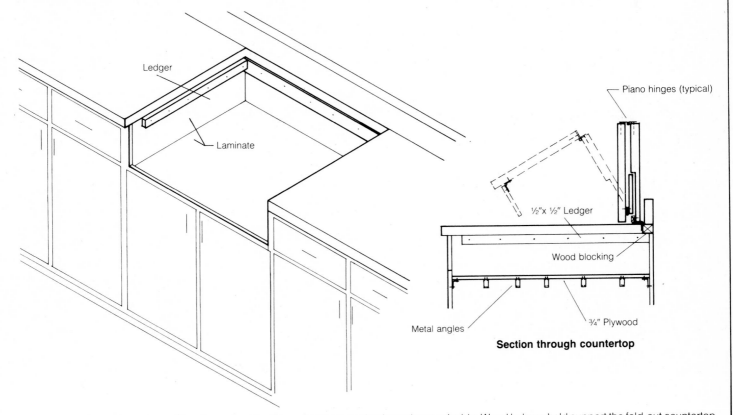

After you have the countertop and framing out, add a plywood bottom and laminate the area inside. Wood ledgers hold support the fold-out countertop.

BONUS SPACE: A SLIDE-OUT COUNTER

If you need countertop space more than you need drawer space, you can add a slide-out butcher block surface. Other materials could be used just as easily as the butcher block: acrylic plastic (synthetic marble), laminated wood, or any material that will accept screws or bolts in the side.

WORK SEQUENCE

First, build the slide-out itself. Then build the framing at the base cabinet front around the dimensions of the slide-out. With a helper holding the slide-out in place, measure inside the cabinet for the distance between slide-out and nearest cabinet support. Install the sliding channels. Slip in the slide-out counter.

STEP 1: PLANNING THE OPENING

The easiest condition is when you are building new base cabinets from scratch. Then you simply frame around the slide-out as required, leaving enough space for a shallow drawer below, if you wish.

Variation: Cutting the Opening

If you are adding the slide-out to an existing base cabinet, where there is no drawer, draw the shape of the slide-out on the face of the cabinet. Drill holes (¼ inch) at each corner; then cut out the space with a sabre saw.

Where there is a drawer where you want the slide-out, you can either build a new drawer after you add the slide-out above the old drawer, or you can try to cut the drawer down to a shallower size.

The framing around a slide-out at the base cabinet face is typical of the framing around drawers and doors, as discussed in the next chapter.

STEP 2: SUPPORTING THE SLIDE-OUT SURFACE

Each cabinet has unique requirements for interior supports. You must have solid backing to which to attach the stationary channel. For the total width of the slide-out add together the width of the slide-out plus the thickness for the particular metal channel you use. You may be able to screw the channel to the side of the cabinet and some exist-ing counter framing. If not, add framing by screwing it to the underside of the countertop.

Product Suggestion

A word is in order about the metal channels sometimes used for drawers and slide-outs. Probably no other piece of kitchen hardware does its jobs as well as the metal channel shown.

The assembly is made up of two metal channels and nylon rollers. One channel is stationary and is attached to the cabinet. The other channel is attached to the moving object: the slide-out or drawer. This piece of hardware is highly recommended, although drawers and slide-outs can be made using dado joints.

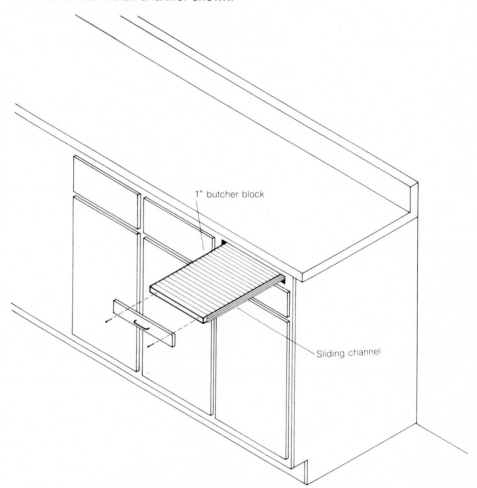

The slide-out can be installed when you build new base cabinets from scratch, or it can be added to existing base cabinets. Sliding metal channels aid ease of operation.

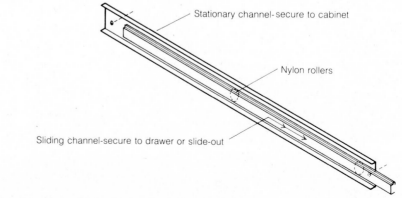

Metal channels are the best way to hang drawers and slide-out counters. One channel attaches to the drawer or slide-out; the other is stationary, mounted inside the base cabinet.

3
CABINETS AND SPECIALIZED STORAGE

Because cabinets are the first type of kitchen storage usually considered by the homeowner, we present two alternative stylings for cabinetry: standard, boxlike cabinets plus a European-style design. The latter also includes details for building a floor-to-ceiling pantry. Specialized projects, created to fit specialized needs and unusual spaces, are then offered. These are usually found within the cabinet, such as an open spice rack that pulls out and slides back in.

One way to store large, flat items such as baking and serving trays, and skillets is upright in these equally positioned slotted dividers.

Adjustable, vinyl-coated, see-through pullout baskets provide easy access for hard-to-store or hard-to-find items.

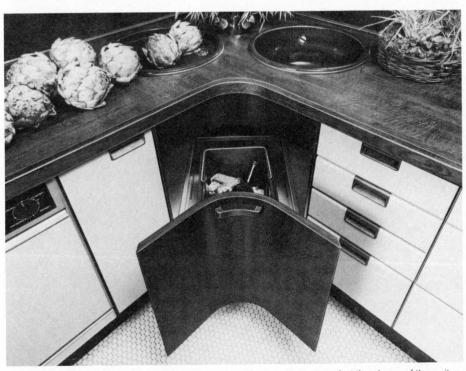

Almost anything can be hidden behind your cabinet front — no matter what the shape of the unit, or the line of the countertop.

KITCHEN PANTRY

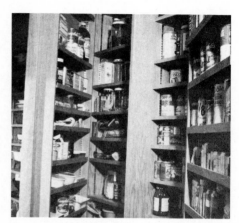

The finished pantry offers many shelf heights and depths for versatile storage. Shelves pull out for ease of use and visibility.

This kitchen was designed by a Wisconsin architectural specialist. Its obvious benefits are maximum use of space and good looks. This project, and the next two projects, show you how to build the basic components.

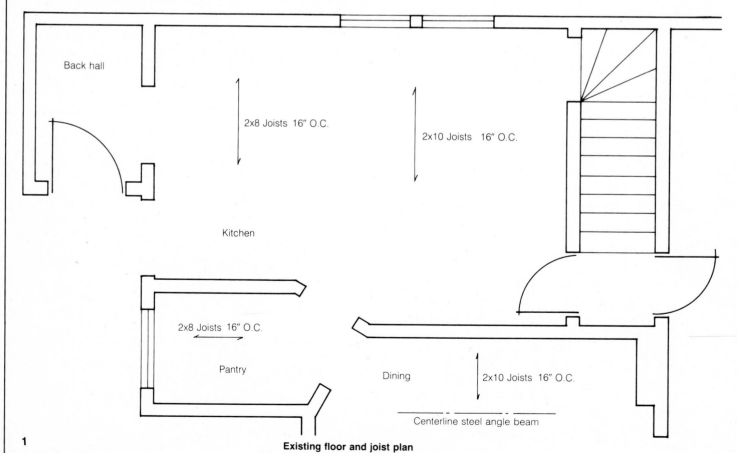

Back hall

2x8 Joists 16" O.C.

2x10 Joists   16" O.C.

Kitchen

2x8 Joists 16" O.C.

Pantry

Dining

2x10 Joists 16" O.C.

Centerline steel angle beam

1   **Existing floor and joist plan**

Renovating an older kitchen often requires moving wall partitions. Before you do any new floor planning, draw the existing floor plan and indicate the direction and size of all joists. Show any other weight that is dependent on wall partitions for its support.

FLOOR-TO-CEILING PANTRY

The pantry, as indicated on the revised floor plan, shows the overall width of the pantry (7 feet 4 inches) within the two enclosing sections of stud wall. The depth of the pantry, overall, is 1 foot 1 inch. The stud wall enclosures are an inch deeper, 1 foot 2 inches. The pantry is the full ceiling height of 10 feet.

Note that the pantry is used for three types of storage: the tall doors at the left enclose compartments for storage of large cans and other bulky items; the two tall doors on the right enclose shelves of less depth because the doors themselves have shelves for smaller cans and other light storage items; the small doors adjacent to the ceiling enclose space for items not used frequently and must be reached using a kitchen ladder.

STEP 1: DRAWING UP PLANS

The first step in building the pantry is to obtain a set of working drawings. Framing carpentry and other rough woodwork, which is covered with some finish material like sheetrock or paneling, is much more forgiving of mistakes and inaccuracies than is interior woodwork with fine materials. So do not spare the details on your drawings. If you cannot draw them yourself, have them done by a professional. The example pantry that follows can be modified to suit your particular space, if it does not fit in its present form. For a Materials List based on these dimensions, refer to the end of this project.

STEP 2: BUILDING ENCLOSURES

Consider the stud wall enclosures shown. They show a stud wall finished with sheetrock. The depth dimension (1-2 inches) is the distance from the finished inside face of the house wall to the finished end face of the short stud enclosure walls. Thus, when you build the enclosures, do not forget to ac-

count for the thickness of the sheetrock. The enclosures use two studs at the wall and two at the ends.

The sill plate is of one 2x4 and the head plate is of two 2x4s, assembled as shown in Illustration 6. To assemble, toenail the studs at the sill and head with three 10d or four 8d nails.

Use a carpenters' square to check the angle of the stud enclosure relative to the house wall; it should be 90 degrees. Nail the sill to the subfloor with approximately eight 10d nails spaced equally over the sill. Next, nail the head plate to the overhead joists, making sure you nail into solid backing; use approximately eight 10d nails, like you did for the sill. You should provide for solid backing at the head (and sill) before you nail the sill and head plates in place. Illustrations 3 and 4 describe typical blocking for head conditions, which also apply to floor joists under the sill.

Remember that the nominal size of

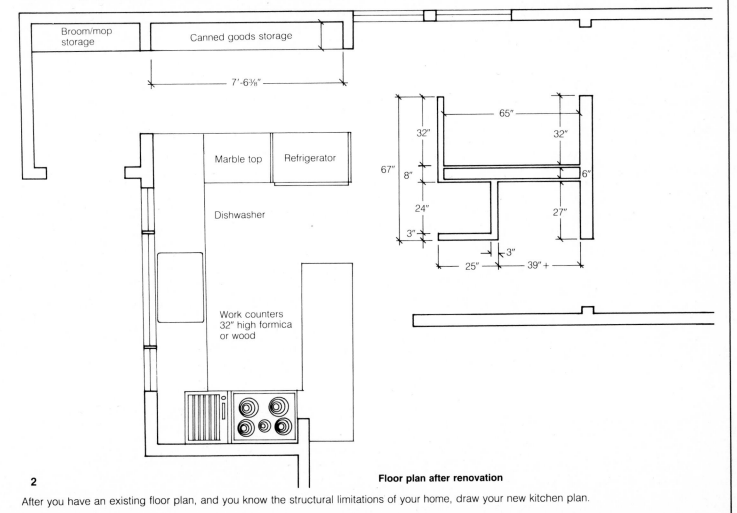

Floor plan after renovation

2

After you have an existing floor plan, and you know the structural limitations of your home, draw your new kitchen plan.

Project continued on next page

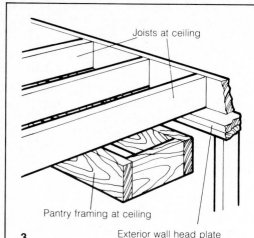

Joists at ceiling

Pantry framing at ceiling

Exterior wall head plate

3

If the pantry is located where its framing runs perpendicular to the supporting joists, the pantry framing may be nailed directly to the ceiling joists (if the house is one-story) or the floor joists (if the house is two-story).

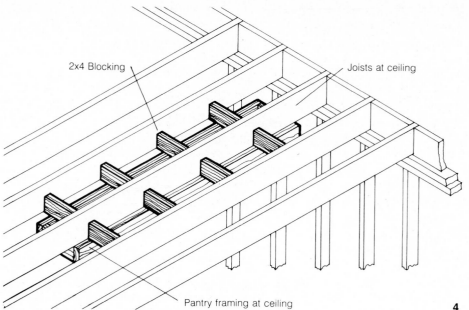

2x4 Blocking

Joists at ceiling

Pantry framing at ceiling

4

If the pantry is located where its framing runs parallel to the supporting joists, use 2x4 blocking between the joists. The blocking should be located approximately 16 inches on center for the width of the pantry. Nail the pantry framing to the 2x4 blocking.

the studs is not the actual size; 2x4s are usually 1½ inches x 3½ inches, but measure all your lumber to be sure of size. The example uses ½ inch sheetrock to cover the stud enclosures; the 2x4 portion of the enclosure, then, will be 1 foot 1½ inches out from the finished wall. When the enclosures are finished, you can begin framing the pantry.

STEP 3: PANTRY FRAMING

The pantry uses 2x6 framing at the top, secured to the overhead joists, and 2x4 framing at the base, secured to the subflooring. Once again, consult Illustrations 3 and 4 to visualize the typical blocking needed to secure the framing at head and sill. Install the framing at the head first. The 2x6 along the house wall can be secured by nailing it to the wall studs with three 10d nails at each existing stud (16 inches on center). Then install the 2x6 cross members at each end, so you will have something to nail the front 2x6 to (lengthways). Nail the end cross members to the short stud enclosure sections with approximately six 10d nails, evenly spaced over the surface of the cross member and nailed into the short stud wall enclosures.

Now, install the front 2x6 framing member, nailing it to the cross members with three 10d nails at each end. Next, install the remaining cross members with three 10d nails at each end of the cross members, toenailing them to

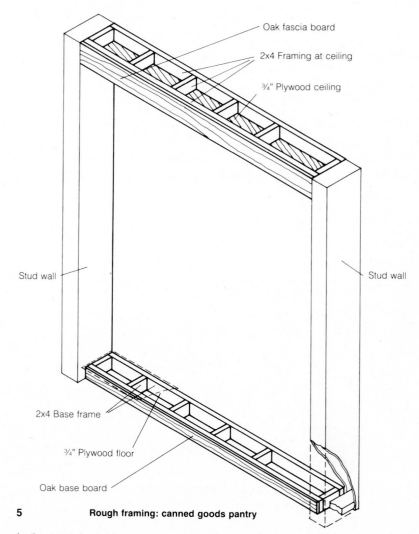

Oak fascia board

2x4 Framing at ceiling

¾" Plywood ceiling

Stud wall

Stud wall

2x4 Base frame

¾" Plywood floor

Oak base board

5   **Rough framing: canned goods pantry**

In the example the pantry is between two short sections of stud wall which are covered with sheetrock. The base and head framing are of 2x4s.

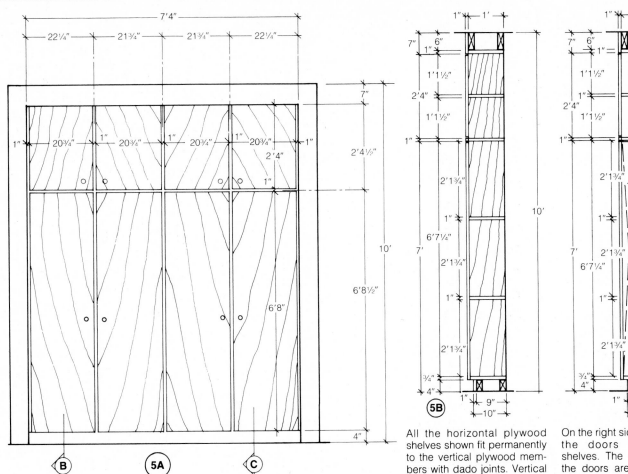

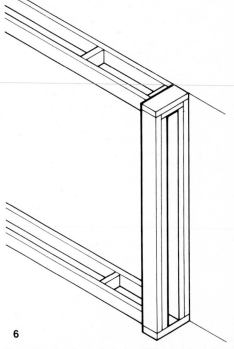

The pantry is built flush to the 10 ft. ceiling. The left two doors of pantry open to a standard shelf arrangement. The right two doors have mini-shelves built into them. All the small doors at the ceiling enclose shelving for infrequently-used items.

All the horizontal plywood shelves shown fit permanently to the vertical plywood members with dado joints. Vertical shelf brackets allow the addition of more shelves.

On the right side of the pantry, the doors have built-in shelves. The shelves behind the doors are only 8 inches deep, to make room for the doors.

the lengthways 2x6 members at the wall, and nailing through the member at the front. Consult Illustration 5 for an assembly view; and Details 5A, 5B, and 5C for dimensions. The length of the members should be very close to 7 feet 4 inches, but cut them to fit precisely the length between the two short stud enclosures.

STEP 4: PREPARING THE PLYWOOD FRAMING GRID

After you install the head and sill framing as described above, prepare the interior plywood framing. First, study the assembly drawing, Illustration 7. The plywood members you see do not move because they provide stability for the pantry. Within these plywood framing members you can add more shelves, using metal pilasters and clips, as described later.

Cut the plywood framing members

to the appropriate sizes, after you have carefully studied the assembly illustrations and Details 5A, 5B and 5C. A note of caution: the plywood framing depth dimensions shown *include* any trim that you may use; therefore, you must *subtract* the thickness of the particular trim you use from the plywood framing. Illustration 9 shows a typical installation of ¼ inch trim, cut to fit flush with the edges of the plywood framing.

STEP 5: CUTTING THE SLOTS

After you finish cutting the plywood framing members, double check them for size before you waste time with the next step, which is to cut the slots for the dado joints. Illustration 8 shows how the plywood framing members are assembled, using dado joints. The dado joints are made with a router. The router is a power tool somewhat similar to a drill; a variety of bits are available

6

The short sections of stud wall that enclose the pantry use two 2x4s at each end (total of 4 per wall) with two lengths of 2x4 at the head (top) and one 2x4 at the sill (bottom).

Project continued on next page

to cut different size slots to accommodate assembly of various size wood members. If you have never used a router, and you are in a hurry, you probably will be better off to have the router slots done by the lumber dealer. If you do the joints yourself, first study the dimensions on Details 5A, 5B and 5C again, then draw the slots on the plywood before you use the router. The slots should be ¼ inch deep and be the width of the plywood thickness.

STEP 6: ASSEMBLING THE GRID

The plywood framing within the pantry is essentially a grid, formed by five vertical members and five horizontal members. The five vertical members are routed to accept the horizontal members, except for the base (floor of the pantry) and the head member (ceiling of the pantry). These head and base members are routed to accept the vertical members. Illustration 7 shows the assembly of the basic framing grid. Within the basic grid, more shelves may be added, as desired.

STEP 7: RECESSING THE PILASTERS

If you want the pilasters and clips recessed, you must cut the slots for them before you assemble the plywood framing within the pantry. The slots are made with a router, just like the slots for the dado joints shown in Illustration 8. The depth of the slots should be the same as the thickness of the pilasters. Illustration 12 shows the recessed pilasters in place within the routed slots. It doesn't really matter, functionally, whether the pilasters are recessed or not. But recessing the pilasters gives a more sophisticated look, for those willing to go to the trouble to get it. Whether surface-mounted or recessed in slots, the pilasters are secured with screws provided with the pilasters (¾ inch #10, if you supply your own). Screw holes are already drilled in the pilasters.

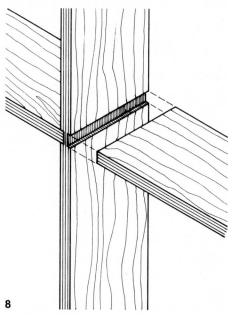

8
The dado joint assures a precise, secure meeting of horizontal and vertical framing members. Use glue to hold the members permanently in place.

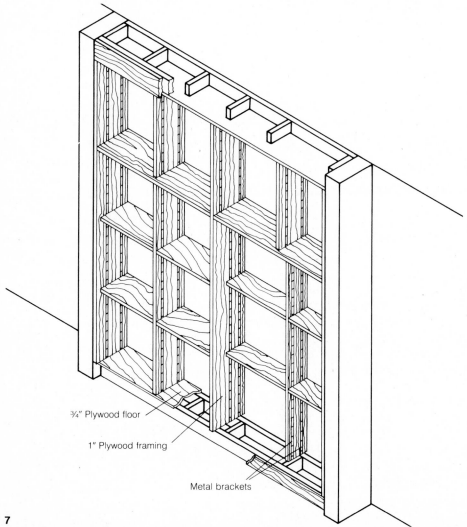

¾" Plywood floor

1" Plywood framing

Metal brackets

7
The interior framing of the pantry is made of 1 inch cabinet grade plywood. The horizontal members fit into dado joints on the vertical members. Metal shelf brackets support additional shelves, as desired.

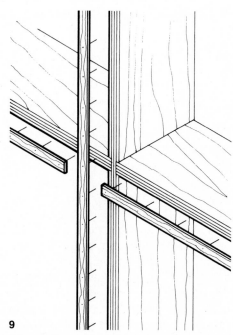

9
Edges of the plywood framing may be trimmed with ¼ inch x 1 inch members of any desired finish wood. One inch finish nails at 4 inches on center can be used to secure the trim, or glue may be used, or both.

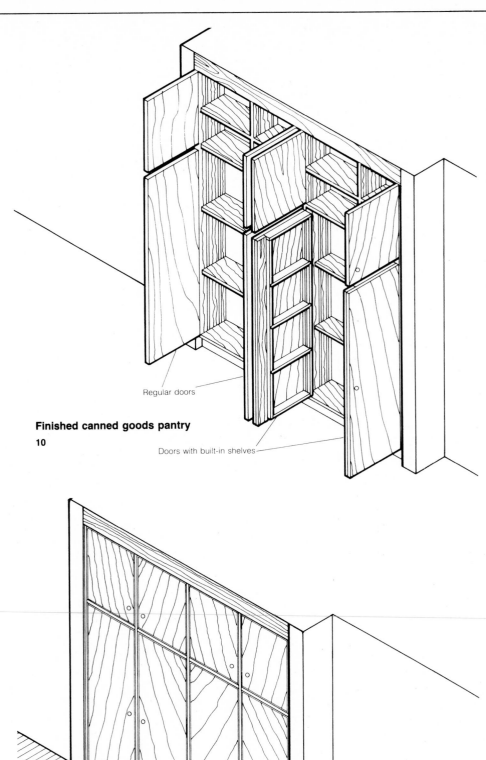

Regular doors

Finished canned goods pantry
10

Doors with built-in shelves

Finished canned goods pantry
11

STEP 8: NAILING THE BASE

To assemble the pantry framing, first install the base (floor) of the pantry. Nail the base to the long 2x4 framing members with number 10 finish nails at 16 inches on center. Put two of the same size nails, equally spaced, into every 2x4 cross member in the framing.

STEP 9: INSTALLING VERTICAL PLYWOOD SIDE MEMBERS

Now install the vertical plywood members at each side of the pantry that fit adjacent to the short stud wall enclosures. Nail the vertical members to the stud walls, again using number 10 finishing nails. The nails should be spaced approximately 8 inches on center, 1½ inches from the edges of the vertical member; this should put the nails solidly into the 2x4 corners within the stud wall.

When using finish nails, buy the kind with "cupped heads", which is a small indentation (cup) in the center of the head. Hammer the nail down to within approximately ¼ inch of the plywood surface, then use a nailset punch to drive the nail the rest of the way into the wood and slightly below the surface. The resulting holes will be filled with a wood filler before final surface finishing is done. This method of nailing into any finish surface avoids hammer dents. The wood filler needed is available with instructions from almost any hardware store.

STEP 10: NAILING THE HEAD AND REMAINING PLYWOOD

The head member is installed next, just like you installed the base member. Then install the vertical and horizontal plywood members, starting at the right side of the pantry. Use a liquid

10 The doors on the right side of the pantry use the horizontal members shown (shelves) as permanent framing, like the left side. Note that shelves use dado joints. Additional shelves may be added as desired, using the metal shelf brackets.

11 The finished canned goods pantry will blend with any furniture style. Plywood with almost any veneer you desire is available at your local lumber store. Exotic woods may be special-ordered. Note the finish trim at the top and base of this pantry.

Project continued on next page

resin (white glue) in the joints, applied per the manufacturers' instructions. There are many good glues available at any building materials supply store or hardware store.

All the horizontal members, excepting one, span ony the space between the vertical members. The exception is the horizontal member that serves as the bottom of the small, upper right-hand storage areas. Illustration 14 shows how this single piece is assembled.

STEP 11: CREATING THE BASIC DOOR

The example project uses 1 inch finish grade interior plywood. Details 5A, 5B and 5C show the required dimensions. Plywood is available with many ve-neers in several typical grades. With interior cabinet work, for other interior work where fine quality wood grain is a must, inspect the wood before you buy it, regardless of the grade.

In studying the illustrations above, note that all the doors fit within the framing, flush with the trim. Check the as-built framing openings with a tape measure to be sure they are the same as your working drawings, and if not exactly the same, correct them if possible. If you cannot correct the differences, note the as-built dimensions on your working drawings. A difference in width in the framing spaces of, say, ⅛ inch, will not be noticeable. However, the difference *would* be noticeable where the door meets the frame if the door size were not adjusted (larger or

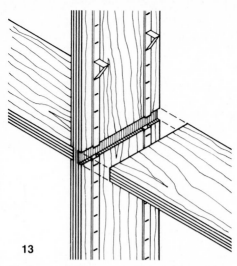

13

Pilasters and clips are used to provide a variety of shelf heights. The pilasters (metal strips with horizontal slots) can be surface-mounted or they may be installed within channels (formed with a router) for a flush appearance.

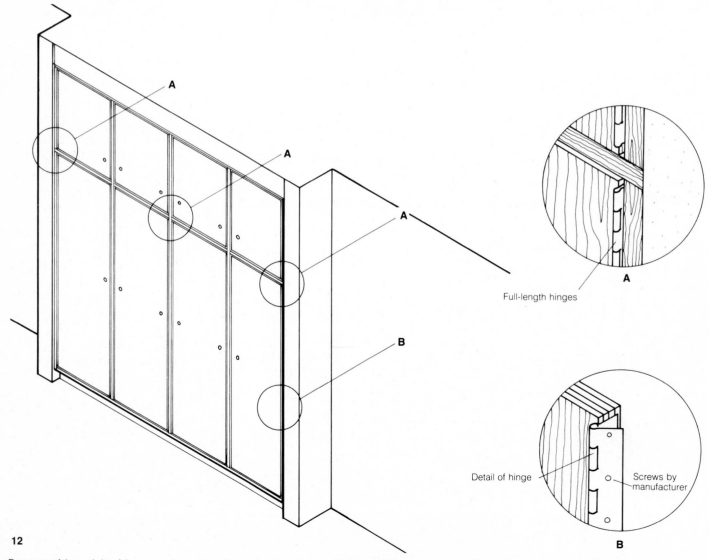

Full-length hinges

A

Detail of hinge

Screws by manufacturer

B

12

Because of the weight of the canned goods on the pantry door shelves, "full length" hinges are used. These hinges are not necessary for the small doors adjacent to the ceiling.

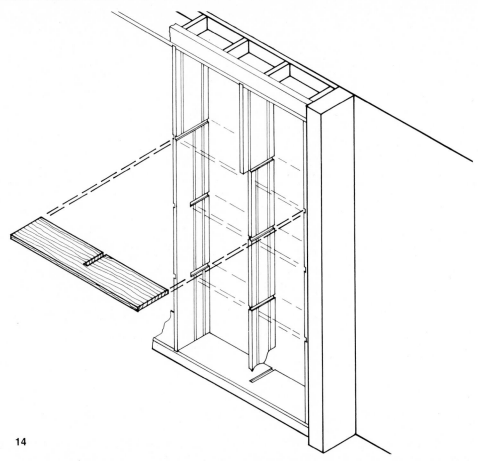

14

The horizontal member that serves as the bottom of the small, upper right hand storage areas (it is also a shelf), is a single piece of 1-inch plywood, spanning two shelves. All the other framing members (also serving as shelves) are half as big as the piece illustrated.

Detail A

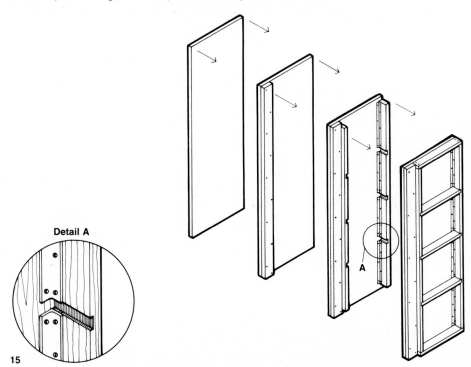

15

The two long doors on the right side of the pantry have built-in shelves. Following from left to right: first attach the edge piece (1x3), then the two vertical shelf supports; then the shelves, including top and bottom member. These shallow shelves are used for small canned goods and other frequently-used items.

smaller, as appropriate). Never fully trust dimensions on working drawings for cabinet work. Always make frequent measurement checks with a tape measure, so that you can make the minor adjustments that are inevitable in woodworking.

As a work procedure, it will be best to cut a door for the particular space it will fit and then fit it into the space as a check. Identify the location of the door on a piece of masking tape (far left door, upper right small door, etc.). Stick the tape to the door, then cut the next door, and so forth. A power saw with a plywood-cutting blade (available at your lumber dealer) can be used for both ripping (cutting with the grain) or crosscutting. Keep the best face of the plywood down when you use the power saw. The plywood is thick enough so that no door supports, other than the full-length hinges, are necessary.

Treating Plywood Edges
Plywood edges for this project may be treated with a veneer tape, which is thin wood that comes in coils. The ve-

To match laminated cabinet surfaces, plywood edges can be covered with laminate strips.

To fill the end grain of plywood to be painted, you can use wood putty.

Project continued on next page

neer tape should be applied per the particular manufacturers' requirements, which is typically a contact cement. Another material for finishing plywood edges is laminated plastic; it is applied with a contact cement similar to those used for counter tops, but, again, follow the manufacturers' instructions. It is not recommended that plywood edges be left unfinished; finish the door edges one at a time, right before you install the doors.

STEP 12: CREATING THE DOORS WITH THE BUILT-IN SHELVES

The long doors on the right, with the built-in shelves, deserve special attention. First, study Illustrations 10 and 15 and Detail 5C. Secure a 1x3 at the edge of the door that opens out. Use 1¼ inch #10 wood screws (all screws used on the pantry are flathead) at 8 inches on center. Stagger the screws (a screw at 1 inch from the left edge, then down and 1 inch from the right edge, and so forth) the full height of the door. The 1x3 fits flush at the top, bottom, and front edge of the door.

Next, install the vertical framing members with routed shelf slots; Illustration 15 shows the assembly steps for the shelf-doors. The vertical members are 1 inch x 4 inches. They are lapped at the top and bottom with shorter pieces of the same thickness, so remember to allow for that thickness (1 inch at top and bottom) when cutting the vertical members (Detail 5A shows the door dimensions). The left vertical member may be screwed to the 1x3 at the edge with 1¼ inch #10 wood screws at 8 inches on center.

Using Metal Angles

The vertical member shown at the right must be secured with a metal angle. The example shows holes staggered along the metal angle at about 4 inches. If you cannot find an angle with these holes, take the angle you buy to a machine shop or auto garage and get the holes drilled at 4 inches on center. Note that the angle fits flush with the edge of the routed shelf slot, so that it does not interfere with the placement of the shelves. Use ¾ inch #10 screws for the metal angle.

Adding the Shelves

There is some variance in the placement of the shelves, depending on your particular needs. However, there should be at least three shelves, besides the top and bottom members, and no space between shelves should be greater than 24 inches. Shelves between the slotted shelves (intermediate shelves) may be installed using metal pilasters and clips, like those described previously. Or, you can buy special clips in a kind of "T" shape that allow you to use only one metal pilaster per side, instead of the usual two.

When the vertical members are in place, attach the top and bottom members to the vertical members with two 1¼ inch #10 screws at each end.

STEP 13: ATTACHING THE DOORS

Now you are ready to install the doors. For this you will need a helper. The doors use full-length hinges (also called continuous or piano hinges) because these hinges offer the great strength which is needed on long, heavy doors, especially the doors with built-in shelves. The shorter doors adjacent to the ceiling could utilize other hinges, but you want the hinges to match, since they are visible. See Illustration 13 for a detail of the hinges. These hinges fit very similarly to the way your room doors fit except for their long length.

Before you attach the hinges, set the door you want to start with in place (any door will do, but it might be wise to do one of the small ones at the ceiling to gain experience) and have your helper hold the hinge in place next to the pantry framing.

Remove the door (with the helper keeping the hinge in place) and mark the position of the hinge on the framing with a pencil. Mark the top and bottom of the hinge, the corners, and all the screw holes. Remove the hinge and place it against the door edge and mark its position there too.

Secure the hinge to the pantry framing, using the screws provided by the manufacturer (they should be ¾ inch #10 — if not, replace them with same). With your helper holding the door, secure the hinge to the door.

Put a screw in every hole along the pantry framing, but when you hang the door just put a couple at the top and bottom and in the middle, until you are sure the door is hung correctly (relative to the pantry framing). Close the door and check it to be sure it fits evenly all around; a visual check is good enough. If no adjustments are needed, install the remainder of the screws into the pantry door. Install the remaining doors the same way.

STEP 14: INSTALLING DOOR CATCHES

There are three commonly used cabinet door catches: magnetic, roller, and spring. All three are readily available at hardware stores for your inspection. Only the magnetic catch will be discussed here because it is the most versatile.

If you look at your existing kitchen cabinets, they probably have magnetic catches. The magnetic part of the catch is screwed to the framing and a small metal angle fits against the door. When the door is closed, the magnet grasps the metal angle and holds the door in place. A look at the magnetic catch is all that is necessary to understand its installation. The good thing about magnetic catches is that the magnet, which "floats" within its bracket, adjusts itself to minor imperfections in assembly, or to door warpage.

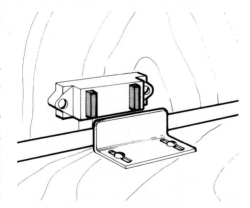

A magnetic catch is one of the easiest catches to install. It can be adjusted by sliding the plate back and forth on the screws.

STEP 15: ADDING THE TRIM

Now, you can install the finish baseboards at the floor and ceiling. These finish boards can be seen in Details 5A, 5B and 5C, with dimensions. Attach them to the framing behind them with #10 finishing nails at 16 inches on center. When the nails are about ¼ inch from being all the way in, use a nailset and drive them slightly beneath the surface of the wood. Fill the nail holes left with the wood filler.

STEP 16: FINISHING

Finish the surface of the pantry as desired. If you use fine-quality plywood veneer, you can wax the wood just as it is. Or, you may stain it first, then wax or shellac it or finish it with varnish. The choices of finish are unlimited but if you use a fine wood, it seems a waste to paint over it. Plywood veneers of the slightly lesser quality than the above can be painted and be very beautiful.

STEP 17: INSTALLING KNOBS

After you finish the pantry, install the door pulls or knobs. Pulls and knobs are very easy to install and come with their own hardware. Typically, a screw is built into knobs and you simply screw them in where you want them. Pulls usually have accommodations on the back side for screws or bolts, run through the doors. The manufacturer typically provides diagrams, but the installation is obvious. Locate the position of the knobs or pulls with a carpenters square.

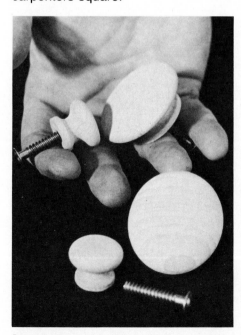

Some knobs and pulls provide the screw but require you to drill a hole in the backside of the pull to mount the hardware.

STEP 18: USING A DOOR STOP

A finishing touch that you may want to consider is some kind of door stop. They are not really mandatory, if you are careful with the doors. However, they are a good idea, especially with children around. Hardware stores have light chain attachments that attach to the door and the framing, on the inside of the pantry, and keep the door from swinging past where you want it to. This protects the door and whatever the door might hit if opened too far out from the pantry.

Another door stop that may be applicable in your situation is a metal stop with a rubber tip. It is likely you have them in your house now, to protect your room doors and the walls behind the doors. These door stops usually fit on the baseboard, but you can buy them for use in higher areas.

These drawers were built to suit the items stored there, with deepest drawer on the bottom and the shallowest on the top.

Materials List

Plywood: 1 inch thick, veneer face of your choice or clear face if you will paint
2 sheets 4x10 feet for doors
3 sheets 4x8 feet (depending upon cost and availability
3 sheets 4x8 feet for framing

Lumber: to match plywood veneer or pine
14 linear feet 1x3 for door edging
38 linear feet 1x3 for vertical members and built-in pantry door shelves
12 lengths 8 feet 2x4 3 for base framing
                       9 for stud framing
as needed 2x4 blocking between floor joists (see instructions)

Wallboard: ½ inch thickness
1 sheet 4x8 for wallcover

Trim: to match plywood veneer or as desired
1 8 foot piece 1x7 for ceiling fascia board
1 8 foot piece 1x4 for baseboard
25 feet veneer tape last column to cover exposed edges of plywood
5 10 foot pieces ¼x1 trim for exposed edges of vertical framing
1 8 foot piece ½x1 trim for exposed edges of horizontal framing

Hardware
190 linear feet metal pilasters as shelf support clip holders
4 per shelf support clips
4 6'8" piano hinges for 4 4'2" doors
8 door pulls of choice

Fasteners
2 pounds 10d common nails
2 pounds 8d common nails
2 pounds 10d finishing nails
2 pounds 1¼ inch brads
100 1¼ inch #10 flathead screws
100 ¾ inch #10 flathead screws

Miscellaneous
wood filler
glue

EUROPEAN-STYLE CABINETRY

BASE CABINET WITH BUTCHER-BLOCK TOP

This base cabinet with butcher-block top is simple and quick to build. For the cabinets that have a laminate top, the construction of the base simply repeats for each adjacent cabinet. See Chapter 2 for instructions on how to create and install a laminate countertop.

Step 1: Building the Base

First, build the 2x4 framing underneath, as shown in Illustration 1. The 2x4 cross members are 16 inches on center. Use 10d nails, about three per joint.

Step 2: Adding End Walls and Floor

Install the two end pieces, made of 1-inch plywood. The notches at the bottom are 4 inches by 4 inches; they provide a foot space when working. This is standard cabinet-building procedure.

If you wish to rout the plywood end walls for interior metal pilasters (Illustration 2), do it now. The pilasters extend from the bottom of the cabinet side to the bottom of the drawer at the top.

Now install the cabinet floor (½ inch plywood), the metal pilasters and the two trim pieces. One of these facing strips goes next to the floor and one flush with the floor of the cabinet.

Step 3: Fastening the Pieces

Secure all the plywood members with ⅛-inch diameter, 1½ inch flathead

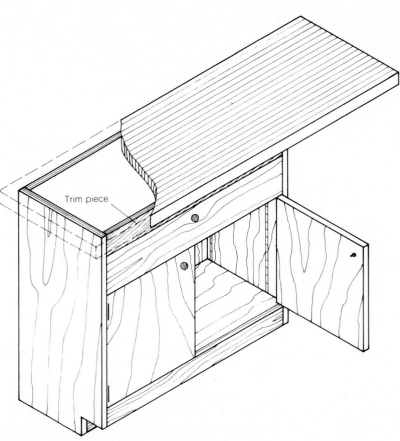

The butcher block top overhangs one end by about one-third of the total length; this is normally the maximum overhang desirable.

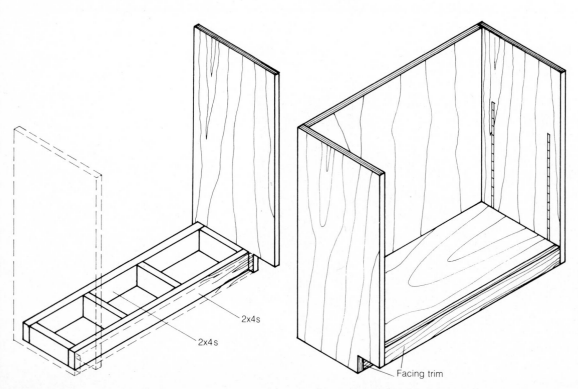

The structure underneath the base cabinet is of 2x4s with cross members at 16 inches on center. Secure it to the floor with 10d nails toenailed through the cross members, close to where they butt the front and back 2x4s.

Heavy plywood veneer, ¾ or 1 inch thick, is a strong material that simplifies construction of cabinets. Metal pilasters and clips allow a wide range of shelf heights.

wood screws. The screws should be counterbored (later, you can fill the holes with wood filler and finish). An alternative to using flathead screws and wood filler is to use a comparable-sized nail. Tap the nails below the wood surface; then fill the hole. This gives a smaller hole to fill and attracts less attention to the fastening method. Unless installed carefully, however, nails can crack the wood. Whether nails or screws, apply them at 4 inches on center. Secure the plywood back to the side pieces (1 inch thick).

Step 4: Installing the Top
Add the top trim piece that spans the front of the cabinet and the butcher block top. Install the butcher block with metal angles (approximately ½ inch wide with 1 inch "legs"). Use flathead wood screws, ¼ inch in diameter and ¾ inch long, to secure the angles to the two surfaces being brought together — the butcher block top plus the sides and front of the cabinet. Install the angles at approximately 4 inches on center around the inside of the cabinet.

Step 5: Doors and Drawers
Drawers are discussed in a later project, "Standard Cabinetry", with doors and hinges. Add doors and drawers.

Step 6: Surface Finishing
Finish the front edges of the plywood veneer as discussed for the pantry. If you have used common plywood, you probably will want to paint the cabinet. If working with a furniture-quality veneered plywood, staining would be preferred instead.

PROVIDING PIPE OPENINGS FOR SINK CABINET
For a new sink cabinet, place the cabinet in position and drill pilot holes down through the bottom of the cabinet and through the floor. Bore holes for the hot and cold water supply lines and for the drain line.

Before enlarging the holes, go down into the basement or crawl space; make sure the pilot holes are not located where the path of the pipe will be interrupted by any obstacle. If a pilot hole is on top of a floor joist, move it a few inches.

Move the cabinet away from the spot and redrill the holes large enough to provide clearance for the sizes of the pipes you will use. When the cabinet is replaced in position, the pipes will be out of sight.

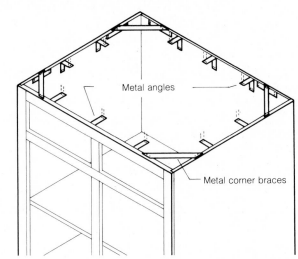

Metal angles offer a good way to secure a countertop. To remove the countertop, loosen the wood screws. Wood supports with screws driven up through the countertop also work well.

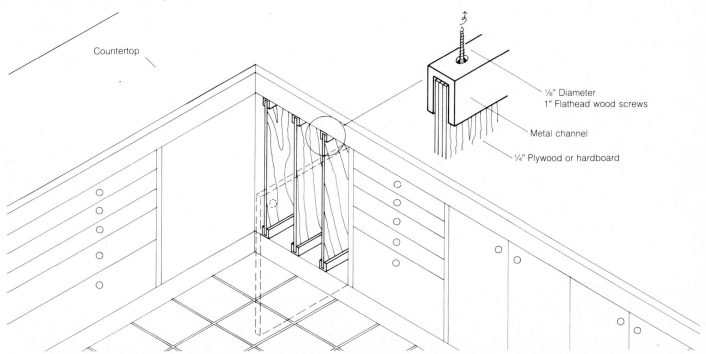

Install framing for metal channels or screw channels directly to interior cabinet walls. Use 1-inch long, ⅛-inch diameter flathead wood screws at the front, middle, and back of each channel. Or, secure narrow strips of wood to the cabinet bottom to hold the panels in place.

CEILING-MOUNTED CABINETS

SUSPENDING THE CABINETS

Ceiling-suspended cabinets need more structural support than cabinets that fit against a wall, because wall cabinets can be secured directly to the wall. Illustration 4 shows the structure above a ceiling-suspended cabinet.

Our example shows one scheme for securing stable ceiling-suspended cabinets. This example shows all the necessary details to handle the situation adequately.

Ensuring Adequate Support

When building the structure that will hold the cabinets from above, keep in mind that the structure is similar to a chain: the structure is only as strong as the weakest connection. What are the connections here? The cabinets themselves are secured to the fur down area (also called a "soffit" or "dropped ceiling"). This is a typical way to handle the space above wall cabinets where it is too high for comfortable usage. The soffit area is built of 2x4s at 16 inches on center, like a stud wall. Unlike a stud wall, this soffit or fur down uses cross braces (1x4s) between each pair of vertical 2x4s. The next major component is the blocking. It is the same depth as the joists; ultimately, the joists hold the weight of the cabinets and all the required supports.

Now, back to the "chain" aspect of this structure. Note that metal straps are used to secure the 2x4 soffit. In turn, blocking members should be secured to the joists with joist hangers. The cabinets hang on the soffit, the soffit hangs on the blocking members, and the blocking members hang on the joists. The cabinets should be bolted (not nailed or screwed) to the soffit.

Step 1: Opening a Sheetrock Ceiling

Remove the sheetrock where the cabinets will fit at the ceiling (and wall, if they touch the wall). Sheetrock is easy enough to remove, but messy. It helps to mark the outline of the sheetrock to be removed. Then chisel through the sheetrock along the drawn line. Remove the sheetrock with a hammer and/or crowbar.

Variation, Step 1, for Plaster Ceiling

If your ceiling is a plaster one, cut the ceiling with a special rotary blade in your power saw, or a reciprocating saw such as the Milwaukee Saws-All. Be prepared for a lot of debris; spread a protective cloth first.

Before cutting, locate the ceiling joists. Cut along the insides of the joists; do not cut any joists. When the opening between the joists has been made, you will be able to add the blocking.

Simpler alternative. Some people will prefer not to open up a plaster ceiling at all. In this case, blocking can be added between the joists if you have access to the joists from above. This is not the preferred method. Although the plaster that has been left in place will be hidden, it could crack if a lot of pressure is put on it.

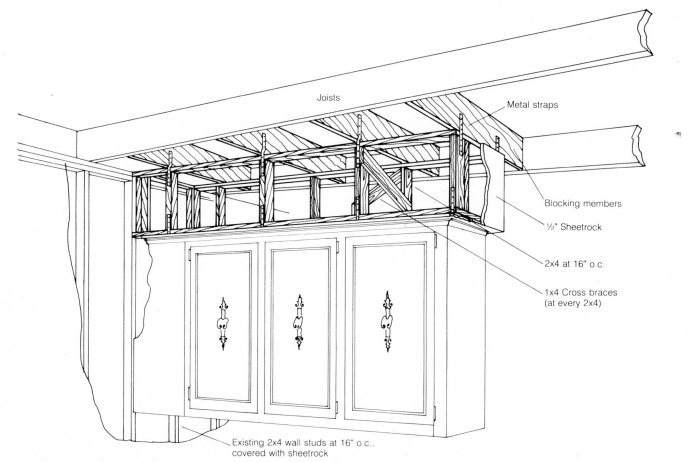

Joists

Metal straps

Blocking members

½" Sheetrock

2x4 at 16" o.c.

1x4 Cross braces (at every 2x4)

Existing 2x4 wall studs at 16" o.c., covered with sheetrock

Because ceiling-suspended cabinets require more structural framework than wall-mounted units, they are more trouble to build. They are, however, excellent for dividing a room without visually closing it off.

Step 2: Nailing the Blocking

Install the blocking between the joists, using joist hangers. The blocking members should be the same depth as the joists and should be spaced 16 inches on center, or less.

Step 3: Building the Soffit

Build the soffit just as you would a short stud wall. You can use nails (10d—4 per joint) to secure the studs at first. Then reinforce with metal straps. The metal straps should be attached at all the joints, as shown. Where possible, at least three strap holes should connect the two members in question. Use ¼-inch diameter, 1¼-inch flathead wood screws.

Step 4: Adding Cross Bracing

Nail the 1x4 cross bracing at every 2x4, with 8d nails (about three at each end of each piece of bracing).

Step 5: Building the Cabinets

Once you have completed the soffit, you can hang the cabinets. All of these cabinets — wall, ceiling-suspended, or base — are modular "boxes", in terms of building them. Note the typical cabinet module for the ceiling-suspended cabinets shown here. The outside end of ceiling cabinets are typically lined up over the edge of the base cabinet below. If you do not have an even number of modules, and you probably will not, then you usually want to place the extra space next to the wall.

In our example, the odd space is used for extra shelves. The doors are not shown on the illustration, so that you can see the shelf arrangement. You could use flush doors, lip doors, or lapping doors with these cabinets. Also, instead of using the odd space adjacent to the wall for shelves (some people leave them open), it could have been covered with sheetrock like the furred down area over the cabinet; most people, however, need to use space more efficiently — not just cover it up.

Materials and assembly. The exposed side of the cabinet calls for ¾-inch plywood and the side that joins the extra space calls for ⅜-inch plywood. The shelves and bottom of the cabinet are ½-inch plywood, fitted into dado joints (slots) ¼-inch deep. They reach all around the sides and back of the cabinet.

Around the sides and back of the cabinet, under the bottom, there is a 1-inch by ½-inch ledger for extra support of the bottom shelf. This ledger is secured to the sides with 1-inch by ⅛-inch diameter flathead wood screws at 4 inches on center, all around. A screw also is placed no more than 1 inch from all corners.

Build the cabinet in two phases: the typical module, and the odd-sized extra next to the wall. Secure the odd-sized cabinet to the ceiling first, then to the wall. Next, butt the typical module against the odd cabinet, securing the typical module at the ceiling, then at the side. Use 1-inch x ⅛-inch bolts at 8 inches on center, all around the inside edges of the cabinets. This will pull the cabinet sections tightly together. (Follow these same butted-attachment steps for base cabinets also.)

Step 6: Fastening the Cabinets

The cabinet is secured to the soffit with ¼-inch bolts that run through a 2x2 ledger around the inside of the cabinet, at the top. The 2x2 is connected to the cabinet sides and back with 2½-inch by ¼-inch bolts approximately an inch from the top edge of the cabinet. These

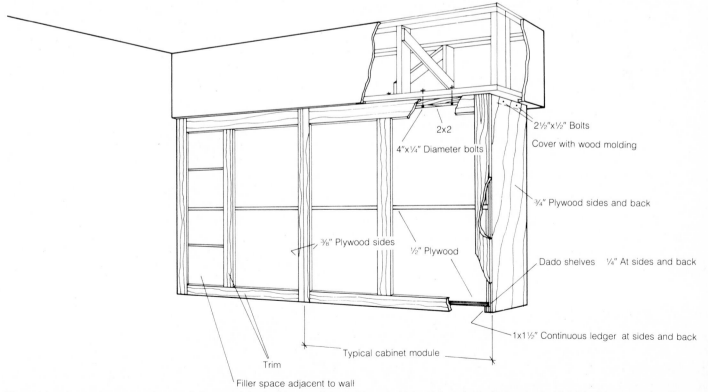

2x2

4"x¼" Diameter bolts

2½"x½" Bolts

Cover with wood molding

¾" Plywood sides and back

⅜" Plywood sides   ½" Plywood

Dado shelves   ¼" At sides and back

1x1½" Continuous ledger at sides and back

Trim

Typical cabinet module

Filler space adjacent to wall

The cabinet hangs from a continuous 2x2 around the inside top of the cabinet, held by ¼-inch bolts. Bolts also hold cabinet to supports above.

Project continued on next page

bolts may be hidden with wood molding later. The 2x2 is connected to the 2x4 supports within the furred down ceiling with 4-inch by ¼-inch bolts that run through the bottom 2x4. These bolts, and the horizontal ones above, are spaced 8 inches on center all around and should be staggered so that they do not hit each other. Do not fail to add bolts at approximately 4 inches from all corners.

At the wall, the cabinet may be secured with ⅛-inch toggle bolts or 2-inch, ⅛-inch diameter flathead wood screws, or similar lag bolts, or similar-sized nails (nails are the least favored). Secure the cabinet to the wall with one of the above fasteners at approximately 8 inches on center, all around the inside edge of the counter, if possible. The important thing is to hit wall studs or other solid backing.

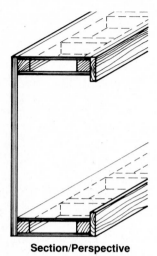

Section/Perspective

A section-through shows 2x2 framing — good for ceiling-suspended cabinets because it is sturdy enough to bolt to ceiling supports.

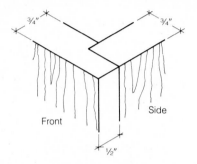

Typical corner joint

The front cabinet trim is notched to receive the cabinet side wall, which is ¾-inch plywood. Trim may vary; shown here are 1x3s.

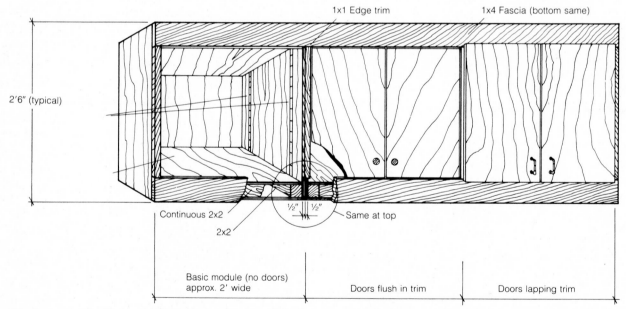

These cabinets are modular. Each one butts to the next. They can be built as separate units and then mounted, or positioned piece by piece to the wall.

Pots, pans and other cooking utensils can be hung from ceilings to create a relatively low-cost accent.

1 A whole wall can be converted to storage of bulky but attractive items, as pictured here. The wood-toned walls echo the wood countertop. This means of storage would not be efficient in a kitchen that is short of space in existing cabinets.
2 Many manufacturers offer hoods that match the appliances in the room and that can be incorporated into the cabinet above the cooking area.
3 This cook emphasizes convenience; she likes everything at hand. The materials and layout enhance the clean lines of the open design.
4 A countertop of slate tile looks beautiful and will withstand heat and years of heavy use.

3

4

1 Custom cabinets of European design can be set into unusual configurations to heighten the impact of layout and of materials.

2 A range hood can become a major decorative focus if chosen with care and imagination, or if purchased as part of the cabinet design. One of the most popular selling points for European cabinet installations is carefully planned integration of all their elements.

3 White painted oak cabinets and wood floor create an English, country, manor atmosphere. Note the open, vertical dividers for plate storage.

1

2

3

4

1 Extra counter space is always appreciated. This setup can be used as a desk or for food preparation. Instructions for the simple pull-out arrangement are given in Chapter 7.

2 The table folds back and tucks into its hiding place to look just like any other cabinet.

3 Ceiling fans are both decorative and effective in circulating air in the kitchen. For installation instructions, see page 148.

4 An old closet, pantry, or other alcove can house a desk with a plastic laminate top to match the counters in the rest of the kitchen.

5 A countertop can be expanded to make room for dining in a small kitchen. Surface material is laminate.

6 An island can be built from scratch (as in the example project in Chapter 7) or from stock cabinets. In either case, a custom look can be achieved with ceramic tile.

7 A counter can be just a layer of laminate over a wood base laid across several cabinets.

5

6

7

Even kitchens that have restricted space can have an area for eating in, as long as the furniture and location are carefully selected.

Real brick was used to create the base for a cooktop. The material is in keeping with the ancient Norwegian provincial style of the home.

1

2

3

4

5

6

1 This unusually shaped island obscures cook-top area even while snackers are seated.

2 The uninterrupted view of the outdoors was the primary factor in designing this kitchen in a rustic way using wood cabinets and a bleached pine floor.

3 A built-in spice rack, coffeemaker, concealed icemaker and downdraft ventilation unit are features of this island.

4 This island, built of stock cabinets with a projecting work surface, is set on casters and is movable. For building details, see Chapter 7.

5 Glass block defines space yet retains visual openness on this large center island accommodating both cooking and serving.

6 A small bar sink installed in an island at the end nearest the dining table allows anyone to get water without disturbing the cook.

7 This suspended hood helps define the separation between cooking and eating areas.

7

1

2

5

3

1 A glassed-in porch with a skylight serves the kitchen as a dining and entertainment area.
2 The cook can converse easily with guests in this kitchen/dining/family room setup.
3 A greenhouse-style addition can provide light, sun and space to a kitchen that faces it.
4 This view shows the kitchen addition from the outside. Construction details for this type of project are given in Chapter 5.
5 A sunroom addition to a kitchen on the north side of a house is a cool retreat; on the south side, it's effective for passive solar heat gain.

4

1 A bar sink can be placed beneath a pass-through with folding doors; the sink aids drink preparation, serving, and dining room cleanup.

2 A cantilevered counter is cheap, and easy to build, but requires adequate support for the extension (at least ⅔ of total length).

3 This shallow pantry utilizes folding doors because a swing-out door would block access and interrupt traffic flow through the area.

2

3

1 Instructions for building this slide-out spice cabinet and the stained glass panel cabinet doors are in Chapter 3.

2 This large, angled island houses the main sink and one of two dishwashers. With stools, it can provide seating for five.

3 Butcher block next to the stove may scorch, but a sanding and reoiling will restore the original surface.

4 Hanging light box over island provides task lighting and a recessed area for plants.

WALL-MOUNTED CABINET

CONSTRUCTION DETAILS

Notch the 2 vertical partitions between the vertical end pieces to fit between the cut 2x4 framing at the top and the 2x2 framing at the bottom. The framing runs all around at the top and bottom of the cabinet and fits against the vertical side pieces, which are not notched.

The bottom of the cabinet attaches to the top and bottom of the 2x2 framing members (use flathead wood screws throughout). The top of the cabinet is similar, except that 2x4s are cut for the framing. However, 2x2s could have been used; size varies according to need. This framing was used so the ceiling sheet of ¼-inch plywood would be ½ inch up from the 1x4 fascia board while leaving the top of the framing flush with the 1x4s. For a cabinet without a soffit, use a ½-inch plywood top as shown in dotted lines at the top. For easier dusting, the top fits flush with the framing members, over a small wooden ledger all around the inside of the framing.

CONSTRUCTION SEQUENCE

Step 1: Preparing the Wall

Find wall stud locations and pencil the location of the 2x4 wall blocking on your wall. Neatly chisel out the 4-inch strip of sheetrock for the blocking. Toenail 2x4 blocking to the studs with 10d nails, 4 at each end, 2 on each side.

Note the wood piece (½-inch plywood or ½x4-inch wood member) that attaches to the face of the 2x4 blocking. This is needed so the cabinet meets solid blocking. Cabinets should not be secured to walls by nailing or screwing through sheetrock, if it can be avoided.

Step 2: Assembling the Units

If you will use a soffit, build it now (shown on page 62). Build the cabinet directly to the wall, piece by piece; or, build the whole cabinet, lift it, and attach it to the wall. The first method is easier if you do not have a strong helper.

Secure the cabinet back to the blocking with ¼x3-inch lag bolts, through the 2x2 bottom framing. Fasten the cut 2x4 and the back sheet at the top into the blocking; you are installing the framing members and the back plywood sheet at the same time. Space lag bolts about 12 inches on center (o.c.), with a lag bolt 1 inch from each end of each framing member.

Cut the sides and partitions. Notch the partitions to fit framing at front and back. If you want the metal pilaster and clips recessed to be flush with the plywood surface, rout them now.

Now that the top 2x4 and bottom 2x2 are in place, secure the vertical sides to the framing at the wall, top and bottom. Use 3 countersunk screws (⅛-inch diameter, 2½ inches long), one on each face of the framing, driven from the framing into the vertical plywood sides. Predrill the holes. These screws should penetrate the framing at such an angle so that they come within ¼ inch of the outside surface of the plywood sides. Countersink the screws so they reach to just below the surface of the framing.

To install the 2 partitions place ⅛-inch diameter, 3-inch long screws from the bottom up through the framing into the plywood. Predrill holes and angle another screw, the same size, through the plywood into the vertical face of the 2x2 framing. Secure the plywood to top framing in the same way, except that you will come down through the framing. You will need longer screws; the screw should penetrate the plywood about 1 inch.

Butt the top and bottom framing at the *front* of the cabinet to the sides of the cabinet and fit into the top and bottom notches of the partitions.

At the bottom, place a ⅛-inch diameter, 3-inch long screw up through the framing member into the partition. Place another screw through the front face of the framing into the partition.

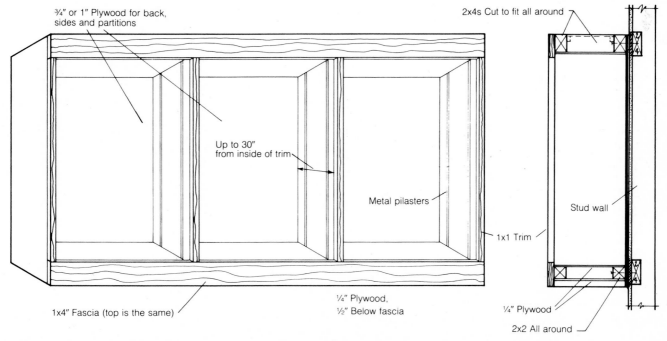

¾" or 1" Plywood for back, sides and partitions

2x4s Cut to fit all around

Up to 30" from inside of trim

Metal pilasters

Stud wall

1x1 Trim

1x4" Fascia (top is the same)

¼" Plywood, ½" Below fascia

¼" Plywood

2x2 All around

The structure for this open shelf system is not complicated, but the resulting, heavy unit requires adequate wall support.

Project continued on next page

Predrill screw holes. Secure the top framing the same way; you will need a longer screw.

During the assembly, make frequent checks with a spirit level. Use a carpenters' square to maintain square corners.

Your next step is to install the connecting framing at the cabinet ends, top and bottom, between the framing at the front and the framing at the wall. This consists of end pieces that complete the framing rectangle. Use 1/8-inch diameter, 2½-inch screws, 4 inches o.c., through the framing into the plywood sides. Angle a screw at each corner, in a predrilled hole, tying together the framing members.

Attach fascia boards to the framing members with 1/8-inch wood screws through the framing members' backs into the fascia boards, about 6 inches o.c. The screws reach to 1/4 inch from the surface of the fascia boards. Predrill for the screws. Wherever possible, add screws, nails and brads about 1 inch from the ends of joining members.

Install the horizontal 1/4-inch plywood, using 1-inch finishing nails about 4 inches o.c., driven through the plywood into the framing. Countersink the nails to within 1/4 inch of the plywood surface.

Step 3: Finishing Steps

If you have a soffit, run screws up through the top framing into solid framing within the soffit. If you do not have a soffit, place a ledger within the top framing and brad 1/4-inch plywood sheet in place.

Next, install the 1x1 trim pieces over the vertical plywood edges, using a wood glue. Cut and install the shelves. Fill any nail holes with wood filler, and finish as desired.

The end of the open shelf could be finished off in any of several ways — from a simple finished sheet of wood to this facing that provides additional storage for small items.

Where dust is not a problem, open shelves show off the items you wish to store. Metal pilasters and clips allow adjustable shelf spacing.

BUILDING STANDARD CABINETRY

TYPICAL WALL-HUNG CABINET

The standard wall-hung cabinet module in our example is secured to a soffit and to the wall.

Step 1: Adding a Soffit

First, build the soffit, as shown, if you do not have one. The 2x4 members within the soffit are 16 inches on center, secured with 5 to 10d nails at the joints. Wait until the cabinet is in place before you install the sheetrock or other finishing material over the soffit.

Step 2: Assembling the Cabinet

Cut cabinet sides, back, and bottom from ⅜- or ½-inch plywood. Use ⅛-inch wood screws, predrilled and countersunk at about 4 inches on center along the edges.

If you wish to install one shelf in the vertical center in dado joints as shown, rout the dado joints before assembling the plywood, then install the shelf. You may choose to use metal pilasters and clips, as discussed in the standard base cabinet and module.

Next, install the front 1x2s with butt and rabbet joints. Use wood glue and brads.

Note the small, continuous ledger under the bottom of the cabinet. The size of this member will vary according to your inside cabinet height. The ledger is typically a 1x1 inch member or close to that dimension. At the top of the cabinet, around the inside, place 1x2s continuously, as shown. Install the metal angles as shown.

Step 3: Preparing the Wall

If you wish additional blocking for extra support, pencil off the area on the wall where the cabinets will fit. If sheetrock or similar material is in place, chisel it out enough to provide solid wood blocking.

Step 4: Attaching the Cabinet

Add the cabinet top (½ inch plywood), using wood screws through the metal angles. It is a good precautionary mea-sure to angle predrilled wood screws through the top framing into the plywood top. Then screw the top to the soffit, running the screws into the 2x4 soffit members. The number of screws is a matter of judgment, but you need approximately one ⅛-inch diameter 1½-inch long screw 4 inches on center all along the 2x4 soffit members. You need to get close, within an inch or so, to the edge of the cabinet, all around. This means you may have to add additional blocking within the soffit (measure the cabinet top against the soffit bottom and add any blocking you need before you hang the cabinet).

Step 5: Finishing the Job

Install the sheetrock on the soffit. Install the cabinet doors and finish the cabinets. Doors are discussed separately, below.

TYPICAL BASE CABINET

The base cabinet in our example is a typical manufacturer's module. There

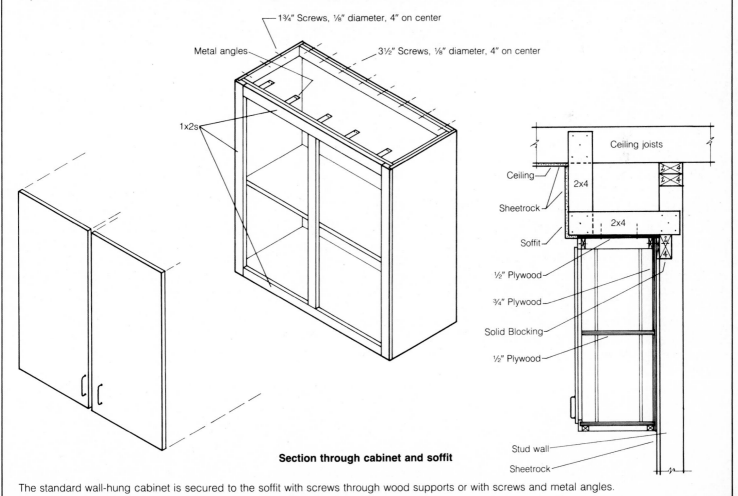

Section through cabinet and soffit

The standard wall-hung cabinet is secured to the soffit with screws through wood supports or with screws and metal angles.

Project continued on next page

is no truly standard base or wall cabinets, as each manufacturer varies somewhat in material use, joinery, and dimensions. The dimensions shown are: cabinet depth 2'0"; height 3'0"; module width 2'5½". The toe space is 4 inches high, and 3 inches deep.

The framing members at the front are 1x2s (¾ inch by 1½ inch members). The plywood sides and back are ⅜ or ½ inch thick. The base under the plywood floor is a simply 2x4 frame all around with 2x4 cross members at 16 inches on center.

If you are building a kitchen from scratch, plan the dimensions of the cabinets around the appliances and equipment you intend to use. Install the wall cabinets before you build the base cabinets, so the base cabinets will not be in your way.

Step 1: Building the Unit
To construct the base cabinet module in the example, first build the 2x4 base. Then install the plywood sides and back (½ inch plywood is suggested). Typically, there is one shelf located in the center of the space below the drawer. The shelf may be glued into dado joints in the plywood sides and back and, if so, you should cut the dado joints before you assemble the sides and back. A more versatile shelf arrangement may be had by installing metal pilasters and clips to vary the number of shelves and vertical spacing of shelves. Use ⅛-inch diameter, 1-inch long flathead wood screws predrilled and countersunk at approximately 4 inches on center.

Install the 1x2s; join them as shown in the illustration, with wood glue and brads. Install the metal corner braces for reinforcement and the metal angles for support of the countertop.

Step 2: Adding the Doors
The easiest door to install simply laps over the edge of the framing; unless you have a strong preference for one of the other door styles, this is probably the best for you. Additional door styles are shown (see below for construction). Do not install the doors until the wall cabinets and countertops are in place; otherwise, they may be scratched or damaged.

Step 3: Installing the Unit
When the module is complete, push it into the desired position and secure it to the wall (assuming it is not freestanding) and floor with wood screws. If the cabinet is not level, use wood shims to level it before you install the baseboard. Shims are small pieces of wood shaped like ax heads. Tap them under the bottom of the cabinets, check for level with a spirit level, and secure the shims with brads nailed through the shim to the floor. Additional modules butt each other and secure to each other from inside, with wood screws.

Step 4: Finishing the Job
The baseboard, wood or vinyl, is installed last. Typical baseboards are 4 inches high and should match other baseboards in the house, continuing around the base cabinets, fitting into the toe space and against the cabinet. Wood baseboards are usually nailed with finishing nails and vinyl baseboards are glued.

STANDARD CABINET DOORS
The door that will be easiest for you to install is called an overlay door. This door is approximately one inch bigger all around than the opening it covers; it simply laps or "overlays" the opening.

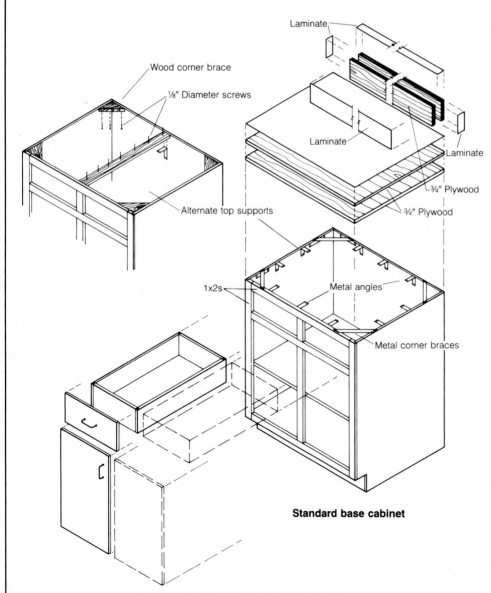

Wood corner brace
⅛" Diameter screws
Alternate top supports
Laminate
Laminate
Laminate
¾" Plywood
¾" Plywood
1x2s
Metal angles
Metal corner braces

Standard base cabinet

The countertop may be secured to a standard base cabinet with metal angles and screws or with wood supports and screws. Either way works well and is relatively easy to remove.

For other door styles, see pg. 87.

Cut the doors from ½ inch plywood. Concealed hinges are suggested for the overlay door. To install concealed hinges, first pencil the location of the hinges on one door, about two inches from the top and bottom. The illustration shows the hinges in place.

Install the hinges on the door. Then attach the door to the cabinet. Then rout the remaining doors and install the hinges. Sand and finish to suit.

STANDARD CABINET DRAWERS
Step 1: Planning the Drawer
The drawers discussed here are typical for many manufacturer-base cabinets. These drawers have routed sides that act as guides for guide strips mounted within the cabinet. Drawers built in this manner will last many years under typical family usage. However, you may wish to install "gliding" hardware (metal channels with nylon rollers), which is discussed in the text for "A Slide-out Counter" and "A Sliding Cabinet Tray." If you do install the gliding hardware, buy the hardware first before building the cabinets.

Step 2: Building the Drawer
To build the drawer, saw the sides and bottom from ½ inch plywood. Rout the sides of the drawer. Rout or cut the rabbet joints for the corner of the drawer. Cut the ½-inch square reinforcement members for the bottom of the drawer. Assemble as shown.

Step 3: Preparing the Cabinet
Cut the drawer guides and try them for size in the routed drawer slots before you install the guides in the cabinet. Then install the guide strips in the cabinet as shown, but use only a screw at the front and back to secure the guide strips. Slide the drawer in. If there are no adjustments, take out the drawer and install the remainder of the screws in the drawer guide strips. Add the overlay drawer front; other drawer front types are shown.

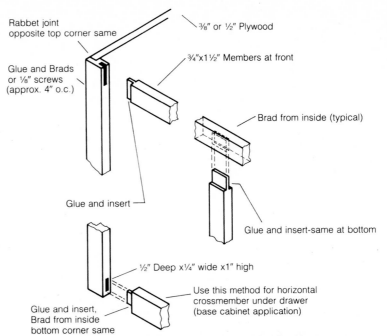

Typical framing joinery at front of base and wall cabinets

The joinery can be formed with a router and a saw. The connections are assembled by applying glue where the parts join, then strengthening the connections with brads or wood screws.

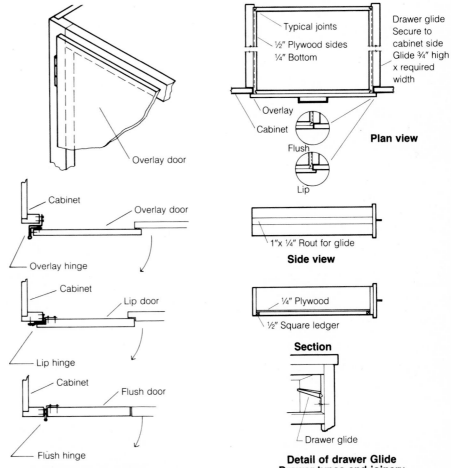

Wall and base cabinets Door and hinge details

There are three popular types of cabinet hinges: the overlay door, the lip door, and the flush hinge.

Detail of drawer Glide Drawer types and joinery

Drawer types have facings corresponding to the basic door types: overlay, lip, and flush. Wood glides are the most typical and are the cheapest solution, but metal slides are recommended.

A SLIDING CABINET TRAY

Because base cabinets are usually 24 inches deep, it is often difficult to reach items stored near the back, especially on the lower shelf. One way to aid the use of and access to the back of the cabinet is to install a slide-out shelf.

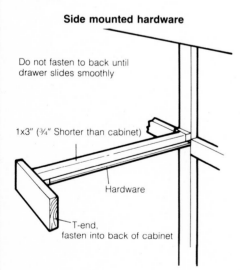

This sliding shelf substitutes for the traditional interior cabinet shelf, allowing access to items at the back.

Side mounted hardware

The shelf is actually a very shallow drawer. The low lip provides a finger grip at the front and the sides hold items in place when the shelf slides out. The shelf moves on side-mounted drawer hardware.

STEP 1: CUTTING THE PIECES
Use ¼ inch plywood or hardboard for the bottom of the shelf. Use 1x4 stock for the back and sides and 1x3 stock for the front. Cut the plywood 1 inch narrower and 1 inch shorter than the interior opening. Cut the side pieces the same length as the depth of the cabinet interior.

Cut ¾ inch long by ⅜ inch deep rabbets on each end of the side pieces.

Hardware preparation

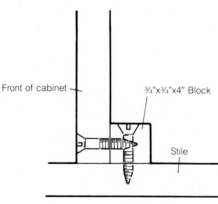

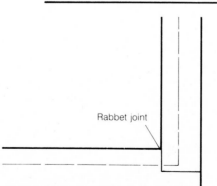

A vertical rabbet in one end of each side piece holds adjoining ends. The bottom shelf rests in horizontal dados.

Cut the front and back pieces ¾ inch shorter than the width of the opening. Cut ¼x¼ inch dadoes ½ inch from the bottom of the front, back and side pieces.

STEP 2: ASSEMBLING THE UNIT
Nail the back and side pieces together with 4d box nails. Slip the plywood shelf into the dadoes to check fit. Remove the shelf and make any needed adjustments; place a thin line of wood glue in the dadoes and reinstall the shelf. Fit the front piece on the unit and nail in place. Allow the glue to dry before installing in the cabinet.

STEP 3: INSTALLING THE HARDWARE
The mounting hardware attaches to the sides of the drawer/shelf. You must provide mounting bars on the sides of the opening to accept the tracks.

Cut 1x3 stock to ¾ inches shorter than the depth of the cabinet. Attach a 4-inch long piece of 1x3 to create a T at one end and attach a ¾x¾ piece of 1x3 stock to create an L at the other end. This makes a secure mounting unit for one side of the cabinet. Make an identical T/L for the other side of the cabinet. If your cabinet has closed sides, you can provide the mounting track support by nailing the 1x3 stock into the cabinet sides.

To install the T/L units, attach the L block to the stile on one side of the cabinet opening. Drive wood screws through the block into the stile. Attach the T section to the back wall. Drive nails through pilot holes to hold the T in place until the hardware has been mounted and the fit and sliding ease of the drawer/shelf has been tested. Test the shelf and remove. Adjust as needed and permanently mount the T end with wood screws.

STAINED GLASS INSERT AND RAISED PANEL DOORS

Making a cabinet door that will accept stained glass (or regular glass) inserts can be done in a variety of ways. The simplest is to construct a door much like the outside frame of a raised panel door, leaving out the center panel and substituting a piece of glass. (See illustrations for how to create a raised panel door.) This consists of taking 4 pieces of wood — approximately 1½ inch x 2½ inches — and making up the outside size of the door. The door can either lay on top of the cabinet frame or be rabbeted into the frame. Hold the frame pieces together either by a mortise and tenon joint or by a dowel. Since mortise and tenon joints require special cutters, we suggest a dowel placed at each of the 4 joints in the frame of the door.

Before assembling the door itself, make the inside grooves for the glass inserts. The grooves should accommodate at least a ¼-inch thickness; this depth varies according to your insert.

The glass is most often held in the frame with small flexible plastic clips

that screw into the frame with a small tip, which overlaps the glass and holds it in place. Enough of these must be used to hold it securely — at least 2 on each side of the typical door and 2 on top and bottom. Another method uses tiny pieces of quarter round molding — about ¼-inch x ¼-inch. If these are used, the recess must be about ½-inch deep so that the glass and molding will not project beyond the back of the door.

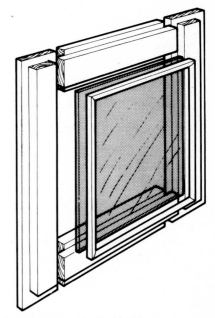

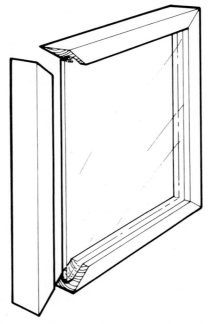

The frame shown for this recessed panel door calls for ¾-inch stock, grooved ¼x ⅜ inch to hold a ¼-inch panel. Use glue, with brads at corners, to hold the panel.

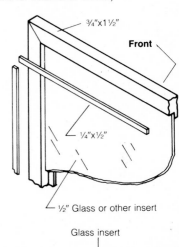

Glass inserts are held with either quarter-round molding and brads or with plastic clips, 2 to each side. Rabbet the door frame ¾ inch at the outside edge. Rabbet the inside ¼x ⅜ inch to receive the inset and molding. (See drawings below for additional views.)

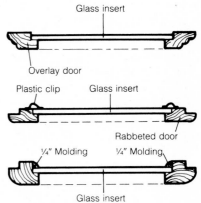

¾"x1½"

Front

¼"x½"

½" Glass or other insert

Glass insert

Overlay door

Plastic clip   Glass insert

Rabbeted door

¼" Molding   ¼" Molding

Glass insert

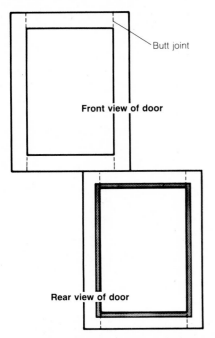

Butt joint

Front view of door

Rear view of door

The door frame is just four butted pieces of wood, into which a thinner insert can be set.

Shown is the frame for the door with stained glass inserts, which is shown on page 80.

SLIDE-OUT SPICE RACK

A slide-out spice rack is basically a drawer installed on its side. Before you build the "drawer", however, consider how you will use the rack. Spices are most conveniently stored on narrow shelves with a depth of 6 inches or less. This is what we show in the example. You may wish to vary that dimension to suit your particular storage needs. Use metal clips and pilasters for the most versatile shelf arrangement. Use metal drawer hardware because this allows for a variety of rack widths and loads. Metal slides are by far the smoothest-operating methods for hanging your rack.

Step 1: Designing the Unit and Choosing Drawer Hardware

After you have determined the uses for the slide-out unit, draw up your plans, and, if possible, determine the probable load of the unit. Then decide on the metal slides you need. Consider the weight when you select the drawer hardware slides; this hardware is usually designed for load capacities of 30, 50, 75, 100, and 150 pounds per pair of slides. Do not over-design or under-design the slides for your rack.

You will have to build the drawer unit to allow for the clearance needed for the hardware. This is usually between one-half and one inch. Your rack will be mounted on the side, so all of the drawer hardware will be mounted on the bottom of the rack. Be sure you purchase hardware suitable for this type of installation. However, depending upon the size of your rack and the type of mounting hardware, you may be able to mount one slide on the bottom and the other one the top.

Step 2: Building the Unit

Construct a drawer unit to fit the framing you have built in the cabinet for the rack, allowing clearances for the hardware. Follow the directions given in the Standard Cabinet project for building the drawer. You may be able to buy a drawer front to match manufactured units. Test fit the pieces before assembly and mark locations for pilasters on the front and back pieces. Rout pilaster recesses. Assemble unit and install pilasters. Cut shelves to fit.

Step 3: Installing the Unit

Attach drawer hardware to the rack unit and to the cabinet. You may have to add a mounting strip to the cabinet. Test fit before installing all the mounting screws in the hardware slides. Remove the unit.

Step 4: Finishing the Unit.

Finish the face and interior of the rack to match your cabinets. Use a sturdy pull handle on the face.

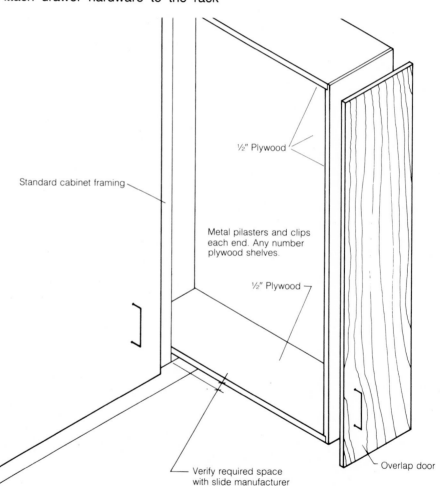

Standard cabinet framing

½" Plywood

Metal pilasters and clips each end. Any number plywood shelves.

½" Plywood

Verify required space with slide manufacturer

Overlap door

Slide out spice rack

The slide-out spice rack utilizes the same construction techniques outlined for standard cabinets. Metal drawer slides are suggested and you should read the slide manufacturer's requirements before you size the spice rack. (For photograph, see pg. 80.)

4
SIMPLE WALL AND CEILING STORAGE

The easiest way to provide storage at low cost and effort is to use open shelves. Less material usually is required for this type of shelving, and construction can be as simple as a shallow box (as shown on this page) to a pivoting cabinet door with shelves fixed to the inside (see next page). Other storage locations for which projects are offered in this chapter include: ceiling beams from which pots and pans can be suspended; pot racks for walls or ceilings; and, recessed dispensers that hold paper goods, or accessories such as a toaster.

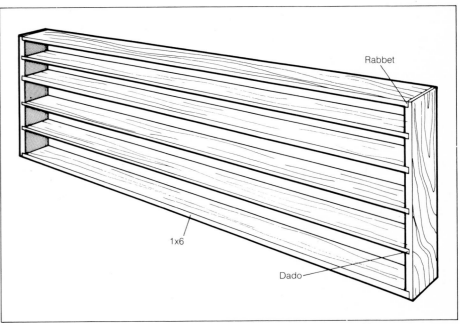

An open shelf can be a frame built of 1x6, open at the back, with 1x6s as shelves. The example shows shelves in dados (grooves), but pilasters also could be used.

A free-standing, open-shelved unit for display, or storage of awkwardly sized items, can be built to fit nearly any space.

These are some of the simplest shelves to install, using painted ½-inch plywood supported by thin metal angles, over which wallpaper has been applied.

PIVOTING SHELF

You can make a pivoting open shelf as shown in the illustrations. The shelves are fixed to the back of flush base or flush wall cabinet doors, which pivot around, bringing frequently used items quickly to hand.

The unit pivots on lengths of metal dowel set into blocks of wood at the top and bottom center of the face. A nylon or similar washer prevents wear. The metal dowel fits into blocking secured to the cabinet framing to complete the installation.

Step 1: Cutting the Pieces

Measure the space for the pivoting unit. Allow 1/8 inch all around for clearance and cut the flush door unit to fit. Bevel edges to allow door to turn in the opening. Cut dadoes to accept shelves as shown. Cut and install shelves as shown. Finish as required to match cabinets.

Step 2: Installing New Framing

Next, install a framing member at the bottom for the bottom dowel to fit into. This framing member can be a short length of 2x4, or a lesser member, about 6 inches long, secured to the existing cabinet framing with wood screws. Drill the dowel hole before you install the 2x4. The dowel can be approximately 1/4 inch in diameter and the hole about 5/16 inch deep.

Prepare the top 2x4 framing member, but do not install it yet.

Step 3: Installing the Shelf Unit

Lift the pivoting shelves onto the bottom dowel. Have a helper hold the shelves in place while you place the top 2x4 and dowel in the proper position. Then secure the 2x4 to the existing framing with wood screws driven through predrilled holes.

Use a magnetic catch on the lower framing and bottom shelf to hold door in place.

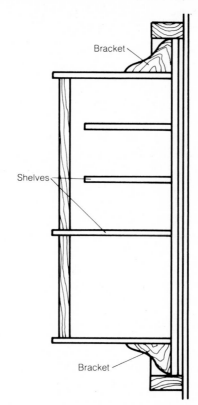

This set of shelves fastens to the inside of a cabinet door. The door edges are beveled so that the entire unit pivots for access to the shelves.

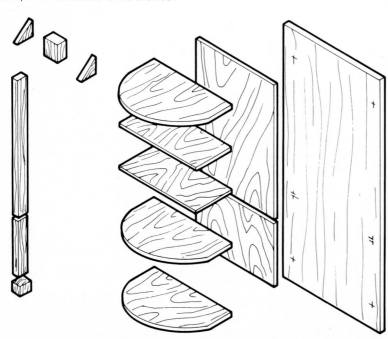

Shelf sizes depend on door dimensions. Cut the pieces from a sheet of plywood.

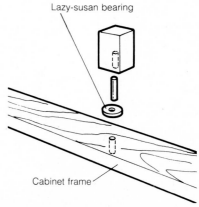

For easy pivoting, use a dowel and washer to connect vertical members and cabinet door to the top and bottom of the cabinet frame.

CREATING A BEAMED CEILING

New beams for ceiling can be made from new or old wood. Simulated ceiling beams offer advantages because they need less support and are easier to install than genuine beams. Boxed beams may also be built and then painted. If your kitchen ceiling is vaulted, use scaffolding to provide a safe and secure place to stand while nailing beam boards.

PLACEMENT OF CEILING BEAMS

Work out a scale drawing of the ceiling, taking into account any fixed soffits, pipe chases or light fixtures. If you want half beams at each side of the ceiling, deduct the amount of space they will take from the total distance. Divide the ceiling by the distance between each beam. Average spacing is often 36 inches, but can be as close as 30 inches or as far apart as 48 inches.

INSTALLATION TECHNIQUES
Method 1: Hollow, Lightweight Beams

These can be made either of wood or styrofoam. Use coated nails or screws to fasten a 1x2 strip (or whatever size fills the recess in the beams) to the ceiling. When the strips run perpendicular to the joists, nail directly into the joists. If the strips are to run parallel to the joists, you must use Molly bolts or wall anchors to fasten the beams to the ceiling, but do not place them under a joist.

Cut the beam to length. Lay a bead of panel adhesive along each side, far enough in so it will not squeeze out onto the ceiling when you place the beams. A finishing nail tacked through the sides of the beam into the strip will help hold the beam in place until the adhesive sets up.

Method 2: Lightweight Plastic Beams

You can install lightweight plastic beams with panel adhesive. Use upright support rods, wedged between the beam and the floor, to hold the beam in place until the adhesive sets up.

Method 3: Heavy Wood Beams

These are supported with 12-inch machine bolts. Drill a ½-inch hole through the beam and through a 2x6 laid across the joists. Secure the machine bolt with a washer and nut.

Method 4: False Beams

Beams are built around a 2x4 nailed to the ceiling with 16d common nails or Molly bolts. Drive the nails approximately every 8 inches. If the beam runs perpendicular to the joists, drive two nails into each joist.

Using 6d finishing nails, nail 1-inch stock finishing lumber onto the sides of 2x4 nailer. The width of the side pieces may be whatever you wish. Nail a 1x4 bottom of finishing lumber between the side pieces, using 4d finishing nails. A good flush fit will be very difficult; if necessary, set the bottom board about ½ inch in from the edges of the side pieces.

If desired, add quarter-round trim where the sides of the beam meet the ceiling. Nail the molding into the side pieces with 2d finishing nails driven at a slight angle. Stain or paint the beams as desired. The size of the beam can be varied by changing the width of the 2-inch stock nailer and the bottom piece of 1-inch stock.

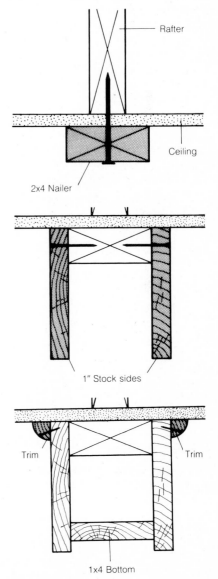

Attach the nailer to the joist; frame the beam with stock lumber. A recessed bottom filler is easier to install than a flush bottom.

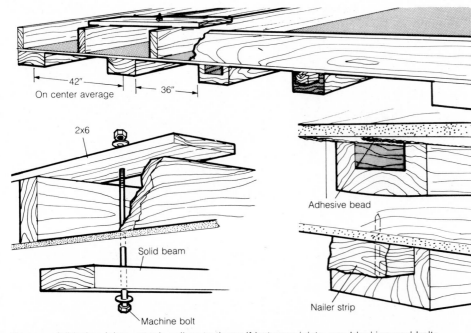

If beams fall below joists, attach nailers to them; if between joists, use blocking and bolts.

INSTALLING BUILT-IN ACCESSORIES

RECESSED PAPER GOODS DISPENSER

Many attractive kitchens look cluttered or are inconvenient because items are either left on the counter or repeatedly taken out of a drawer and put back. There are wall-mounted dispensers for wax paper, foil and plastic wrap; however, these still add a cluttered look.

Recessed dispensers provide both quick access and a neat look. These stainless steel units provide reachable storage for towels or wax paper and foil. A large unit provides recessed storage for all three. The units fit between the studs on an interior wall.

Installing the Unit

Locate the studs at the position for the recessed dispenser. Determine the most convenient height for the bottom edge of the dispenser. Mark this with a level line on the wall. To install a towel dispenser or a waxpaper/foil dispenser, measure up 8⅜ inches and then make another level mark. A combination dispenser for all three items requires an opening 14⅜ inches high. All units require an opening that is exactly 14⅜ inches wide, which is the space between the studs. Mark the vertical lines between the previously marked horizontal lines.

Use a drill to make starter holes just inside the corner marks. Use a sabre saw or keyhole saw to cut out the opening.

The dispenser slips into the appropriate opening snugly. The frame, integral with the dispenser, overlaps the opening. Two screws come with the dispenser and fit a hole on each side face of the unit. Drill pilot holes in the stud and drive screws into place to hold the unit securely.

HIDDEN TOASTER

One manufacturer of kitchen appliances makes a toaster that builds into a wall. It is a four-slice model that requires its own circuit because it pulls 1600 watts when all four slice sections are in use.

The opening for the toaster is 14½ inches wide, the space available between studs installed 16 inches on center. The opening is 8⅜ inches high.

The toaster is, however, deeper than the standard 3½-inch space from one interior wall to another, so you must "borrow" ³⁄₁₆ths of an inch from the other side of the wall. If the other side is paneling, you may be able to mark the inside, remove the paneling and rout this small amount from the panel. If you have wallboard, you may try the same thing, or simply replace that panel with a thinner sheet of wallboard. Instructions come with the unit.

To help you keep accessories from cluttering up the countertop, Modern Maid offers a toaster that can be recessed into the wall and slides out for use.

Paper goods can be stored in a metal-lined recessed dispenser, such as this one by Keystone Marchand. Other sizes also are available.

You can build a utensil hanger in nearly any shape you like, and of many materials. But you should give some consideration to the shape and material that will work best in your kitchen. For example, if you wanted a utensil hanger over a rectangular work island with a Jenn-Air Grill-Range, a rectangular shape would work better with the island than a round one, and a metal hanger is safer above a heat source than a wooden hanger.

The round utensil hanger shown in our example is a ¼-inch steel band with ¼-inch hanger hooks welded on the sides, as shown. Any diameter from one foot to two feet (or even a little more) would work. The hooks should be spaced according to the size of the utensils you will hang, typically 4 to 6 inches apart.

Inside the round metal hanger, four equally spaced metal eyes are welded to the sides. Chain, cable, or wire is secured to the metal eyes as shown. The chains, or other support lines, are connected at the center with a metal ring about one inch in diameter. Then the support line continues up as far as you need, to connect with a swivel-eye. The swivel-eye is connected to an eye-bolt, as shown.

These hanging lines are typical for the four example utensil hangers shown. It is recommended that you run the ¼ inch eye-bolt through solid backing through the ceiling and bolt it in place; 2x4 blocking is adequate.

The other metal utensil hanger is rectangular in shape. Typical dimensions are approximately one foot wide and three feet long.

The remaining two examples are of wood. One is simply a length of 2 inch diameter wood dowel with hanging hooks secured underneath. The other

wood example is an octagon approximately one foot to 18 inches from face to face. It is built of 1x3s. The joints are

formed as shown and glued together; small, countersunk wood screws are suggested at the joints.

Pots and pans attach to this wooden grid by means of a dowel or pipe along the outside — hooks could be substituted for the dowel.

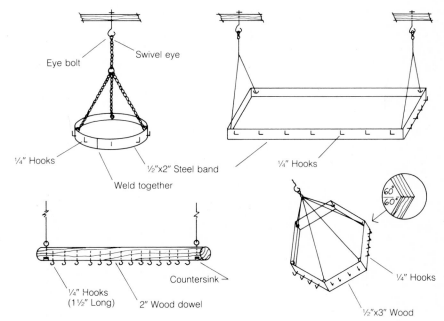

The top two example racks are of metal; the bottom two are of wood. The straight wood dowel at left can attach to the wall or be hung from the ceiling.

CHAPTER 5: ATTACHED WALL GREENHOUSES

The greenhouse floor in our example is a 4-inch concrete slab resting on a 10-inch wide concrete foundation wall. The foundation wall, in turn, rests on a 16-inch wide by 12-inch deep concrete footing. The foundation wall is keyed into the footing. The depth of the foundation wall depends upon local frost conditions; the top of the footing should be below the local frost line. Check with your local building department for this dimension.

With the help of the chart, determine the dimensions of your greenhouse slab (A and B in the illustration).

STEP 1: KEYING THE FOOTING
Dig trenches for and pour the footings forming a key in the top of the footings. The key is approximately 2 inches wide at the top and 1½ inches wide at the bottom. The key should be about 2 inches deep and can be formed with wood cut from a 2x4. Grease the wood key form before you press it into the footing (See Illus. 3).

STEP 2: POURING THE FOUNDATION
Allow the footing to set completely. Then build formwork and pour the foundation wall. (See Illus. 5.)

Step 3: Preparing the Floor Slab
Allow the foundation wall to set completely. Install 4 inches of gravel at a level such that when you pour the floor slab, the top of the greenhouse slab will be where you want it. The top of the greenhouse floor slab may be level with your house floor, or you may want to drop the greenhouse slab down a little (but not more than a comfortable step — 6¾ inch maximum). Obtaining the level you want will entail either removing some soil or building up some soil (be sure to compact according to the building department specifications) before you pour the slab.

When you have the gravel in place, cover it with Visqueen or a similar vapor barrier, tucking the plastic down several inches below the top of the foundation wall.

Next, install 6x6 No. 10 wire mesh over the vapor barrier, raising it about an inch and a half with small stones.

The mesh should go out to approximately 1½ inches from where the slab will be (slab is flush with face of foundation wall).

Pour the slab, finish smooth or rough as you choose, and let it set completely. Depending on weather, the slab will take about a week to set.

Foundations require hard physical work and they are important. If you do not have experience with concrete foundation, and you do not have time to learn, you may want to subcontract the foundation to a small general contractor or a concrete contractor specializing in foundation work.

4/12 ROOF SLOPE

A	B	C	D
11′ 4¾″ 16′ 2¾″ 12′ 8½″ }	7′ 9⁹⁄₁₆″	2′ 5¾″	9′ 1⅞″
12′ 10¼″ 19′ 1¾″ 16′ 4¼″ }	7′ 9⁹⁄₁₆″	2′ 5¾″	9′ 1⅞″
13′ 1¾″ 16′ 3½″ 19′ 5¼″ }	7′ 9⁹⁄₁₆″	2′ 5¾″	9′ 1⅞″

5/12 ROOF SLOPE

A	B	C	D
11′ 4¾″ 16′ 2¾″ 12′ 8½″ }	7′ 7³⁄₁₆″	3′ 0³⁄₁₆″	9′ 8⁵⁄₁₆″
12′ 10¼″ 19′ 1¾″ 16′ 4¼″ }	7′ 7³⁄₁₆″	3′ 0³⁄₁₆″	9′ 8⁵⁄₁₆″
13′ 1¾″ 16′ 3½″ 19′ 5¼″ }	7′ 7³⁄₁₆″	3′ 0³⁄₁₆″	9′ 8⁵⁄₁₆″

6/12 ROOF SLOPE

A	B	C	D
11′ 4¾″ 16′ 2¾″ 12′ 8½″ }	7′ 4½″	3′ 6⅛″	10′ 2¼″
12′ 10¼″ 19′ 1¾″ 16′ 4¼″ }	7′ 7½″	3′ 6⅛″	10′ 2¼″
13′ 1¾″ 16′ 3½″ 19′ 5¼″ }	7′ 4½″	3′ 6⅛″	10′ 2¼″

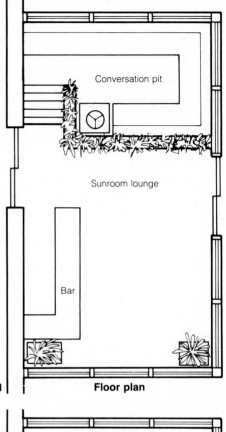

Floor plan 1

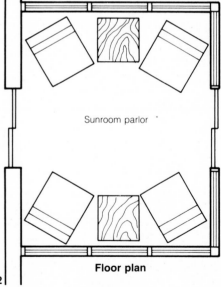

Floor plan 2

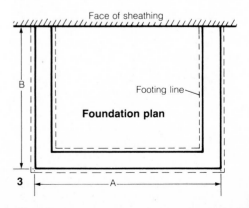

Foundation plan 3

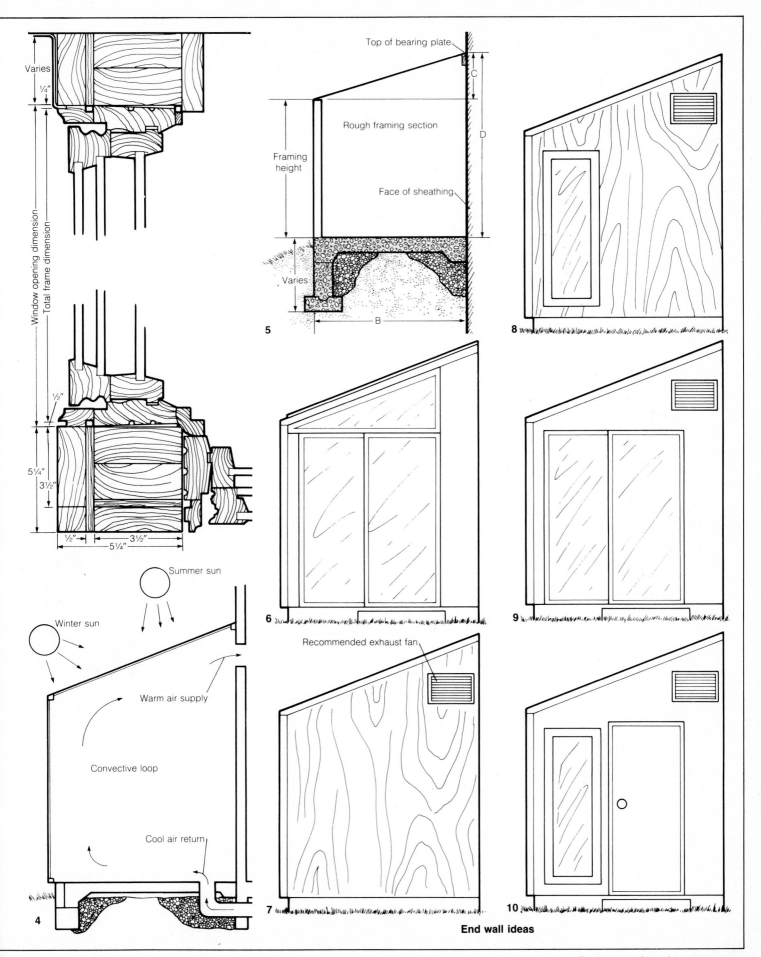

Varies

¼"

Window opening dimension

Total frame dimension

½"

5¼"
3½"

½"   3½"
5¼"

Summer sun

Winter sun

Warm air supply

Convective loop

Cool air return

4

Top of bearing plate

C

Rough framing section

D

Framing height

Face of sheathing

Varies

B

5

6

Recommended exhaust fan

7

8

9

10

End wall ideas

Project continued on next page

STEP 4: INSTALLING FRAMING

First install the rough framing. Before you begin, study Illus. 12, 13 and Illus. 19 through 28, noting how the greenhouse components relate to the rough framing.

First, install a 2x4 base plate at the sides and at the front, omitting the 2x4 where the doors exist at the front (see Illus. 29). The base 2x4 can be installed with a rental nail gun: space the steel studs (nails) according to your local building code.

Now, fill in the void above the 2x4 base plate with solid wood blocking until the appropriate sill height is reached (see the sill detail in Illus. 12).

Secure the vertical 2x4s to the wall using 10d nails or comparably sized screws at about 6 inches on center vertically (see Illus. 12 and 24). Stagger the nails or screws from one side of the 2x4s to the other. These vertical mem-

bers must be secured to solid backing so, unless you are lucky and there is a wall stud right behind the vertical 2x4s, you will have to remove enough siding to place solid blocking in the wall, as in Illus. 25.

Study the rough framing in Illus. 23, which shows the construction of the horizontal ledge above the vertical framing at the wall, which you just installed. Secure this horizontal member as you did the vertical members at the wall, being sure there is solid backing behind the horizontal member and providing the backing where it is missing (use 2x4s).

Now cut two vertical 2x4s with trim pieces cut to fit flush to adjoining components. First, refer to Illus. 12 and 27. Then secure the vertical 2x4s together with 10d nails at approximately 8 inches on center on each side. Toenail this vertical member at the sill with two

10d nails on all four sides. Use a 6-foot length of 2x4 to hold the vertical member in place by nailing the 2x4 to the vertical member and wedging the length of 2x4 into the ground. Secure the 2x4 at the ground with a 2x2 stake

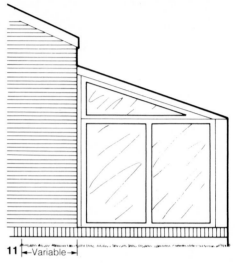

11 ← Variable →

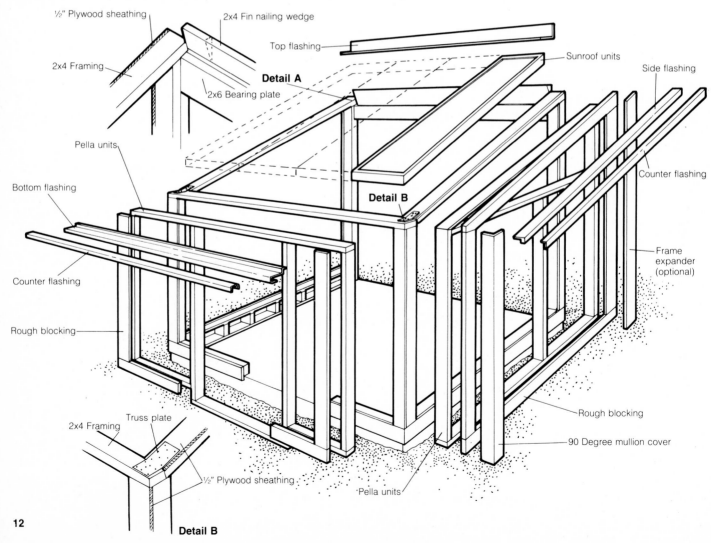

12

Detail B

about one foot long. Pound the stake into the ground next to the temporary support, so that it will not slip.

Install the slanting member across the top of the vertical member that you just built to the horizontal member at the wall. Use several 10d nails at each end.

Build the opposite side wall framing just like the side wall framing discussed above. Then install the horizontal member that connects the vertical corner members at the front (door) wall. This is a 2x4 and it must be angled as shown in Illus. 12 Detail B and Illus. 20. A metal truss plate may be used. If you do not use the truss plate, nail the front horizontal member to the vertical member with five 10d nails. Then toenail the slanting member with three 10d nails at the top and three underneath.

Next, nail the two intermediate members shown in Illus. 19 and 20. These members are 2x4s and should be secured together similarly to the vertical members discussed, then toenailed at the front and at the wall with 10d nails similarly to the procedure just discussed for the corners.

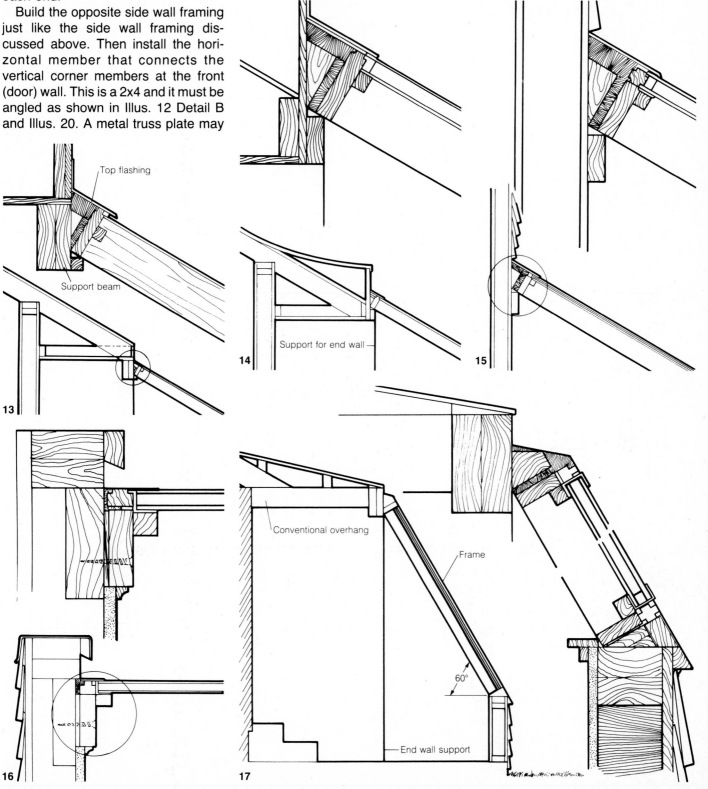

13

Top flashing

Support beam

14

Support for end wall

15

16

17

Conventional overhang

Frame

60°

End wall support

Project continued on next page

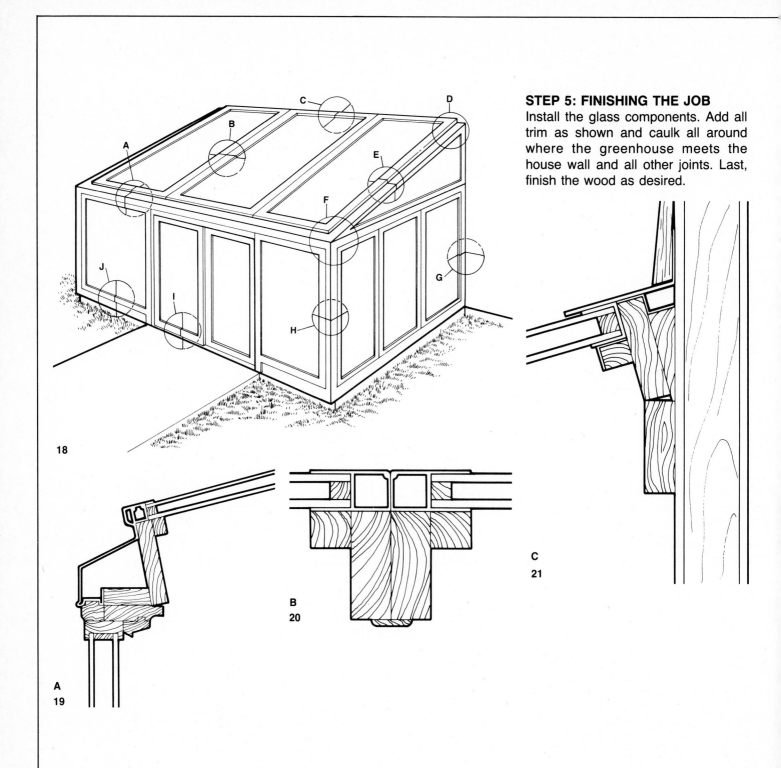

18

A
19

B
20

C
21

STEP 5: FINISHING THE JOB
Install the glass components. Add all trim as shown and caulk all around where the greenhouse meets the house wall and all other joints. Last, finish the wood as desired.

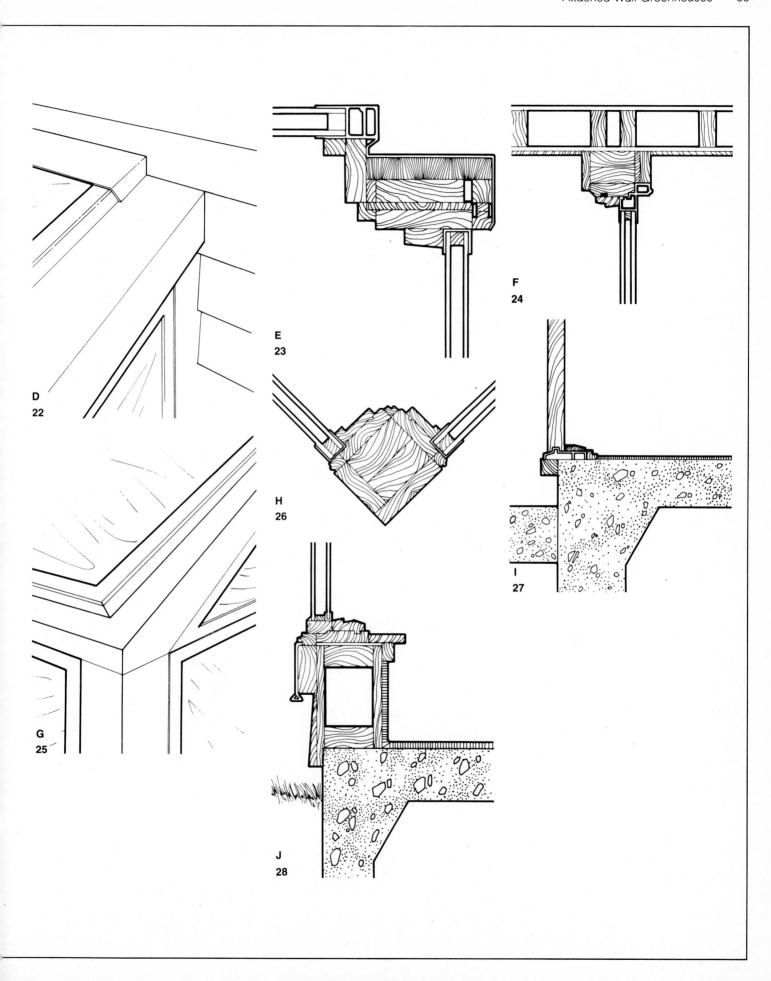

D
22

E
23

F
24

G
25

H
26

I
27

J
28

6
SKYLIGHTS AND WINDOWS

WINDOWS

Windows let in light and air and are an unappreciated but potentially important contributor to kitchen design. Window projects offered here include a bay window, stained glass windows, a lean-to-window greenhouse, and 3 skylight configurations.

ADDING A SKYLIGHT

A skylight, if properly planned and located, can provide five times more natural light than wall windows of equal size. Venting models, when placed near the ridge, allow warm, stale air to escape through the skylight while drawing cool, fresher air in through lower openings.

Location

In warm climates, place the skylight on the north or east, to lessen heat gain in the summer. In cold climates, locate the skylight on the south and west to help increase heat gain in cold winter months.

Types and Options

Use bronze tinted or translucent white models to filter the sun in warm climates. In cold climates, use clear, colorless skylights for unobstructed sunlight, unless privacy is important. In that case, use white translucent. Most skylights come in single glaze, for moderate climates, or double and triple glaze for warm and cold

climates. The dead air space(s) between the double or triple glazing greatly increases the insulating value of the skylight.

The two most common types of skylights are the domed and flat models. Other styles, such as the pyramid, round dome, and half-cylinder shape, are avail-

able. The sizes vary greatly and most are geared to neatly fit 16 inch or 24 inch on center rafter framing with a minimum of carpentry.

If you will be using more than one skylight, divide the skylight area by the number of skylights to determine the size of the individual units.

SKYLIGHT SIZE GUIDELINES

Room Size (Sq. Ft.)	Skylight Area (Sq. Ft.)
up to 80	4 (2'x2')
80-100	5 (2'x2½')
100-140	6 (2½'x2½')
140-160	8 (2'x4')
160-225	10 (2½'x4')
225-340	16 (4'x4')

Even kitchens with plenty of windows are getting skylights to enhance appearance and improve ventilation.

INSTALLING A BAY WINDOW

Bay window units are available in various forms from different manufacturers. They range from small box bays with 6-inch projections scaled to fit into standard window openings, to enormous bays utilizing window sections 8 feet high and 4 feet wide, extending several feet from the house wall.

It is possible for you to install your own bay window to meet your specifications, but you must be willing to do some careful work preparing the opening and assembling the bay unit. Manufacturers do provide specific installation information, including size of rough opening, assembly and installation. A small unit will come pre-assembled and require little extra preparation and no support beyond secure attaching to framing, like any other windows. Larger windows require support at the base. The larger the bay, the more extensive the support required. These directions are for a window with a rough opening of between 6 and 12 feet and a projection of between 1 and 3½ feet.

STEP 1: PROVIDING STRUCTURAL SUPPORT

Because the outside walls of a home are load-bearing, you must provide temporary support for your ceiling joists while you are working. Place a piece of carpeting or quilted material on top of a length of 2x4 at least 4 feet longer than the opening you will be making. The 2x4 at the ceiling runs parallel with the wall you are opening. Wedge the 2x4 against the ceiling of the room with additional, vertical 2x4s.

The supports should be placed approximately 18 inches from the wall to be opened. Make every effort to position the 2x4 at the ceiling under a joist, if the joists run parallel to the wall you are opening. If you are not sure of the location of the joists and you do not want to open the ceiling to find out, place several 3 to 4 foot pieces of 2x4 above and at right angles to the long 2x4 at the ceiling — flat against the ceiling. This will distribute the pressure and give good support. If the floor of the room is wood parquet or fine planks, use additional padding at the base of the posts to protect the floor. The carpet on the 2x4 will protect your ceiling.

STEP 2: OPENING THE WALL

Outline the proposed location of the new window on the wall. If a small window is now located in this space, remove it first. Cut away the wall finish material along the outline. You may use a circular saw set to the depth of the wall covering to cut this material, or use a hammer and chisel. If the width of the opening is not flush with framing studs, enlarge the opening to reach the nearest studs on each side.

Cutting the Exterior

If you have wood siding, drive nails through from the inside of the opening to mark the corners of the opening on the exterior. Use these nails as guides to mark and cut the exterior siding. If you have masonry siding, you will have to remove the bricks or blocks by chipping out the mortar between the units. Begin at the top of the opening area and work down. Remove more brick or block from each side than the final opening space; you will have to fill in the masonry later. Now cut the wall studs.

STEP 3: FRAMING THE OPENING

Your opening must be large enough so that you can slip a finished window unit in place. Establish the required height of the bottom of the installed window, the final width and height. Install dou-

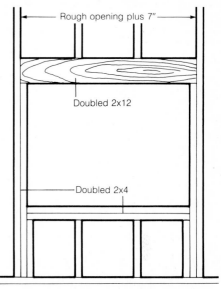

The framing for a bay window opening is similar to a standard window except for the size.

A bay gives the appearance of added space to a small area. Here, the addition of a bay provides a spacious look and generous natural light to a small dining area created from a breezeway.

Project continued on next page

bled studs at either side of the opening between the top and bottom plates. Position these so that the opening is 7 inches wider than the final rough opening.

Install additional, jack studs on each side of the opening. These jack studs will support the doubled 2x12 header at the top of the opening, with extra space for shimming the window. Install a doubled 2x4 sill on jack studs at the height required for the rough opening.

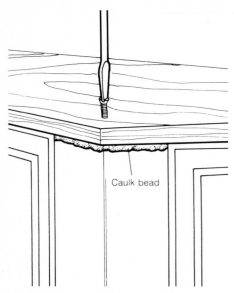

The bay is held at mullion blocks to the head and seat boards. Caulk seals joint.

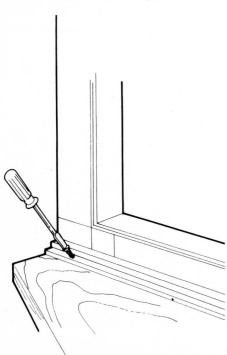

Prefabricated windows are joined in head and seat boards through the framing. Always use screws for greatest security.

STEP 4: CUTTING THE PLYWOOD SUPPORT

The bay window will rest on a plywood support base of 2 thicknesses of ¾-inch plywood. The base extends from the inside of the framing sill to the outside edge of the window sill in the unit. Cut this support from two sheets of ¾-inch plywood. The interior edge will lie parallel with the inside of the wall framing; the sides will follow the angle of the bay.

The exterior edge is cut to match the line of the sills of the finished bay. Use 1¼-inch No. 8 wood screws to join the two layers. Attach the plywood support to the rough sill with 3½-inch No. 10 wood screws.

Additional support is provided by wood block brackets attached to the house with screws or masonry anchors, by conventional framing set on poured concrete footing, or masonry. Have this support designed by an architect or engineer and build as directed. Wood brackets will be sufficient for a window extending no more than 3 feet from the house wall. An extension of 18 inches or less will need no extra support. Attach brackets as shown by counterboring holes for screws or masonry anchors.

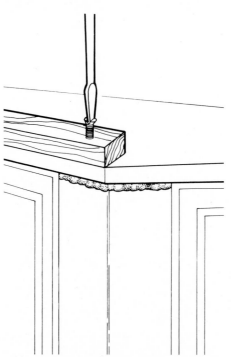

Attach 1x2 boards around underside of seat board to allow space for insulation. Unit is shown turned upside down.

STEP 5: CREATING A BAY WINDOW

If you have bought a bay that is complete, you will only have to follow the installation directions. However, if you are putting together a bay from individual windows, you will have to create the bay even though it is essentially a bay window kit that you have purchased.

Preparing the Mullions

The windows are joined on either side of the center with blocking mullions. In

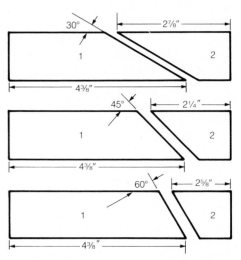

Cut mullion blocks for bays as shown here. Install as shown in first drawing on next page.

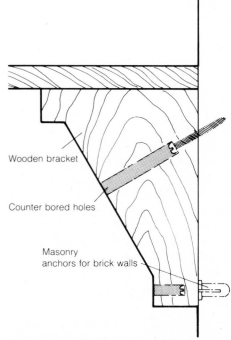

Wood support brackets are needed for large windows that are not tied to floor joists. Use masonry anchors to attach to brick wall.

some cases these will be supplied by the manufacturer; in other cases you will have to fabricate the mullion blocks yourself. Your bay may be as small as 4 feet high or as large as 6 to 7 feet high, so the mullion blocks will have to be ripped from lumber long enough to reach the entire height of the window. Refer to the drawings illustrating how to rip the mullion blocks and cut these pieces to the length appropriate for your installation.

Use corrugated fasteners to join mullion blocking. Tack mullion blocks into place with small casing nails. The window frames must touch on the inside face of the bay. The gap in the mullion blocking that is visible on the outside will be covered by mitre-cut molding.

Cutting Head and Seat Boards

Now cut head and seat boards from ¾-inch plywood. If there is no pattern provided, you will have to create one by placing the windows, held together by the mullion blocking, on the plywood and then scribing the outline on the board. The head board, which reaches from the line of the finished interior wall surface to the outside edge of the window frame, covers the top of the windows. The seat board only reaches to and follows the inside of the window frames.

Nail 1x2 boards all around the perimeter of the underside of the seat board. Place insulation between the plywood support and the seat board.

Assembling the Bay

Set the bay unit in place on the plywood support and run a bead of caulk around the top. Install the head board, using 2-inch No. 8 flathead screws driven into the mullion blocks and into the window frames at 12 inches on center.

Invert the unit and place the sill board against the bottom of the unit. Check for level and plumb. Shim as needed and attach with 3-inch No. 8 wood screws driven at an angle through the seat board into the mullion blocks. Caulk the joint. Attach insulation to underside of the seat board. Turn right side up.

Attach a strip of 1x1¼ wood around the perimeter of the headboard. Mitre and butt the joints over the mullion blocks.

STEP 6: SETTING THE WINDOW IN PLACE

Slip the unit into place. The outside edges of the windows should just touch the exterior wall sheathing. Check for level and plumb and shim as needed. Attach to plywood support by driving wood screws through the perimeter of the seat board into the plywood support. Drive wood screws through the head board into the header at the wall framing and into joists if installed for roof. Install additional blocking between the sides of the window unit and the wall framing as shown in the drawing. Use a 2x4 at the window frame and a 2x2 between the double jack studs and the new 2x4. Caulk all joints well.

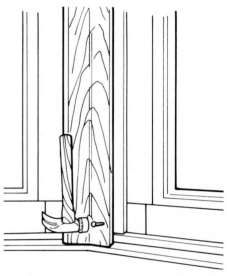

Typical Mullion

30° 45° or 60°

Mullion blocks butt together as shown. Gap is covered by mitre-cut molding on the outside. Note side framing and molding trim required.

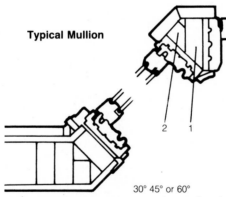

Dashed line show possible roof construction

Jamb extension   Head board

Seat board

Plywood support

Brackets

Bay is insulated above head board and below seat board. Molding trims joints. All joints between window and framing are caulked.

STEP 7: FINISHING THE INSTALLATION

Caulk and flash all exterior seams in the unit and between the unit and the walls. Some units come with side mounting brackets, which should be installed for more stability in the connection to the house. When the unit is secure, flashed and sealed, cover interior and exterior seams with molding. The interior wall finish will cover the gap between the blocking and the windows.

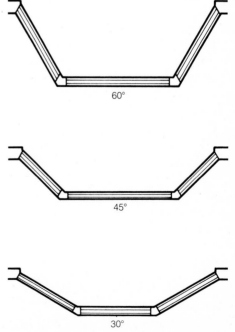

All interior joints are caulked and then covered with appropriate decorative molding to complete the bay installation.

60°

45°

30°

Bays are usually installed in one of these configurations. Required mullion blocks for each of these is shown on the previous page.

ADDING A SKYLIGHT

Step 1: Selecting the Site
Determine whether your rafters are 16 or 24 inches on center, then select a skylight of the proper area, determined from the chart, that will fit your framing.

Step 2: Marking the Opening
Use the opening measurements given by the manufacturer, adding 3 inches to the front-back dimension to allow for the headers, and mark the four corners on the inside of the roof. Drive a large nail up through the roof at each corner; so they can be found on the outside.

Step 3: Creating the Opening
Remove the shingles to within at least 10 inches of the opening on all sides. Pull the roofing nails out carefully and salvage as many shingles as possible for replacement once the skylight has been installed. Remove the building felt in the immediate area of the opening. Snap chalklines from nail to nail to form all four sides. Remove the nails; then cut the opening.

Step 4: Framing the Opening
Use any rafters that were cut or new lumber of equal stock to provide a header at the top and bottom of the opening. For larger skylights, where more than one rafter was cut, add a double header at top and bottom. (Adjust your original marks.)

Step 5: Inserting the Skylight
Apply a 4-inch-wide layer of roofing mastic or roofing cement around the opening. Re-lay the shingles at the bottom to within 2 inches of the open-

ing. Set the skylight into place, pressing firmly into the mastic. Nail as directed only by the manufacturer.

Step 6: Finishing the Opening
The flashing will extend over the shin-

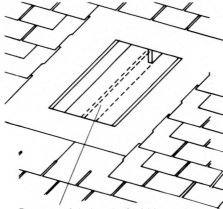
Remove roof deck and rafter(s) in opening
Roof decking and intermediate rafter must be cut out for opening for the skylight

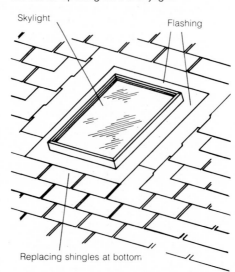
Skylight　　Flashing
Replacing shingles at bottom
Skylight, usually with integral flashing, is set into the opening and roof repairs begun.

gles at the bottom. Replace the shingles at the sides and top. They will go over, but will not be nailed into, the flashing. Finally, refinish the inside with finish materials to match the ceiling.

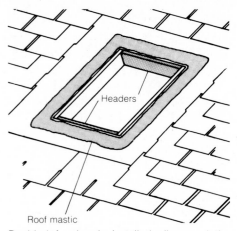
Headers
Roof mastic
Doubled framing is installed all around the opening. Roof mastic seals the joints.

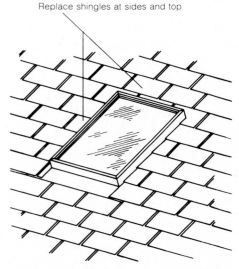
Replace shingles at sides and top
Shingles cover flashing on the top and sides of the skylight. Adhesive holds shingles.

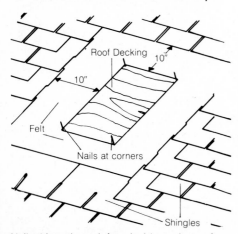
Roof Decking　10"
10"
Felt
Nails at corners
Shingles
Nails driven through from inside mark area from which shingles and decking are removed.

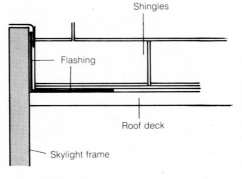
Shingles
Flashing
Roof deck
Skylight frame
Sides (top)
At the top of the skylight the shingles cover the flashing to direct rainwater down the roof slope. The flashing overlaps the shingles at the bottom of the skylight for the same reason.

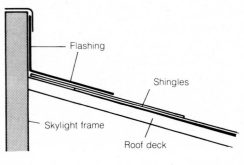
Flashing
Shingles
Skylight frame
Roof deck
Bottom

BUILDING A LIGHT WELL (SHAFT)

In homes that have an attic you will probably need to install a light well or light shaft. The only time this is not called for is when the skylight is going into a vaulted ceiling.

Types of Light Shafts

There are three basic types of light shafts (or wells) and all are easily constructed. They are the straight well, the splayed light well, and the tilted light well.

While the straight shaft is very easy to build, it does have a drawback. The resulting hole in the ceiling is smaller than the skylight, reducing the amount of light that comes in. Also, the shaft tends to focus the light in a smaller area. To circumvent this problem, use a splayed light well.

How to Build a Splayed Light Well

The construction is the same as for a straight well, except the front and back of the well slants at an angle as it goes down, so that the well gets larger toward the ceiling. Keep the sides as near vertical as possible. If they become too wide, it may weaken the ceiling structure since additional joists have to be cut. Mark the shaft with a plumb bob as before, but move the front marks further forward and the rear marks further to the back to reach the desired splay. Then construct the well as before, except that the studs will be at an angle to conform to the two different size openings.

How and When to Use a Tilted Well

There may be places in the home, often a hallway, where a skylight cannot be directly overhead because of a ridge or other obstruction. In this case use a tilted light well. Once the skylight has been installed, construct an opening in the ceiling where you need the light, so it is as near as possible to the desired area. Then construct the well

as before, except the entire well now will tilt to bring the light to the ceiling opening.

How to Build the Straight Well

The first is the straight well. Hold a plumb bob at each corner of the skylight and mark the corner on the attic floor below. Cut out the opening, providing headers between the joists at front and back, just as you did for the roof. Then use 2x4 studs to frame the sides of the opening. Place two at each corner, so that there is a nailing surface in each direction for finish materials. If the space between the corners is less than 32 inches, place a single stud in the center. If more than 32 inches, place studs at 16 inches on center. Toenail the studs with 10d common nails to the rafters and headers above and the joists and headers below. Install insulation between the studs of the light well. Then apply finish materials to the inside of the light well.

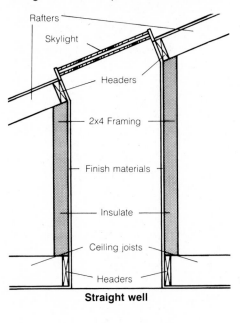

Straight well

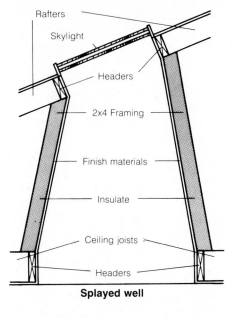

Splayed well

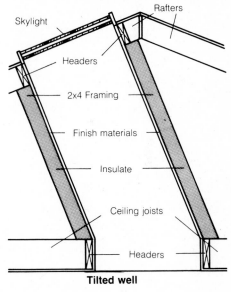

Tilted well

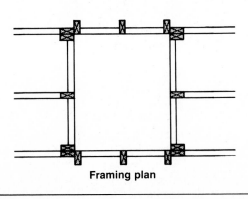

Framing plan

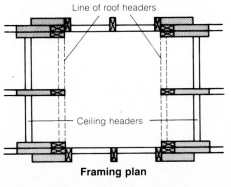

Framing plan

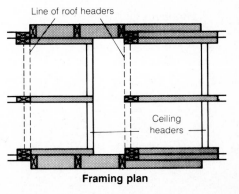

Framing plan

CREATING STAINED GLASS WINDOWS

Stained glass windows can add beauty and individuality to a kitchen, and also provide privacy without the need of curtains, drapes, shutters or blinds that keep out the sunlight.

It is possible to buy stained glass windows, or to have them custom made, but that is expensive. If you have any talent at crafts, there is no reason why you cannot create your own stained glass window.

TOOLS AND MATERIALS

For a genuine stained glass window, you will need lead "cames" from a local hobby shop or a mail order company. The cames are the lead shapes with cross-sections of "I" or "C" shapes. You also will need low-temperature solder formulated for use with lead cames. This is different from the usual 50-50 or 60-40 lead-tin solder used for ordinary metal work. Its formulation is two parts lead, one part tin and two parts bismuth, and it melts at around 235 degrees F.

If you are really skilled at soldering, and not many of us are, it is possible to use another type of solder along with the soldering iron (not gun) to just heat the solder so it flows and blends with the lead cames. This, however, is a touchy operation.

WORKING WITH STAINED GLASS
Creating a Pattern

If the stained glass window is to replace an existing clear glass window, the first step is to carefully measure the existing window and then transfer the dimensions to a sheet of paper. If the window is old and obviously out of square, use a large sheet of wrapping paper over the window to create a "rubbing" that clearly outlines the shape on the paper. Mark both the pattern and window to indicate the top.

Draw your stained glass pattern inside the lines you have made on the paper. The lines should be the thickness of the center section of the cames, which is about 1/16 inch. Pattern ideas can come from stained glass windows you have seen or from books on the skill of making leaded or stained glass windows. Try to use simple, bold designs. Small details are

difficult to execute. Number all the component pieces.

When the pattern on the paper is complete, transfer it to light cardboard using carbon paper. Put the carbon sheet between the cardboard and the pattern and trace the lines. Cut out the various shapes of cardboard; then place them back on the paper pattern. Incidentally, if you cut out the cardboard shapes with a jigsaw, the

thickness of the blade will create the necessary spacing to allow for the cames (see illus. 2 and 3.)

Cutting The Glass

Purchase the stained glass in the colors you have chosen for your pattern and place each of your cardboard patterns on the glass. Pull the glass cutter toward you with a steady pressure. After scoring the glass — you actually

Stained glass work requires careful and precise work. Check your window; if it is out of square, take a rubbing of its outline using a dark crayon.

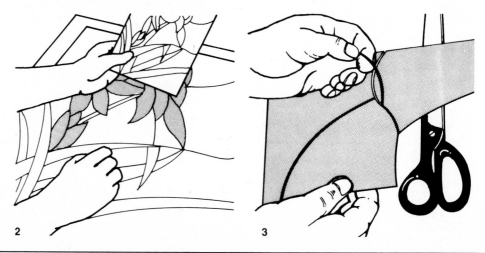

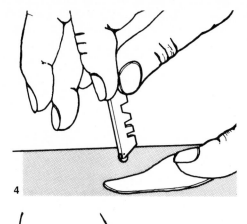

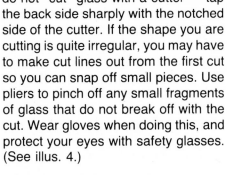

do not "cut" glass with a cutter — tap the back side sharply with the notched side of the cutter. If the shape you are cutting is quite irregular, you may have to make cut lines out from the first cut so you can snap off small pieces. Use pliers to pinch off any small fragments of glass that do not break off with the cut. Wear gloves when doing this, and protect your eyes with safety glasses. (See illus. 4.)

Putting the Pieces Together

When all the pieces are cut to size and shape, place the original drawing (called a "cartoon") on a worktable. Take two straight boards and tack-nail them in an L-shape. The boards should be the length and width of the window you are creating. Uncoil the lead cames. Then straighten them by clamping the end of each one in a vise and pulling on the other end with pliers. Cut C-shaped cames to fit to the lengths of the two outside edges of your window and place them against the two boards. Cut the cames with a sharp knife, razor blade in a holder, or a chisel. Fit the first piece of glass into the grooves in the corner. Cut cames to fit around each piece of glass. Finish the final two edges with two lengths of C-shaped cames. (See illus. 5.)

Oleic acid is used as flux with the low-temperature solder. Apply the acid to each joint with a brush. Then hold the soldering iron on each joint, moving it around as you apply the solder. When the entire joint is covered, remove the iron. Repeat this operation on each joint. Finally, turn the assembly over and repeat the soldering of each joint on the other side of the window. (See illus. 6.)

Finishing the Surfaces

Mix turpentine or paint thinner with putty or glazing compound to create a paste-like consistency. Use a stiff-bristled scrub brush to force the compound into the cames. Do not smoke while doing this; the mixture is flammable!

The final step is to sprinkle a mixture of "whiting" (white lead available at art supply stores) and sawdust over the window and rub with a stiff brush. As white lead is poisonous, wash your hands thoroughly and dispose of all waste materials so children and pets cannot contact it. Because of the hazards of white lead, it is probable that there is a substitute for the lead available where stained glass supplies are sold. We would recommend any suitable substitute over the poisonous white lead, even if the substitute is more expensive or the white lead is available. Both sides of the stained glass window should be treated in the same manner.

The finished window now can be installed in place of the existing clear glass pane, or it can simply be fitted onto and against the clear glass for added strength. Hold the new window in place with molding that is attached with screws if the stained glass is applied over existing glass. The screws will allow easy removal for cleaning of the clear glass about once or twice a year.

SIMPLER ALTERNATIVE

You can make "imitation" stained glass windows using flat strips of lead sold in hobby shops. The strips bend to fit around shapes in the design. The spaces inside the "cames" are painted with translucent lacquers that closely imitate the colors of real stained glass. The imitation stained glass windows must be on the inside (house side) of the clear glass, not on the surface exposed to the weather. This form of "stained glass" is quite moisture-resistant and long-lasting, although it will not have the brilliance of real stained glass.

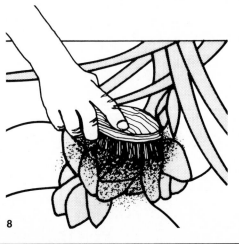

BUILDING A LEAN-TO-WINDOW GREENHOUSE

The simplest way to build a window greenhouse is to build it *around* the window. When you build the greenhouse around the existing window, you do not have to be concerned about fitting the greenhouse members to the window framing. Read all the instructions before you buy any materials. The example greenhouse is built using standard lumber sections (2x6, 2x4, 2x2s). Study Illustrations 1, 2, 3, 4, and 5. This design will work best with an existing window that opens into the kitchen.

STEP 1: FIGURING DIMENSIONS

Measure the outside frame and sill dimensions of your window, outside the house. The greenhouse framing will fit around the window framing. Illustration 1 gives an idea of how the framing fits around an existing window. You may build the greenhouse taller and/or wider, as you like, but do not build it so big that you cannot reach all area within it comfortably. Also, it is not anticipated this design will be used for windows wider than 4 feet. However, if you have wider windows, or a series of windows together, you could duplicate this

design structure and butt the window greenhouses, side by side, for as great a length as you desire.

STEP 2: CUTTING THE FRAMING

The top framing member is cut from a 2x6. The notch is 1 inch x 4 inches. The bottom framing member is a 2x4 with a 1x2 inch notch, cut as shown in Illustration 2.

The vertical framing members are 1x4s that fit between the top and bottom framing members. In addition to being notched horizontally to accommodate the greenhouse framing members, they also are notched vertically so that they fit flush with the vertical framing at the sides. You will need a power saw to do the notching, or you can pay the lumber dealer to make the cuts after you have cut all the members to fit around the window.

STEP 3: NOTCHING THE FRAMING

Before you install any portion of the framework, you need to prepare the 2x2 members to accept the glass and the floor. For ease of construction, buy all the members a little longer than you need. The 2x2s, for instance, should

be about 6 inches longer than you will need them; you can figure the rough lengths with a yardstick or carpenters' rule.

The glass on all three sides fits into notches at the edges of the 2x2s and is held in place with a small (½ inch square) member secured with 1-inch x ⅛ inch diameter screws. These small members are called "glass stops" (see "Step 9"). The glass stop at the bottom of the panes should be beveled slightly so that it drains water. Facing any side of the greenhouse, the notches cut in the 2x2 members are ½ inches wide and 1 inch deep. This size allows you to use ¼-inch glass and have the ½-inch member flush with the edge of the 2x2, as shown in Illustrations 2 and 5. Cut the notches with a power saw.

STEP 4: MARKING FLOOR DEPTH

Decide how deep you want the greenhouse floor to be. Typically, the depth of the floor from the house will be from 12 to 16 inches. Mark the depth on two of the 2x2s that you will use for the horizontal members at the bottom of the greenhouse.

STEP 5: FITTING THE FRAMING

You will need a helper for this step. Have the helper hold one of the horizontal 2x2s at the bottom in place. The

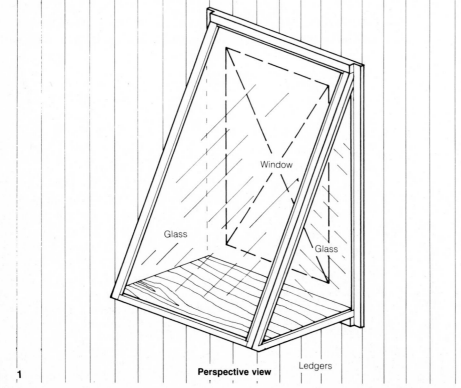

1

Perspective view

A lean-to greenhouse does not offer as much shelf space as standard types, but it allows lots of light into the house and keeps the plants off the window sill.

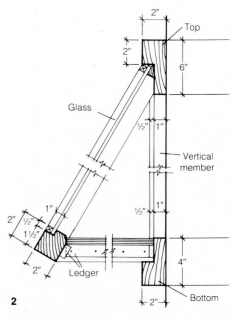

2

The greenhouse framing consists of 2 sloping 2x2s, 2 horizontal side 2x2s, and 1 horizontal 2x2 across the front.

piece should be pencil-marked on top to the same depth as you want the floor (Step 4). Hold the horizontal member perpendicular to the wall, flush with the top of the 2x4 bottom framing member at the wall. Illustration 3 shows the finished 2x2 at the bottom; this is how you want the helper to hold the pieces now.

While the helper holds the horizontal 2x2, you hold the sloping 2x2 as it appears in Illustration 3. Let your 2x2 fit outside the horizontal 2x2 against the end of the 2x6 at the top and you can

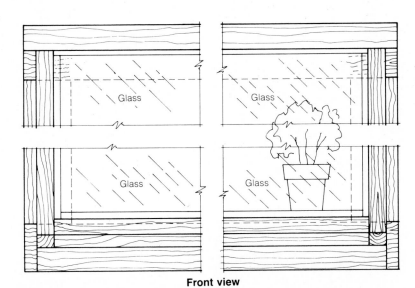

3   **Side view**

The 2x2 framing fits into notched 2x stock members at top and bottom and flush to the 2x stock members at the sides.

measure and pencil-mark the angles on the horizontal and sloping member you must cut (see the circled areas on Illustration 3). This sounds much more complicated than it actually is.

Cut the sloping 2x2 and the horizontal 2x2 so they will fit together as shown in Illustration 3. Check the fit by holding the pieces in place as they appear in the illustration. If they fit properly, use them for patterns to cut the 2x2s at the opposite end. Do this by laying the cut members on the uncut members, respectively, and marking the angles. Then cut the members to fit as you did the first ones.

STEP 6: BUYING THE FASTENERS

The top and bottom framing members are centered over the window framing and are fastened to the house. The fastener used depends on the exterior wall surface. For wood surfaces, use a 4-inch flathead wood screw of approximately ¼-inch diameter (non-corrosive screws and nails used for all exterior work). For brick, use ¼-inch diameter toggle bolts long enough to get through the 2x6 and the brick (usually about 6 inches).

You will need to drill holes through the 2x6 and the wall surface, regardless of the fastener you use. The fasteners should be installed approximately 8 inches on center, with a fastener about an inch from each end.

STEP 7: FASTENING THE PIECES

Mark the locations of the fasteners on the framing and drill the holes. Countersink all the fastener holes about ¼ inch. Secure the top, bottom, and vertical framing members to the house and caulk all around the framing at the joints and where the framing meets the house.

Next, install the 2x2 members at an angle as shown. Use 2¾-inch long, ⅛ inch diameter flathead woodscrews where the 2x2s meet each other. Use another two screws where they meet the 2x6 at the top and the 2x4 at the

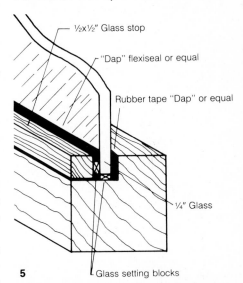

5

Glazing requires a firm edge on the frame to support the glass, resilient material to hold the glass and a sealant to keep out water.

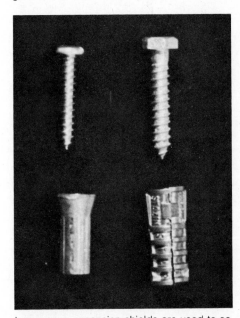

In masonry, expansion shields are used to secure the 2-inch thick framing to the house. In wood, long screws usually are preferred.

4   **Front view**

The framework attaches to 2-inch framing at the house wall. A ½-inch plywood bottom and ¼-inch glass completes the greenhouse unit.

Project continued on next page

bottom. When the 2x2s are in place they will form a triangle at each side of the greenhouse.

STEP 8: INSTALLING THE FLOOR

The floor fits flush with the top of the horizontal 2x2s and butts against the front horizontal 2x2 (not yet installed). The floor is supported by ½ x 1 inch ledger that runs continuously around.

First, install the floor ledger at the sides and house wall; the front ledger will be added later. One inch long ⅛ inch diameter flathead screws at 4 inches on center will be sufficient. Remember to install the ledger ½ inch down from the top of the 2x2s, to allow room for the ½-inch floor. The screws need not be counter sunk.

When the floor support is in place at the sides and house wall, cut the half inch plywood to fit and lay it in place on the ledger attached to the house and at the sides. Do not secure it yet.

You will note in Illustration 2 that the bottom corner of the floor corresponds with the corner formed by the 2x2s. Using the floor as a guide, pencil-mark the corner of the floor onto the 2x2 members at each end. Now, remove the floor and hold the front 2x2 in place. The pencil mark will show you the angle at which you must cut the front 2x2 in order for it to fit flush with the floor, as shown in Illustration 2.

Cut the front 2x2 member to fit between the sloping 2x2 members and install it, using two 3-inch flathead woodscrews with ⅛ inch diameters. Drill a ⅛ inch hole about half-an-inch shorter than the screw before you drive the screws in (this is good practice for the whole project). Be careful not to hit the other screws already in place.

Now cut the front ½ x 1 inch ledger and install it as you did the other ledger members.

With the front 2x2 member and the ½ x 1-inch ledger installed, lay the floor in and screw it down with 1 inch, ⅛-inch diameter flathead screws at 4 inches on center, all around the floor. Caulk all the joints with an exterior caulk.

STEP 9: ADDING GLASS STOPS

Now, you need to cut the small, angu-lar member "glass stop" that fits behind the glass at the top. You can see the member in Illustration 2, right behind the glass where it meets the 2x6.

It is simple to make a pattern for the shape of this member. Hold a piece of cardboard into the notch of the 2x6 and pencil-mark the angle onto the cardboard. Cut the cardboard and trace its shape onto a 2x2 and cut it to fit between the sloping members. Nail the angular member to the 2x6 with 1-inch brads at 2 inches on center.

Produce enough of the ½ inch square members to hold the glass in place. These members can be made by ripping half-inch strips off another ½ inch member (or off the ½ x 1 inch pieces you notched out in Step 3).

STEP 10: ADDING THE GLASS

Preparing the wooden frames to accept the glass is one of the most important steps for a watertight glass fit, and for avoiding cracked glass, especially in areas of extreme weather.

Materials Needed

Glass installation calls for use of a rubber tape, sealant, rubber pads called "glass setting blocks," wooden units called "glass stops," plus wood screws and glass.

This window greenhouse, a standard design rather than a lean-to, comes in a kit available from Lord and Burham.

Taping the Frame

First, study Illustration 5. The illustration shows the glass/frame assembly. Be sure the wood frame is clean and dry, then install rubber tape ("Dap" or an equal brand) against the permanent part of the window frame. Follow the manufacturers' instructions for application of the tape. The tape is a resilient band of protection for the glass, and it fits continuously around the frame.

Placing the Glass Setting Blocks

These are little rubber pads the width of the glass (typically ⅛ inch or ¼ inch — ¼ inch is used in the example) and about 4 inches long. They are installed at the corners of the window frame, horizontally and vertically. (However, again, follow the manufacturers' instructions about locations and applications of sealants, glass stops and glass setting blocks).

Sealing the Frame and Placing the Glass

Install a coating of Dap "Flexiseal" sealant under the areas where the ½x½-inch wooden glass stops will be. Note that the glass is less than the frame dimension, all around, by the thickness of the glass setting blocks. Install the ¼-inch thick glass on the setting blocks. Be sure the Flexiseal is uniformly distributed over the frame surface.

Install rubber setting blocks against the glass exterior, as you did for the interior side of the glass, to protect the glass against the wood glass stop (½x½ inch). Add the glass stop, using 1-inch long, ⅛-inch diameter screws at 4 inches on center. Fill the gap that remains between the glass stop and the glass with Flexiseal. Bead the Flexiseal up against the glass and curve or angle it so that water will drain.

It does not matter whether you install the front or side panes first.

CONSTRUCTING A STANDARD WINDOW GREENHOUSE

The standard window greenhouse utilizes construction similar to the lean-to greenhouse and, like it, the standard greenhouse fits around the window. Read through the instructions for the lean-to greenhouse (preceding project) before you begin this project.

DIFFERENCES FROM LEAN-TO MODEL

Aside from the shape, one difference between the standard window greenhouse and the lean-to is that in the lean-to an aluminum or corrosion-proof metal angle holds the glass in place where the sloping glass meets the corner. This is used only at the top of the greenhouse and is secured to the wooden structure (see Illustration 3). Wooden block glass stops are used for the rest of the greenhouse.

Another difference between the construction detailing of the two greenhouses is the glass-sealing method. The lean-to greenhouse uses a notch in the 2x2 members so that the "higher" part of the 2x2 is inside the greenhouse with the glass pressing against it. This is generally a more secure, watertight method than the one shown for the standard greenhouse in this example

ple (see the plan view in Illustration 5). However, notching the 2x2 members is a good deal more trouble than simply "clamping" the glass between the glass stops, as shown here in the standard greenhouse. Again, either method will work; pick the one that seems best for your skills and timetable.

Before you begin work on a window greenhouse, or even decide which one you want, read through the instructions for both of the projects a time or two, referring to the illustrations.

CONSTRUCTION PROCEDURES

Here, in brief, is the work sequence. First, cut and prepare all the members that fit around the window next to the house. Mark the location of the fasteners on the framing and drill the holes. Secure the framing members to the house and caulk all around the framing at the joints and where the framing meets the house.

Step 1: Sizing the Greenhouse

Measure the outside frame and sill dimensions of your window from the exterior of the house. The greenhouse framing will fit around the window framing. Illustration 1 shows the finished

greenhouse in perspective. The greenhouse example is designed to be approximately 4 feet wide by 5 feet tall. These are not critical dimensions, but the greenhouse should not be much larger than the above if using 2x2 members.

Step 2: Notching Horizontal Framing

Cut the top framing member from a 2x6. Notch it (see Illustration 2) 1x4 inches, from the bottom.

Cut the bottom framing member from a 2x4. Notch it 1x2 inches, measured from the bottom. Also, notch the 2x4 every 4 inches on center as shown in Illustration 4, to provide ventilation. This is discussed again in Step 7.

Step 3: Preparing Vertical Framing

The vertical framing members, which fasten to the house wall between the top and bottom pieces, are 1x4s. The horizontal greenhouse members butt the 1x4s. Vertical 1x3s run between the horizontal 2x2s for added support. The vertical 1x3s screw to the 1x4s with 1½-inch long, ¼-inch diameter flathead wood screws at approximately 6 inches on center. Place a screw about 1 inch from each end, so that the bottoms of the 1x3s extend 1 inch below the 2x2s.

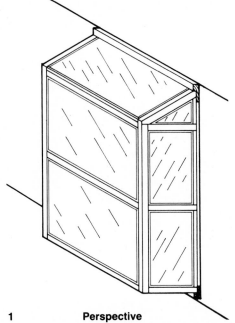

1   Perspective
The standard window greenhouse has a slanted "roof", typically with a slope of about 30 degrees. It calls for a shelf in the middle, and a floor. The top framing member is a 2x6, the bottom member a 2x4; vertical side members are 1x4s and 1x3s. Remaining members are 2x2s.

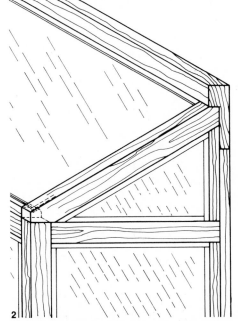

2
The sloping 2x2 must be notched as shown to fit against the 2x6 top member. Glass used is ¼ inch thick and is held in place with ½-inch square wood glass stops, secured with flathead wood screws. Use Dap or a comparable sealing system to waterproof the glass.

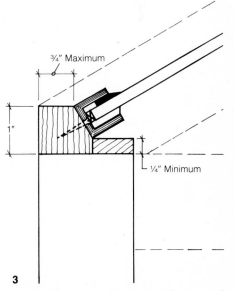

3¾" Maximum
1"
¼" Minimum

3
An angle of non-corrosive metal makes a good glass stop. This one is ⅛ inch thick and ⅝ inch deep by ½ inch wide (inside dimensions) to hold the ¼ inch glass and still have room for the sealant system, as shown.

Project continued on next page

The glass stops are ½ inch square wood members. Use the Dap sealant system per the manufacturers' instructions or an equivalent sealant system.

Step 4: Securing the Framing

The top and bottom framing members are centered over the window framing and fastened to the house wall. The fastener used depends on the exterior wall surface material. For wood surfaces, use 4-inch flathead wood screws of approximately ¼-inch diameter — noncorrosive screws and nails should be used for all exterior work. For brick, use ¼-inch diameter expansion shields approximately 6 inches long, depending on your particular wall; check with your hardware dealer. Drill holes through the 2x6 and the wall surface and install the fasteners

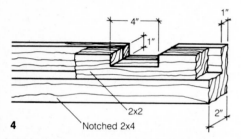

4

The greenhouse can be vented into the house. A simple vent system can be made by cutting notches in the members below the floor and building a narrow (1 inch wide) "door" in the floor that opens with a piano hinge. The vent is covered with noncorrosive screen.

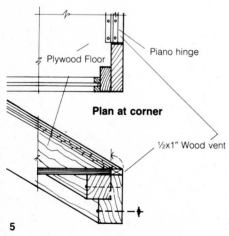

5

Section/perspective at corner

This illustration shows the piano hinge used on the vent "door", which is made using a ½ x 1 inch strip of wood. On the notches in the members below the door, screen is installed to keep out insects. In the plan view, note the ½ inch square glass stops that are attached (screwed) to the 1x3, which in turn attaches to the 1x4 at the wall.

approximately 8 inches on center, with a fastener about an inch from each end. Secure in the vertical 1x4s same way. Countersink all fasteners about ¼ inch.

Step 5: Sealing the Framing

Caulk around outside edges of the framing, where it meets the house, and at all joints.

Step 6: Planning for the Shelf

Decide on the floor and shelf depth. The shelf is not an option, it is needed for strength and rigidity, just as the floor is needed. The shelf is located in the middle of the greenhouse, supported by the horizontal 2x2s. See Illustration 1 for its location. Use ledgers, as shown, for floor support. Typical depths are somewhere between 12 and 16 inches; 16 inches should be taken as a maximum for the structural members used in this design.

STEP 7: ADDING THE 2x2s

This is similar to fitting the framing for the "Lean-to Greenhouse". You will need a helper. Have the helper hold the horizontal 2x2s in their final position while you pencil-mark them on top for the proper length and to the depth you want for the floor.

To mark sloping 2x2s at the top of the standard greenhouse, hold them in position to measure and mark them against the horizontal 2x2s they meet. Let the sloping 2x2 fit outside the horizontal 2x2 to mark the necessary angle.

Note that, unlike the lean-to greenhouse, the 2x2 members in the standard greenhouse design are not notched for the ½ inch square glass stops.

STEP 8: INSTALLING FLOOR AND SHELF

The floor is ½-inch exterior plywood, as is the shelf. The floor fits on top of the horizontal 2x2s and receives reinforcement from a ½x1 inch ledger that runs continuously around the horizontal members, similarly to the lean-to ledger.

First, install the ledger flush with the top of the 2x2 members; use inch-long,

⅛-inch diameter flat-head screws at 4 inches on center. Place the ledger ½ inch below the top of the 2x2s to allow room for the floor, whose top surface is flush to the top of the 2x2s.

When the ledger is in place, cut the ½ inch plywood floor and secure it with wood screws. Provide for the hinged vent, as shown in Illustration 5. Install the shelf similarly, drilling ¼-inch holes in the shelf at approximately 1 inch on center, for ventilation.

Step 9: Placing the Glass Stops

Install the glass stops closest to the inside using 1-inch long, ⅛-inch diameter screws at 4 inches on center (see Illustration 5, plan view). Use Dap or an equivalent sealant system for the glass when you install the glass and the outside glass stops (see Illustration 3).

Step 10: Reinforcing the Greenhouse

It is assumed that no large, heavy plant pot will be used in this greenhouse. "Large and heavy" is subject to definition and judgment, but typically a 6-inch diameter pot is about the maximum suitable size. If heavier pots are to be used, reinforce the bottom of the greenhouse with 2x4s secured to the floor of the greenhouse at the front (with ¼-inch diameter screws). Run the braces down to a point about a foot below the bottom horizontal member. At this point, the braces (four of the 2x4s equally spaced should do) can be connected to a horizontal 2x4 secured to the house, like the top and bottom members of the greenhouse.

Step 11: Finishing the Unit

This greenhouse may be finished with transparent or opaque stain, with paint, or with a varnish or other exterior wood finish.

7
ISLANDS, BARS
EATING COUNTERS

Most homeowners immediately assume that a work surface must a be counter, or an eating area consisting of the standard table and chairs. In large kitchens, however, a central island often provides the ideal answer to the need for additional working space. In small kitchens, eating bars and counters that fulfill dining needs can be arranged so they take up little floor space.

Some of the projects included in this chapter have been shown in photographs presented earlier in the book. For example, the pull-down counter, which is hidden as part of a cabinet, is found on page

70. The large butcher-block topped island is shown on page 14. Additional projects are: a small, laminate-topped work island, a butcher-block work table that also can double as a serving cart if casters are added, and an eating bar positioned so that it can also see use as a food preparation area.

Variations on the basic projects can be worked out to suit different space availability and desired configurations. In almost all cases, standard stock cabinets can be used as the basis for a work island, rather than having to build the cabinet units from scratch.

This smaller island provides snack space for two or three people as well as a safe tile working surface around the range top.

An island can be designed to serve several functions. This unit provides ample space for family dining on the lower counter while the higher area is a useful working and serving counter.

A variety of counters and peninsulas define the work and dining spaces in this kitchen. Chopping block is handy to both sink and stove.

BUTCHER BLOCK WORK TABLE

MACHINING PROCEDURES
Creating the Butcher Block Top

A butcher block top is made by cutting strips of wood and gluing the face surfaces of the strips together. This places the edges of the board, which are the toughest and most durable sections, outward to become the work surface.

Use 8/4 stock for the strips. The 8/4 pieces will be 2⅞ inch thick to create a top 2¾ inches thick once you have planed the table. The planing is carried out after the table has been glued together. The ⅛ inch usually is sufficient to allow for any misalignment that occurs during the gluing process. You will need 13 pieces of 8/4 by 2⅞ inch stock. When they are face-glued together, they create a butcher block top 2¾ inches wide and 2⅞ inches thick.

The same type of allowance is needed for the length of the boards; an extra 1 inch has been added to the length of the boards. Therefore, the top requires 13 pieces of 8/4 stock, each 2⅞ inches thick x 39 inches long.

Gluing the top. A professionally equipped shop may have the table and large bar clamps needed to glue the whole top at once. It is undoubtedly tempting to try this method, but it is better to use a more lengthy process and to glue the strips one after another, allowing each newly added strip to dry

before adding the next. Hold sections being glued with bar clamps in order to apply even pressure along the entire length of the boards.

Glue up only as many strips as you can plane level at one time. If you have a 24-inch planer, do the entire top. Otherwise, glue the boards in sections, plane each section and glue the sections together. When gluing the last joint between the two or more planed-to-size sections, they must be perfectly aligned and all excess glue wiped clean.

It is advisable to clamp the various

pieces level while applying pressure with bar clamps. To hold the boards even, use a C clamp at each end of the section being glued. Place newspaper along the seams at the ends and place short lengths of 1x3 at right angles to the seam on both the top and bottom and use the C clamp.

Cutting to Size

Once you have glued the top together, use a table saw to cut it 22¾ inches wide x 38 inches long. Router the top edges with a ½ inch radius and the bottom edges with a ¼ inch radius.

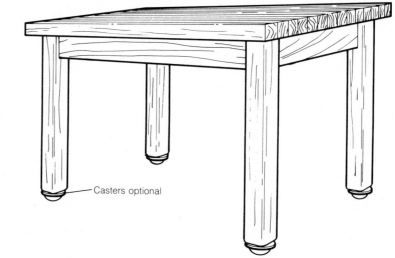

This work table can be built to your size requirements. The example here is 28 by 22¾ inches. Casters can be added, as can a shelf at midheight on the supporting legs.

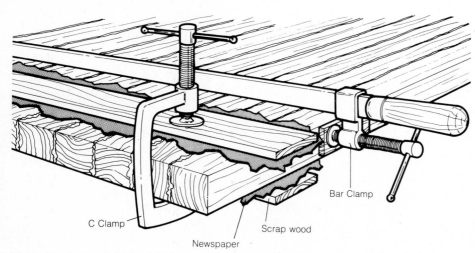

When clamping together the individual strips to form the butcher block top, be sure to use protective scraps of wood and newspaper to protect the surface of the table.

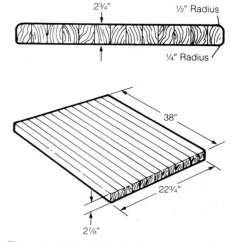

The edges of the table top perimeter are routered ½ inch, and the bottom edge ¼ inch, for a smooth, rounded edge on both sides.

You will end up with a ½-inch radius curve along the edge.

Making the Aprons

Two of the table aprons are 3 inches wide and 15½ inches long; the other two are 3 inches wide x 30¾ inches long. Both are cut from 5/4 stock. The back of all the aprons are machined with both the standard table top fastener groove (a table saw kerf ⅜ inch deep and 11⁄16 inch down from the top edge) and the standard leg brace groove (a table saw kerf ⅜ inch deep and 2¼ inches from the end of the apron). See drawings for details.

Creating the Legs

The legs are also made out of pieces that must be glued up to size and then machined down to the finished dimension. Each leg is made from two pieces of 6/4 stock 2⅞ inches wide by 33½ inches long, cut for gluing. Again the excess width and length is to accommodate any misalignment during the gluing operation. Follow previous gluing instructions for clamping these pieces.

Once the glue has set and clamps have been removed, cut the legs to exact size on a table saw. Round the edges with a router to ¼ inch radius. Drill a hole 1½ inches from the top end of each leg for a standard leg brace lag bolt. The hole is at right angles to the length of the leg.

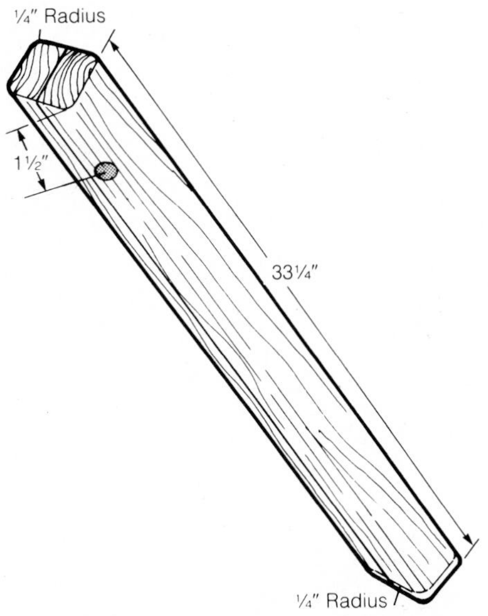

Glue leg from two 2⅞x33½ inch pieces and trim to 2⅝x33¼ inches. Rout all edges, including at the foot end, to a ¼-inch radius.

SANDING THE TABLE

The top must be rough sanded and finish sanded on all sides except the bottom surface. The aprons are sanded on the outside or "seam" surface and the legs all around.

ASSEMBLY STEPS

Joining the Apron Sections and Legs

Install 5⁄16 inch x 3½ inch hanger bolts into the legs. Center No. 1914 Stanley leg braces onto the aprons and attach with two ¾ inch No. 8 screws set in predrilled holes, as shown.

Place the top upside down on an assembly table and position the apron assembly roughly in place. Attach the legs to the leg braces by inserting hanger bolts through the center holes in the braces. Slip each washer on and tighten it with a hex nut. The subassembly of legs and aprons should be square.

Adding the Top

To assemble onto the bottom surface of the top, center the leg and apron unit, using the 1 inch overhang as a guide only. Fasten the top fasteners to the top on either side of one leg. Then measure and check the position of the leg diagonally across from the first; install the top fasteners. The entire assembly should now be square and ready for the rest of the top fasteners to be attached.

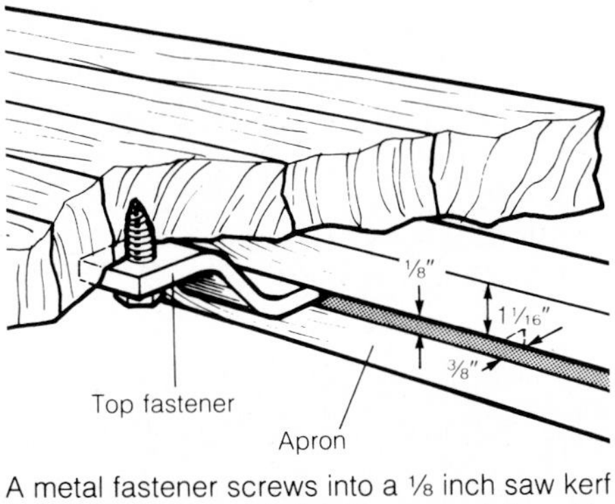

A metal fastener screws into a ⅛ inch saw kerf (or width of saw blade) to connect the side apron to the underside of the table top.

Adding Levelers or Casters

Finally, install the standard adjustable leveler glides in each leg according to the details shown in the accompanying specifications and drawing.

Materials List

Lumber:
8/4 stock 13 pieces 2⅞″x39″ for table top
5/4 stock 2 pieces 3″x30¾″ for side aprons 2 pieces 2″x15½″ for end aprons
6/4 stock 8 pieces 2⅞″x33½″ for legs

Hardware:
14 pieces Top fasteners (K.V.-324) (from Block Iron & Supply Co. or equivalent)
4 pieces Leg braces (#1914 Stanley) (from Craftsman Wood Service or equivalent)
4 pieces 5⁄16″x3½″ Hanger bolts with nuts (from Craftsman Wood Service or equivalent)
4 pieces Washers for the above hanger bolts
4 pieces No. 29 adjustable glide 1″ stem, 15⁄16″ diameter pad and ¼″ diameter stem with No. 20 threads. (from Stom Illinois Fiber Specialty or equivalent)
4 pieces "T" nuts ¼″x20″ with 3 spurs (from The Karl D. Engle Co., Inc. or equivalent)
1″ No. 8 flathead slotted wood screws

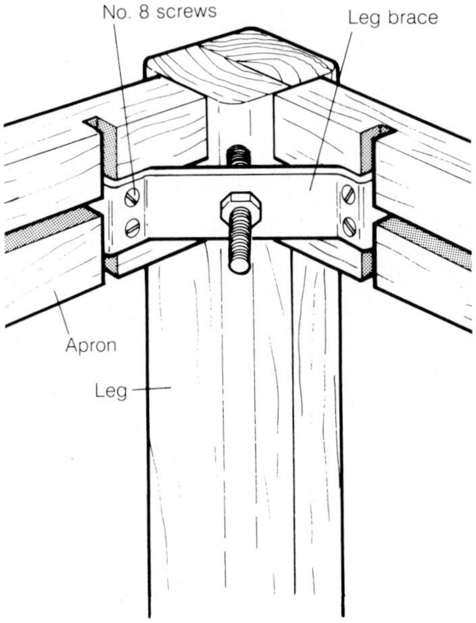

A corner hanger fastener braces the table and also connects to the table legs.

Project continued on next page

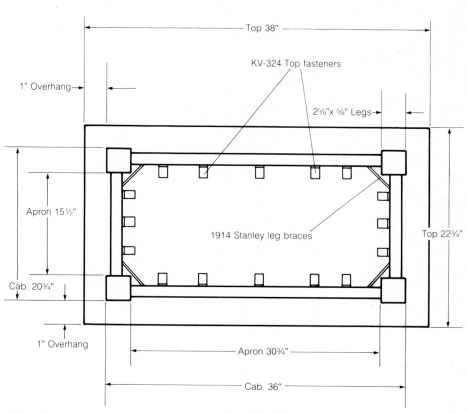

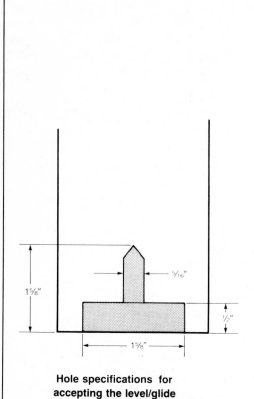

**Hole specifications for
accepting the level/glide**

Drill a hole in the bottom of the legs to receive an adjustable glide. Center the hole and drill in two sections as shown.

The butcher block top is supported by the legs and apron and held by screws driven through the top fasteners. Spacing as shown here will make the top very solid.

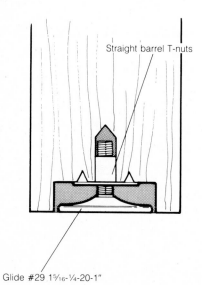

Glide #29 1⁵⁄₁₆-¼-20-1″

The glide is held as shown. If your floor is not level, adjust the glides to compensate for the difference and make the table even.

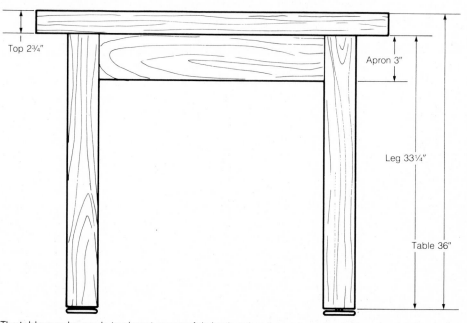

The table may be made to almost any useful size but the dimensions shown here should remain the same. Glides make the table easy to move on a smooth surface. Add casters if desired.

BOOKCASE FOLD-DOWN COUNTER

A combination bookcase and countertop unit can be conveniently located near the kitchen.

With the counter folded away, the unit takes very little room from the dining area.

MATERIALS

This unit is versatile enough to serve more than one purpose. It may be used as a kitchen planning desk, a small eating or serving counter, or an extra food preparation surface. Although it is probably most logical to cover the surfaces with laminate if the unit is in the kitchen, there is no reason you cannot paint the unit or even build it of fine hardwood and give it a stain and varnish finish. The system also may be scaled to a variety of sizes to fill a specific space. The maximum size is limited to 4x8 feet or 4x10 feet, the sizes of standard plywood sheets.

Construction Details

The sides of the unit may be constructed from ¾ inch plywood or standard 1x6 stock. The back is made of ¼ inch plywood. The shelves may be either plywood cut to size or stock lumber. The counter surface should be of ¾ inch plywood. The "leg" of the counter is of ½ inch plywood.

The counter is attached to the bookcase unit with hinges. The leg and counter are attached with special telescoping hinges that provide support when open but allow the unit to fold flat when closed up as the cover of the upper section of the bookcase.

If you wish to laminate the unit, do this by laminating the surfaces before assembly. However, do not laminate the ends of the permanent shelves that fit into the dadoes, unless you cut the dadoes wide enough to accept the laminated boards. To cover joints, laminate the exposed front edges after the basic bookcase unit is assembled.

Project continued on next page

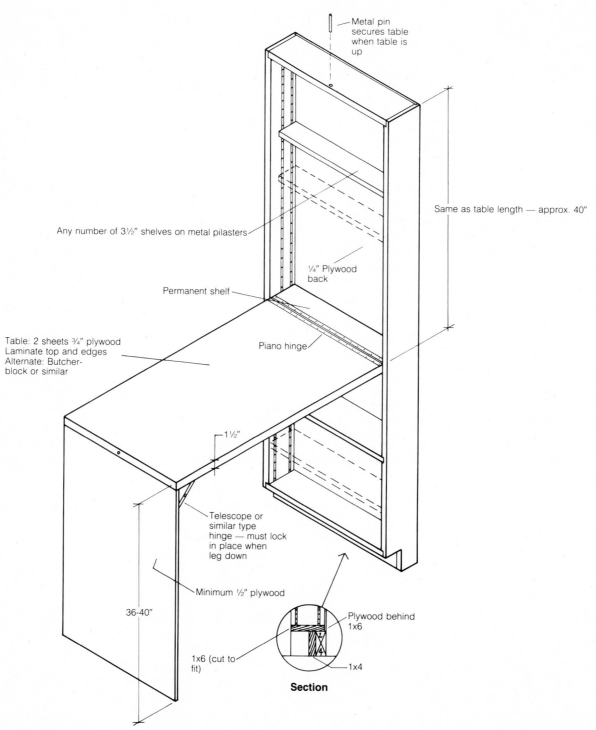

Metal pin secures table when table is up

Same as table length — approx. 40"

Any number of 3½" shelves on metal pilasters

¼" Plywood back

Permanent shelf

Table: 2 sheets ¾" plywood Laminate top and edges Alternate: Butcher-block or similar

Piano hinge

1½"

Telescope or similar type hinge — must lock in place when leg down

Minimum ½" plywood

36-40"

Plywood behind 1x6

1x6 (cut to fit)

1x4

Section

Construction of the unit is not difficult and the size may be altered to fit any space. The unit may be secured to the wall by driving screws through the plywood back into the studs.

CONSTRUCTION PROCEDURES

Step 1: Cutting the Lumber

Cut the 1x6 sides to the length needed for the height of your unit. Cut rabbet joints and dado joints as shown in the illustration. Rout dadoes to accept metal pilasters to support the shelves in the upper section of the unit.

Step 2: Cutting Top, Bottom and Shelves

The lower shelves of this unit are fixed. Measure carefully so that the shelves will fit in the dadoes cut in the side pieces. Cut the top and bottom pieces to fit in the rabbet joints. A slight variation in the length of the shelves or top will mean that the unit will not assemble square.

Step 3: Creating the Base

The unit sits on a base made of 2x4s. Cut the front and back pieces so they will fit between the sides of the unit. Install blocking between the front and back 2x4s to create a secure base for the unit. The base is slightly less deep than the bookcase unit in order to provide the toe space.

Step 4: Cutting the Back of the Unit

The plywood should cover the entire back, against the wall. Cut it from ¼-inch plywood.

Step 5: Assembling the Basic Bookcase

Install the pilasters in the routed recesses. Be sure the strips are aligned so your movable shelves will be even when installed. Attach the sides and the top. You may use countersunk No. 6, 1½-inch long flathead wood screws and fill the heads with wood putty, or use oval, round or pan head screws and leave them exposed. Drill pilot holes so the wood will not split.

Install the three permanent shelves in the lower part of the bookcase. Set the unit on the 2x4 base and attach with wood screws, countersunk and filled.

Attach the ¼-inch plywood back with brads or 4d finishing nails. Drive nails into the sides, top, bottom and permanent shelves.

Step 6: Building the Counter

Cut two pieces of ¾-inch plywood to the size required for the counter surface. Glue these two pieces together. Use a good, contact type or other wood glue. Clamp sheets together until thoroughly dry. Laminate if desired.

Cut the leg/support section. This will be the same size as the counter. Laminate as desired.

If you do not laminate these pieces, use veneer tape or other thin trim strips to give the edges a finished look.

Step 7: Installing Counter Section

Attach the leg to the counter with appropriate (telescoping hinges, if available, or piano hinges) hinges so that the two sections will fold flush. Attach the counter to the uppermost permanent shelf with piano or other appropriate hinges.

Step 8: Installing Closure Pin

Brace the counter up in the closed position. If the unit is less than 8 feet high, drill through the top and the edge of the leg section. Drop a metal rod or dowel through the hole to keep the unit closed. The dowel, of course, must be long enough to be gripped safely to pull out when you want to open the unit. If the unit is too tall for you to reach the top conveniently, drill the holes in the side above eye level.

Remove the pin and open the counter. Locate the hole in the leg and measure the location when it rests against the counter. Drill a hole through the counter to match the hole in the leg section. Place the metal rod or dowel through this hole to lock the counter and leg securely when the unit is open.

Step 9: Creating Movable Shelves

Cut (and laminate if desired) pieces of 1x3 stock for movable shelves in the upper part of the unit. Install pilaster clips as needed to support the shelves.

You may install a protective rail for each upper shelf (as shown in the photo on page 70) by drilling ¼-inch diameter holes ⅜-inch deep just above and in front of the edges of the movable shelves. Then cut the dowels ¼ inch longer than the width of the opening. The dowels will bend enough to allow installation.

Materials List (for unit 8 feet high and 4 feet wide)

Lumber: for sides, top, shelves and base 1x6 stock 8 feet long: 4 pieces for top, sides, and permanent shelves
1x3 stock 8 feet long: 2 pieces for movable shelves
2x4 stock 10 feet long: 1 piece for base

Plywood: for back, counter and leg
¼ inch plywood 4x8 sheet: 1 piece for back
½ inch plywood 4x8 sheet: ½ piece for leg
¾ inch plywood 4x8 sheet: 1 piece for counter

Dowels: for protective rail for movable shelves and anchor pin ¼ inch diameter dowel 4 feet long: as many pieces as needed

Hardware: for assembly
No. 6 flathead wood screws 1½ inches long: 20 - 25 pieces
Note: you may use oval, round or panhead screws for decorative effect.
Metal pilasters and clips: four pilaster strips to length required and as many clips as needed (four per shelf)
Hinges: Piano hinge to attach counter to basic unit shelf, telescoping (bracing) hinges or other suitable hinges to hold leg and counter. Use at least two to attach counter and leg.

SMALL WORK ISLAND WITH OVERHANGING COUNTERTOP

Work islands make large kitchens more efficient. Usually, work islands are attached to the floor. The work island in our example is raised on casters and may be moved about the kitchen as desired, serving as a preparation surface and storage area, and doubling as a bar or breakfast table with the addition of a foot rail.

The cabinets shown in our example are standard base cabinets that may be bought from stock or built as described in Chapter 3 of this text. Base cabinets are usually secured to walls,

with the back out of view. However, since the back of our portable cabinet is visible and is not attached to the wall, it will need to be ¾ inch plywood and will have to be finished. You can employ the typical methods of securing the countertop and securing the base cabinets to the framing underneath, but it is suggested that you increase the number of supporting members at the top and bottom of the cabinet. This is a matter of judgment, depending upon the length and depth of your cabinet.

STEP 1: BUILDING THE FRAMING
To build the work island, first build the 2x4 framing as shown in the illustration. The example work island is approximately 6 feet long by 2 feet deep. The 2x4 framing is simply two long members with cross members a maximum of 16 inches on center. A three-inch recess between the framing and the cabinet is shown all around at the base.

STEP 2: PROVIDING FOR CASTERS
At the ends of the framing, you must

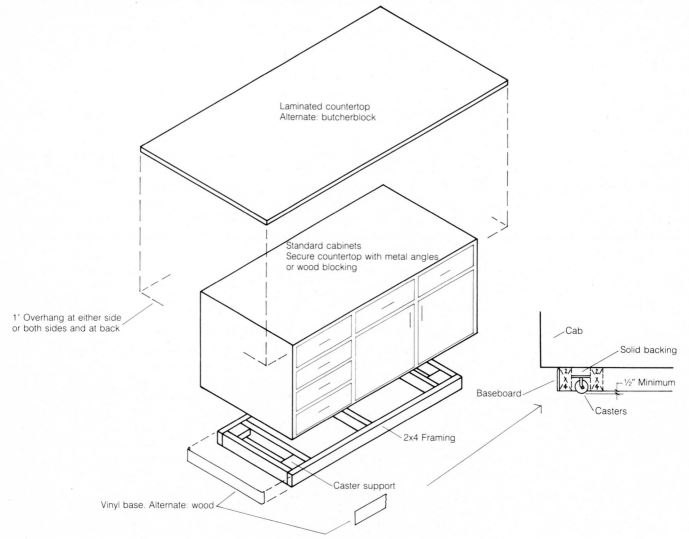

Laminated countertop
Alternate: butcherblock

Standard cabinets
Secure countertop with metal angles
or wood blocking

1' Overhang at either side
or both sides and at back

2x4 Framing

Caster support

Vinyl base. Alternate: wood

Cab

Solid backing

½" Minimum

Baseboard

Casters

Small island with laminated countertop
To assemble the island, first construct the framing, which rides on casters. Then add the cabinets and the countertop of your choice.

provide a place to secure the casters, if you need them. The method shown in our example will accommodate most casters. At each end simply add a 2x4 cross member as shown, then secure solid blocking (2x4 blocks or similar) at an appropriate height for your particular casters. The casters should be bought before you add these supports. The caster supports shown in our example raise the framing (and thus the cabinet) off the floor a minimum of ½ inch. Your caster may need a little more space, depending on the floor surface; carpeted areas may require a little more room to avoid dragging of the cabinet. Secure the casters to the caster supports. Bind the caster wheels, using wood shims, to keep the framing base in place while you secure the cabinet.

STEP 3: ATTACHING THE CABINET
If you buy a stock cabinet, the base framing will already be provided. In this case, beef up the existing framing with 2x4 or similar members and add the casters similarly to the method above. Add the vinyl or wood baseboard before you secure the cabinet to the framing. Secure the cabinet to the 2x4 framing using conventional methods: we suggest metal angles or wood blocking with flathead wood screws.

STEP 4: ADDING THE COUNTERTOP
Next, secure the countertop, using the conventional methods as discussed in Chapter 2. The countertop shown is made of two sheets of ¾ inch plywood glued together, then covered with laminate. A butcher block counter 1½ inches thick is a good alternate. For the cabinet shown, 6 feet by 2 feet, a one foot overhang is about right. You could make the overhang less, but making it more would require additional framing support under the overhang, and it would begin to look peculiar with a longer overhang. Generally, the overhang seems to look best if it is approximately ⅓ the total length area: in our example, the total depth of the countertop is three feet, one foot of that being overhang. This is not a firm rule, just a rule of thumb. (Another variation is to overhang the counter at each end.)

STEP 5: INCLUDING A FOOTRAIL
The overhang provides a good dining surface or bar, especially with the addition of a footrail. Brass or other metal footrailing should be adjusted so that it is a comfortable height for your family members and the type seating you intend to use. If your stools have metal foot rests, you do not really need a foot rail on the cabinet. Before adding the railing, finish the surface of the cabinet as desired.

If you do use a footrail on the cabinet, secure it to the cabinet with bolts and provide solid backing within the cabinet. Try to get a minimum of 2 inches of support blocking for the bolts; that is, if you use ¾ plywood for the back of the cabinet, the addition of a band of 2x4 blocking inside the cabinet would be adequate. Footrailing typically comes with its own vertical supports, which lessens the need for interior cabinet supports for the railing; however, the vertical supports rest on the floor, defeating the portability of the unit. If you do not use casters, this is of no consequence. If you wish to be able to roll the cabinet about, provide interior support for the railing as described above and omit the vertical railing supports that come with the railing.

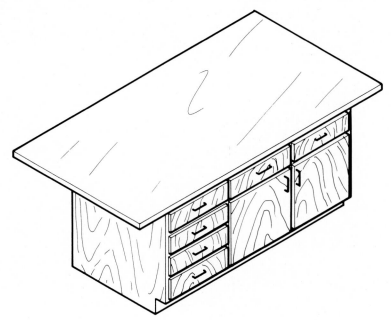

The top of this island extends out on all sides by 1 foot. This overhang makes the structure a useful eating and work area. The cook can move the island wherever he wishes.

LARGE WORK ISLAND WITH SINK AND DISHWASHER

The work island in our example is basically two sets of standard base cabinets butted together at their backs. The countertop shown is butcher block, but laminated plywood, real or man-made marble, or any other material suitable for countertops could have been used.

The sink shown is stainless steel. You could use any type of sink you desire, installed as described elsewhere in the text. The installation of grills, rangetops and so forth, follow the same installation procedures as outlined for other countertop insets described elsewhere in the text.

If you buy stock cabinets, choose units built to accommodate your appliances, like the dishwasher shown in our example. If you build your own cabinets, it is essential that you first select the appliances that you want, then build the cabinets to accommodate your particular appliance dimensions. Appliance manufacturers supply installation brochures and/or details showing what spaces and support are recommended.

Be sure before beginning that you have room for an island as large as this. If your space is limited, you may have to custom build your cabinets or modify any stock cabinets.

CONSTRUCTION PROCEDURES
Step 1: Locating the Island

Before you can determine the exact size of the island and counter, you will have to measure the space available for the unit. Remember that you will have to provide enough room on all sides for two people to pass easily and to allow all doors and drawers to open without jamming against nearby cabinets or walls. If you have a large, country kitchen or a combination kitchen-family room, this type of island is probably suitable for you. When you have determined the most logical and useful size, mark the proposed location on the floor. Try to walk around the area for several days to get used to the size and shape of the island and to see if the location interferes with basic traffic patterns.

Step 2: Check the Access for Water and Power Lines

You will have to extend the water and drain lines to the island if you wish to have a sink and/or dishwasher installed there. Have a plumber check your basement or crawl space to find the best path and manner of providing the extension. You may find that the drain extension requires a slope that will bring the line to the main stack in such a way that it cuts off easy access to your laundry area or furnace. Water supply lines are seldom a problem because water is moved through these pipes under pressure; however, drains work by gravity or by the force of a pump.

Power lines are usually not a problem unless the installation is unusually awkward. If your electrician has to spend five or ten minutes wriggling in and out of a confined area as he performs each step of the installation, you will pay a great deal for this extra time. Checking on the possible difficulties of the installation before making any final plans or purchases can save you a great deal of money.

Step 3: Purchase Your Appliances

If your island design will fit in the space, and if the water, drain and power lines can be installed at a reasonable cost, choose the appliances you wish to have in the island. Our example shows a sink and a dishwasher, but you may install a range top, a trash compactor, or simply use the unit for storage and a work surface. Once you have chosen the appliances you want to have in the island, check the available space once more to see if you will be able to use stock cabinets for all sections, and, if not, whether you will have to build — or have built — some special size units. Once you have made your decisions about appliances and are certain about the models you want, you may either purchase the models with delivery scheduled for a later date, or arrange for delivery and store them.

Obviously later delivery is more convenient, but whatever you do, make sure to get the installation instructions and owner's manual at the time of purchase so you can double and triple check the manufacturer's specifications for size, access and hookup.

Step 4: Building or Purchasing the Cabinets

If your cabinets are stock units, you will probably want to buy stock cabinets for the island. However, if you wish to build your own, follow the basic directions given in Chapter Three and build

A large center island can provide extensive storage and working space and may adapt to contain any number of appliances such as a range top, trash compactor and dishwasher.

the units to your specifications. Because the units will sit back-to-back, it would be advisable to rabbet the back framing so that the plywood panels on the back will be flush with the framing.

Step 5: Installing the Island
Place the base unit(s) for the island in position. Rough in the plumbing and electrical connections. Position the cabinets on the base and attach as required.

Step 6: Installing the Appliances
Under counter appliances should be installed at this point. It is easier to slide appliances into position and to hookup connections for a dishwasher or trash compactor before you add the countertop.

Step 7: Adding the Countertop
Your countertop may be, as mentioned above, any practical material of your choice. Remember, however, that if you use a heavy material such as marble or ceramic tile, you have to provide additional bracing to support the weight. Follow directions for installation given in Chapters Two and Three for fabrication and installation.

Cut openings for and install your sink, range or special insets as required. There are directions provided with the appliance, sink or inset material.

Step 8: Finish the Cabinets
Stock cabinets may be prefinished; however, the cabinets that you have built, or any unfinished stock cabinets, must be finished. Do this in whatever manner is appropriate and practical for your cabinets.

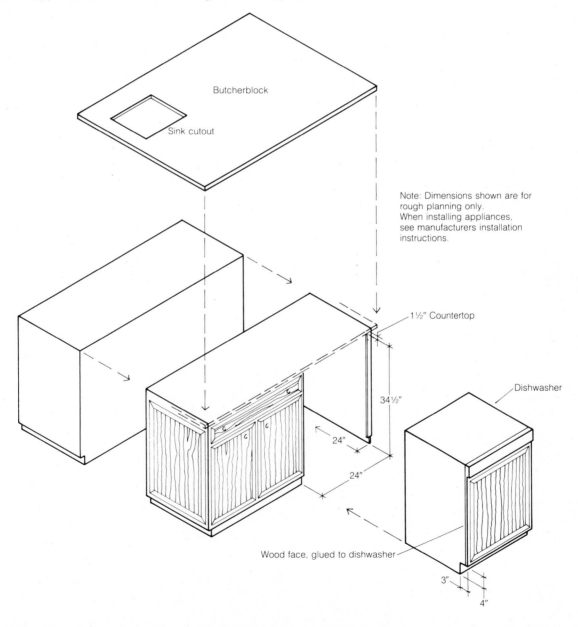

Large work island with sink and dishwasher
The construction of the island is limited only by the space available and the space required for the proper installation of the appliances.

SERVING COUNTER

The serving counter in our example is a clean and light design that functions as both a dining and work counter equally well. The instructions that follow describe a prefabricated butcher-block surface for the serving counter, but you may use laminated plywood or similar construction with other materials if you wish.

The unit shown was built with an angle, but you may use the same basic instructions to create a straight counter.

The serving bar is 36 inches high and two feet wide. It is supported at the

A very compact kitchen has considerable working and serving space when an angled counter, such as this one, is installed. Wall end support has extra storage.

end with a "leg" of the butcherblock with the same dimensions. At the wall the serving counter fits between two vertical supports that may be made of butcherblock, laminated double sheets of plywood (like a laminated countertop), or stock lumber. The serving counter butts the wall and is connected to both the wall and the two vertical supports with a 1x2 ledger that runs between the vertical supports and along the wall as indicated in the plan view illustration.

The vertical supports create the sides of a shelf unit. The supports may be fitted inside with metal pilasters and clips to vary the number of shelves and the spacing for your needs.

CONSTRUCTION PROCEDURES

Step 1: Designing to Fit Your Space

First, determine the materials you wish to use for your counter. Then measure the space carefully. Compute the materials you will need from a plan drawing. Purchase the materials needed. **Note:** if you wish to construct the butcherblock counter yourself, follow basic instructions for this project given on pages 114-116.

Step 2: Cut Your Materials to Size

Carefully check all the measurements. Do this before you mark the boards and other materials and before you make any cuts.

Step 3: Install Wall Support Sections

To assemble the serving counter, first install the vertical supports and the 1x2 ledger as indicated in the plan view illustration. Be sure you secure the led-

ger and the vertical supports to solid backing. Use ¼ inch by 3 inch flathead wood screws to attach to studs.

Step 4: Install the Counter

Place a sawhorse near where the end leg will be located. Lift the serving counter onto the horse and the ledger on the wall. Secure the serving counter at the wall, angling ⅛ inch by 2 inch flathead wood screws up through the ledger into the serving top.

Now, install the leg, using the metal angles indicated in the assembly view illustration. These metal angles, or braces, may be decorative if you wish

— they come in many styles and several materials, including brass. Use at least 4 of these angles, two close to the edges and the other two equally spaced between the edges. Quarter-inch x 1 inch flathead wood screws are adequate.

Secure the leg to the floor, angling ¼ x 3 inch flathead wood screws through each end at several points along the edge.

Step 5: Finishing

Last, install the trim per the illustrations, then finish as desired.

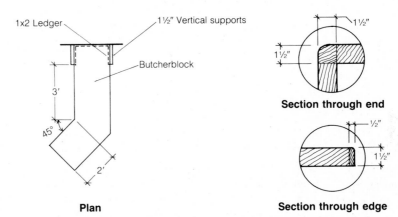

Plan

This plan view and section show details of wall end support and finish of leg end. Counter run must be sturdy enough and short enough to stand without center support.

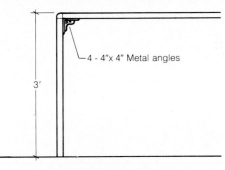

Partial front view

The leg of the counter matches the counter surface and is held in place and braces by four metal angles secured with screws.

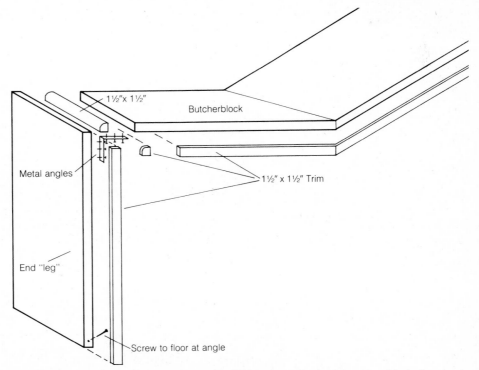

Metal angles hold leg and counter together. Filler strip and edge trim are added when basic construction is complete. Surface finish is to your choice.

8
UNDERCOUNTER PROJECTS

To increase the versatility and convenience of your food preparation and sink areas, consider adding facilities to the area under and around the counter. The most popular such addition is, of course, the dishwasher. The dishwasher installation presented here is actually a conversion from a portable to a built-in, a situation that occurs frequently. The other items fall into more of a "luxury" category: a bar sink, an instant hot-water dispenser, and a serving cart that rolls under the counter and is disguised with a front panel to match the rest of the cabinetry.

A bar sink can be located away from your regular run of kitchen counter for added convenience.

An under-counter serving cart may be disguised behind a false front that matches the style of your cabinetry (project on page 130).

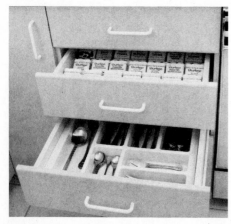

Drawer and utensil dividers keep spices and silverware neatly arranged and easy to reach.

A bar sink can eliminate problems when entertaining (installation instruction on page 134).

For extra counter space, a slip-out work surface can be fastened to the cabinet interior.

INSTALLING A DISHWASHER

A portable dishwasher may be a short-term answer to dirty dishes for many families. However, it is often inconvenient in the long run to have a unit that must be stored in a closet or left standing when not in use, and set awkwardly next to the sink when in use. Furthermore, because the portable is attached to the sink faucet, the kitchen sink cannot be used while the washer is running.

Most portables are "convertible" for under-counter installation. Installation on one side of the sink, convenient to the storage location of the dishes, solves most of the problems of a portable dishwasher.

A built-in dishwasher requires its own 20 amp circuit. You should have an electrician handle the wiring because of the dangers inherent in electrical connections near water.

STEP 1: PREPARING THE OPENING

If you are remodeling and installing all new cabinets, leave space for the dish-

A dishwasher should be convenient to both the sink, for rinsing off the dishes, and the wastebasket or trash compactor, for scraping material that will not go through a disposer.

The standard dishwasher is 24 inches wide and will fit below a standard countertop. The convenience makes up for the loss of cabinet space.

Project continued on next page

washer and span this opening with the countertop. If you are installing the dishwasher in an existing kitchen, you will have to sacrifice a 24-inch section of base cabinet, either a drawer or a shelf section.

Pull out the drawers and remove hardware. With a saw, cut through the facing and kick plate to the floor. A reciprocating saw will make this job relatively simple. If the unit is a shelf and door cupboard, remove the door and the shelves and cut out the facing.

If you are doing major remodeling, install the dishwasher before adding the countertop. This is an easier installation.

The dishwasher is made to slip under a standard-height cabinet. If your counter is higher than usual, you will have to install a filler strip when the dishwasher is in place.

If your flooring takes up much room, as may be the case if several layers of flooring have been laid over the years, you will probably have to cut some of this away to get the dishwasher into position.

STEP 2: AN OPENING FOR PIPES

Make sure that the dishwasher fits into the space intended for it before doing any of this plumbing work. Make any adjustments necessary. Cut an opening in the side of the cabinet between the dishwasher and the sink compartment. The opening should be large enough to allow passage of the supply and drain lines.

STEP 3: MAKING PLUMBING CONNECTIONS

You must provide a hot water connection and a drain connection. Because a dishwasher is usually located adjacent to the sink, it is relatively simple to make the connections to the hot water supply line and the existing drain.

However, there are some adaptations necessary.

Connecting to the Water Supply

Purchase a T-fitting with a shutoff valve and enough copper tubing to reach from the connection at the pipe to the connection at the dishwasher. Use compression fittings for these connections. The dishwasher installation manual will specify the correct tubing size and should have the compression nut attached to the intake. Check this carefully before starting.

Turn off the water and drain the line. Cut the supply line below the shut off and attach a T-fitting with compression nuts and rings. Attach a shutoff valve for the dishwasher to the T-fitting and a new supply line for the dishwasher to the valve. Again, use compression fittings. Turn by hand until tight. Then give an additional quarter turn with a wrench. Do not overtighten or you will crack the tubing. Run the supply line to the dishwasher, but do not hook it up. Place a large bucket under the supply line and turn on the water to check new connections for leaks. Shut off the water. Tighten the connections as needed.

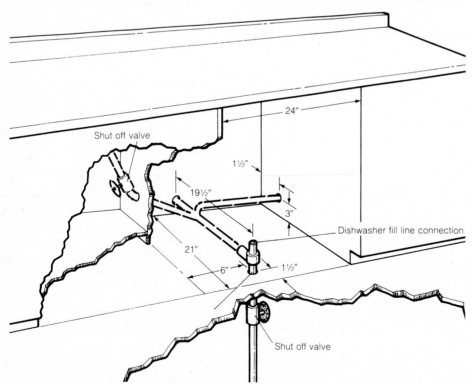

The water line for the dishwasher can be run directly up from the basement or from the line under the adjacent sink. Use the most convenient path; include a shutoff valve.

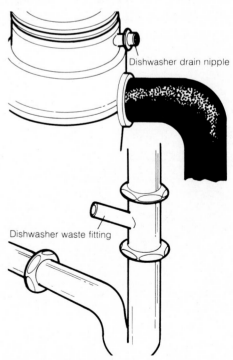

The drain line from the dishwasher may connect to a new fitting in the sink drain line, above the trap, or to a disposer.

Connecting the Drain Line

The drain is a rubber or plastic hose that is resistent to high temperatures. It attaches to the dishwasher drain outlet with a hose clamp. Run the line through the opening in the cabinet. It is strongly advised, even if local codes do not specify or require it, that you run the drain to an air gap connection or create a loop that will bring the line above the level of the sink. Otherwise, if your sink drain becomes obstructed, the foul water will backup into your dishwasher. You may either purchase a prefabricated air gap that connects above the sink to the hose, or loop the hose as high as possible under the sink cabinet to create this loop.

You may install a drain fitting above the P-trap on the sink drain or into your disposal. There is usually a connection provided. The drain fitting will fit on the drain line with regular pipe retaining nuts. The section has a projection on which the flexible drain hose will clamp tight.

STEP 4: FINISHING THE INSTALLATION

Hook up the electrical connection. Connect black wire to black, white wire to white. Use wire caps (wire nuts) to seal the connection. Attach green ground wire to the screw provided and replace cover.

Level the dishwasher by turning the levelers on each leg. Use wood screws to attach the dishwasher to the countertop.

Turn on the water and the electricity to the special circuit for the dishwasher and run the unit through one cycle. Check for any leaks. Install the kick-plate cover that hides the plumbing and electrical connections.

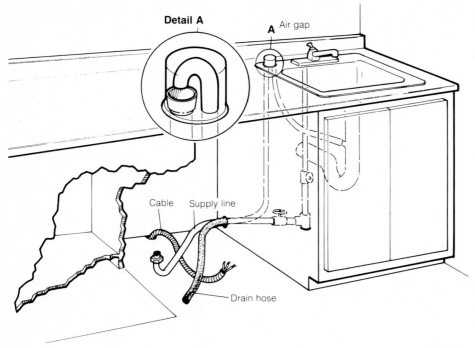

Detail A

A Air gap

Cable   Supply line

Drain hose

Dishwasher connections are a power cable, on a separate circuit, a supply line and a drain hose, which should have an air gap to prevent sink drain back up into the dishwasher.

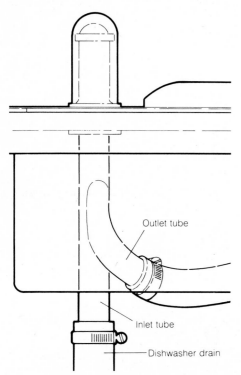

Outlet tube

Inlet tube

Dishwasher drain

A prefabricated air gap is installed in the spray hose opening or in another created in the counter top. Many codes require their use.

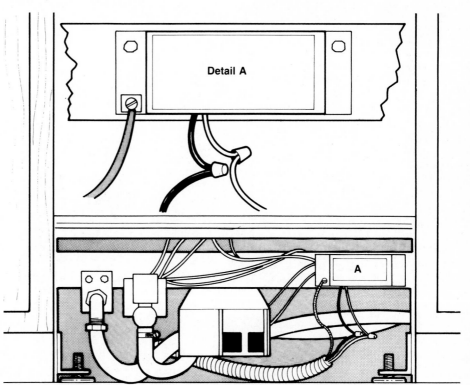

Detail A

A

Shown, left to right, are the standard hookups for the water supply line, the drain line and the power. Note the fittings and hookup of each. Wire attached to screw is the ground wire.

PORTABLE SERVING CART

The serving unit described here fits under the countertop, blending in with the face detailing of the base cabinet. It can hardly be distinguished from a cabinet door.

You will note that the serving unit is just a box mounted on casters. All the plywood shown should be at least ¾ inch and preferably 1 inch. The shelf at the top is permanent and necessary for stability. This shelf is for the most-used items: salads and dressings, table spices, etc. Metal pilasters and clips in the lower portion of the serving unit allow you to adjust shelves as you need them.

You can plan for the cart when putting in your cabinets by leaving the required opening. Otherwise you will have to remove part of the existing cabinetry.

STEP 1: PREPARING THE OPENING
Before you build the serving unit, pencil off the area to be cut on the cabinet face, if necessary. But do not cut out the framing yet. Before you saw out the base cabinet front, add any new framing you need, as indicated in the illus-

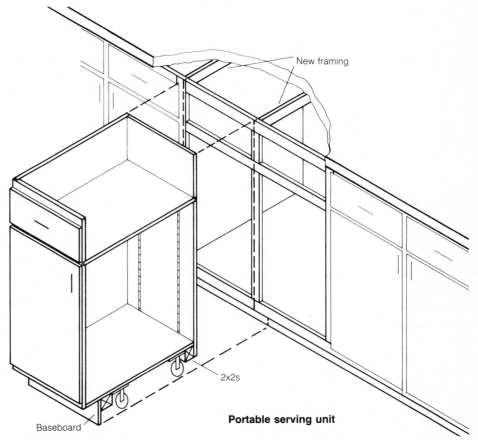

Portable serving unit

This portable unit contains two permanently fixed shelves. Metal pilasters accept support clips for movable shelves. Unit may be a portable bar, a baking center, or server.

tration. Remove the floor of the base cabinet where the serving unit will be and add new framing as required. By anticipating the new framing you need, and adding it *before* you cut the existing framing, you are less likely to weaken the existing cabinet structure.

If you are building the serving unit along with the base cabinet from scratch, you simply frame for the serving unit as you build the base cabinet.

STEP 2: CUTTING THE PIECES

Cut the sides and back from a sheet of ½-inch plywood. The depth of the cart will be the depth of the counter (usually 24 inches) less the thickness of the front. The height of the pieces will be the height of the counter, less the thickness of the countertop and the caster height. Also cut strip for a toe space to match the rest of the cabinets.

STEP 3: BUILDING THE CART

To build the serving cart, assemble the ½-inch plywood components using the construction techniques discussed for base cabinets in Chapter 3.

The shelf fits into dado joints on all three vertical plywood pieces. Predrill for ⅛-inch screws, 4 inches on center, to hold together the vertical pieces and bottom.

The dummy drawer and cabinet door can either be glued to the vertical plywood or screwed from behind with ⅛-inch flathead wood screws. You may be able to buy this front to match existing cabinets. If not, be sure to test stains before applying them, for the right color.

At the bottom of the serving unit, 2x2s are used for reinforcement and to hold the front baseboard in place. This baseboard must be approximately ¼ to ½ inch off the floor. The casters should be purchased at a quality hardware store. Do not buy cheap casters. The casters come with their own base plates and usually the screws or bolts for their attachment.

STEP 4: CUTTING THE OPENING

When the serving cart is finished, measure its as-built dimensions and substitute these actual dimensions for the proposed dimensions you used earlier. This gives a close fit. Use a sabre saw to cut out along the dashed line (as in the illustration). Then slide in the serving unit, making any necessary adjustments for a precision fit.

This unit, manufactured in Europe, matches the cabinet run. The shelving used here is a pull-out wire rack style. Interior provides storage and the top an extra work or serving surface.

Materials List

1 sheet ½″ plywood
4 casters
4 2-foot strips of metal pilasters
4 support clips
2 pieces 2x2 cut to the width of the cart
Door/drawer handles
Wood screws No. 8 1½″ long
4d or 5d box nails

INSTALLING A HOT-WATER DISPENSER

There are two types of hot water dispensers: a flash heater that simply heats water passing through it as the tap is turned on, and other units with small tanks. However, we will discuss installation of only tank units because they are more commonly found in kitchens.

The tanks heat one-half gallon of water to boiling and hold it at 190°, a temperature that is ideal for making tea, instant coffee, instant soups, and drip coffee. The tank fits under the sink; the dispenser tap may attach to the hole that is usually available for the spray hose on most modern sinks. If installation must be made in the countertop, the dispenser tap can be inserted in a 1¼-inch diameter hole drilled in the countertop and the lines run through any cabinet wall.

SYSTEM COMPONENTS
The Tank

The tank unit consists of the tank inside a container shell that attaches to a wall. The tank contains a heating element and an adjustable thermostat to compensate for differences that occur in the heating levels because of elevation above sea level. The tank unit also contains a power cord with a three-prong (grounded) plug. The unit must be plugged into a grounded outlet. It cannot be attached to a three-to-two adapter or the thermostat fuse may malfunction.

The Dispenser

The dispenser unit contains the tap, the water feed lines and the vent line. The dispenser is approximately 4 inches high, but there is a model that accepts an extension sleeve to raise the dispenser tap another 4 inches, if installation requires extra clearance.

Water Supply Lines

The unit may be attached to either a hot or cold water line. If attached to the hot water line, the water will heat faster and the tank will be less likely to be troubled with lime-deposit build-up. The unit comes with a drain plug to minimize such lime deposits.

INSTALLATION PROCEDURES

Remove from the sink the spray hose attachment or the plug in the spray hose opening. If your sink does not have this feature, you will have to drill and clean a 1¼-inch hole in your countertop. If there is a cabinet side in the way, drill holes and run tubing through holes to the space under the sink. Do not attempt to drill a hole in the sink.

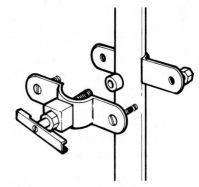

Saddle valve taps a supply line and seals the hole while as a connection to the new line.

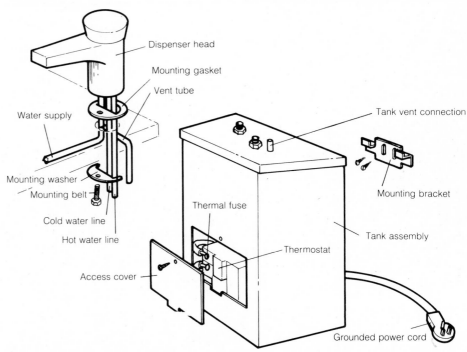

Water held just below boiling in half-gallon tank provides enough for instant coffee, tea, bouillon, and quick soups and drinks.

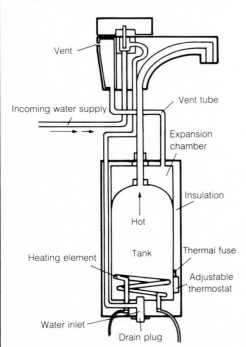

Water in small tank heats and holds at 190°. Vent/expansion chamber are safety features.

Installation is relatively simple. The tank hangs on a bracket under the sink. The faucet usually fits through the spray hose opening. Standard length tubing is attached.

Mounting the Dispenser

Remove the dispenser tap from the package and carefully straighten the copper tubing. One good way to do this is to lay the unit on a hard surface and run your hand along the tubing several times. When the tubing is straight, slip it through the opening or drilled hole. The dispenser unit should sit on the mounting gasket that covers the hole. The mounting screw attaches to this gasket. A mounting washer then slips over the screwhead from the underside of the sink or counter, positioned so the screw shaft is in the slot. Tighten the screw to hold this part in place.

Attaching to the Water Supply

There are three sections of copper tubing, two ¼-inch and one ⁵⁄₁₆-inch, and one plastic tube attached to the tap. The longer piece of ¼-inch copper tubing attaches to the water supply. You will have to attach the supply line of the dispenser tap to either the hot or cold water supply pipe. Depending upon local codes and the type of pipe involved, this may be as simple as attaching a self-piercing saddle valve to copper pipe or as complicated as cutting out a section of galvanized or plastic pipe and installing a gate valve connection with compression fittings.

Connecting a saddle valve The saddle valve attaches to the main supply line and the supply tube for the dispenser is attached to the saddle valve. A hole must be predrilled in galvanized pipe. Shut off the water and, using a hand drill, drill a small hole. Attach the saddle valve. Place a pan under the connection and turn on the water to clear the line and check the seal. Then shut off the water again.

Installing a gate valve. A gate valve is attached by cutting a short section of pipe from the supply line after you have shut off the water. Then insert a T-section into the supply pipe and attach with compression fittings at either end. The gate valve attaches to the T with a compression fitting. Place a bucket under the open end of the gate valve and turn on the water supply, keeping the gate valve shut. Check for leaks at the compression joints. Tighten the nuts on the compression joints to close off leaks. Check the fittings each day for three or four days, tightening the nuts a little every day until the joints are completely sealed. Open the gate valve to flush that pipe, run the water into the pail.

Hooking up the supply line. When the saddle valve or gate valve line has been cleared, attach the supply line to the valve connection: slip the nut from the valve over the end of the supply tube and insert the end of the tube into the supply valve. Tighten the nut on the tubing to the ferrule on the supply valve. Place a pail under the other tubes from the dispenser tap and turn on the water. The water should run out the second ¼-inch tube. Flush the line and shut off the water.

Installing the Tank

The tank may be placed on either the back or on a side wall below the sink. The maximum distance below the sink that it can be placed is limited by the reach of the copper tubing. This is usually 16 inches or less. Hold the tank in the position in which you want it installed and mark the location of the top on the wall.

Attach the mounting bracket with screws. The bracket should be located on the wall so that the top of the bracket is one inch below the mark for the position of the top. Hang the tank on the mounting bracket.

Attaching the Lines

The copper lines from the dispenser attach to the tank connections with compression fittings. The plastic vent tube attaches with a small hose clamp.

Flushing out the Lines and the Tank

Except for the electrical connection, the installation is complete. Before plugging in the unit, however, you must fill and flush the tank. Turn the knob or handle and hold in the on position until water flows out of the tap. This will take a minute or more. Let the water flow for a short time; then shut it off.

Final Steps

When you are sure that the tank is full, plug in the cord. The tank will take about 15 minutes to heat. If water drips from the spout, turn on the tap and run 4 or more cups of water out to relieve pressure on the expansion chamber. The unit will make a bubbling noise as the water reaches the proper temperature.

The thermostat is set for boiling, to assure purity, and then to hold the water at 190°. However, the thermostat is set for sea level. At elevations appreciably above sea level, you may need to lower the thermostat to prevent constant boiling. The thermostat access is through a removable plate on the front of the tank. Also, lower the thermostat setting if the tap releases steam when water is drawn.

If the unit does not work, check the circuit breaker. If it is on, set the thermostat higher to see if the water heats.

Maintenance Precautions

Unplug the unit if you are going to be away from home for several days. If you are going to be gone for several weeks or you are shutting a summer home for the winter, run the dispenser tap until the water becomes cool, unplug the unit, shut off the supply valve and remove the tank drain plug to drain the water in the tank. Replace the drain plug. **Always fill the tank with water before connecting the plug to the power source.** *Because the water dispensed is scalding, care must be taken to prevent misuse by children or the elderly.*

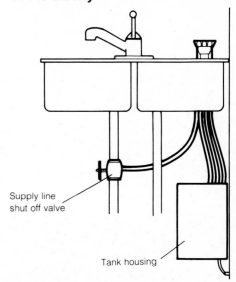

Supply line shut off valve

Tank housing

For fastest and most economical heating, attach supply line to hot water line. Provide a separate shutoff valve to the tank.

INSTALLING A BAR SINK

Because a bar sink is so much smaller than a regular kitchen sink, it is easier to install than a larger and more complex plumbing fixture.

These sinks are meant for auxiliary use, to aid in preparation of drinks while entertaining, so that the cook is not interrupted or inconvenienced during meal preparation. They also provide quick access to water and beverage service in family or recreation rooms. A bar sink is small enough to fit into a confined area, such as the end of a run of counter or even in a small cupboard or closet.

Sinks are available in enameled cast iron, but the majority of the bar sinks are in a lightweight acrylic with a stain-resistant finish. There are faucet units designed especially for the sinks. Each sink comes with a template to use in marking the countertop for the cutout.

You will need to provide supply pipe to bring water to the location of the sink and drain pipe to carry the waste water away. Assuming that you have reached this stage, either by doing the

If your space is large enough, you may install a bar sink with a cutting board and cups to hold condiments.

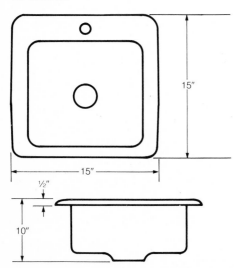

A standard bar sink is only 15 inches square and will fit in small spaces. The 10 inch depth allows adequate depth for washing glasses.

pipe work yourself or having a professional "rough in" the pipes to this point, the actual installation is one of the simpler tasks available to the do-it-yourselfer. Be sure shut-off valves to the supply lines are closed before beginning work.

STEP 1: MARKING THE COUNTERTOP

Lay the template on the countertop. Check the position so that the cutout (sink location) is correctly placed. Insure that the supply and drain pipes can reach the sink for the hookup. Draw the outline on the countertop; remove the template.

STEP 2: CUTTING THE OPENING

Drill a hole at each inside corner of the sink outline; the holes should just touch the line drawn on the countertop. Use a sharp keyhole saw or a sabre saw to cut exactly along the line as marked. It is better to cut fractionally inside the line and to use a rasp to trim back than to cut outside the line. This could result in an edge too narrow to support the sink.

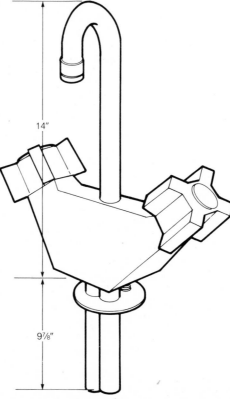

The faucet designed for the bar sink installs through a single opening. Supply lines attach to main lines with compression fittings.

STEP 3: FITTING THE SINK

Test-fit the sink in the opening. Then trace the outside edge of the sink rim. Pull the sink out of the hole and assemble and attach the drain fitting and strainer. If there are adhesive strips on the underside of the sink rim, remove protective paper, set the sink into position and press down. If your sink does not have these strips, apply adhesive as specified by the manufacturer. Fit the sink into place and press down.

STEP 4: SEALING THE SINK

Apply caulk, as specified or supplied, around the rim of the sink. Press to seal edges and wipe excess caulk from the counter before it dries.

STEP 5: INSTALLING THE FAUCET

Insert the faucet unit into the sink. Acrylic sinks come with a single opening to accommodate the faucet unit designed for them. However, you may use standard faucet units by drilling holes in the sink rim at the spacing and to the size required.

The basic bar sink faucet unit has the supply pipes next to each other, so you will have to bend the tubing to some degree to reach your roughed-in supply pipes. Attach the supply lines with reducing nuts and compression fittings.

STEP 6: ATTACHING THE DRAIN

The drain pipe should be hooked up to the roughed-in drain and include the trap unit. These sections are held together by tightly fitting retaining nuts. The drain unit that comes with the sink is sealed at the sink by a rubber gasket provided with the unit.

STEP 7: CHECKING THE CONNECTIONS

Turn on the water at the shut-off valves to check for leaks at the pipe joints. If there is any leakage, shut off the water and tighten the connections. Do not overtighten. Keep checking every day for a week. If there are any leaks, tighten the nuts a little each day. Do not turn more than a quarter turn each day, or you may crack the tubing or the compression nuts.

9
ALL ABOUT WALLS

Before you can add, remove, or otherwise modify the walls in your home, you must understand the structure of a wall. We will deal only with interior walls.

ANATOMY OF A WALL
Materials in a Typical Wall

Wood framing. The most common wall construction is the wood-framed wall. This is made up of 2x4s (often pressure-treated) for a bottom plate, a double 2x4 top plate, and 2x4 studs at 16 inches on center. In some cases, the wall will have framing 24 inches on center. In very old homes the spacing may vary.

Surface finish materials. Most post World War II homes will have surfaces of gypsumboard (also called wallboard, drywall, plasterboard, or carry the trade name Sheetrock). Prefinished paneling also is commonly used. Plaster is occasionally used today, but it is not as common.

How to Identify Bearing or Load-Carrying Walls

Most interior walls are just room dividers; they can be removed without structural problems. However, some may be load-carrying or "bearing" walls. A bearing wall usually will run the length of the house and be roughly in the center. However, it can jog, and the function may not be obvious. The bearing wall helps cut down the span of the ceiling joists, allowing use of shorter lengths of lumber.

Depending upon the size of your house, or the type of soil under it, you may have more than one interior bearing wall, or you may have none at all. This often can be determined by looking at the construction plans for your home, if they are available. You may also be able to tell by looking in the attic.

An interior wall that runs perpendicular to the ceiling joists (joined either by lapped joints or butt joints) is a bearing

wall. Interior walls running parallel to the joists rarely are bearing walls. Homes framed with roof trusses normally have no interior bearing walls.

If you are unsure about the location of load-carrying walls, or if there has been a considerable amount of settling, have an expert look at your home.

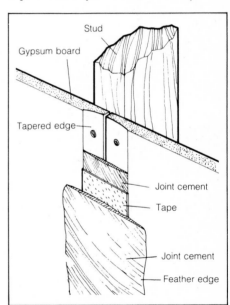

Wallboard joints are taped, spackled, and sanded to produce smooth seams.

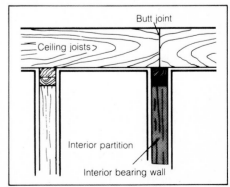

An interior bearing wall will support ceiling joists that run perpendicular to the wall.

Wallboard gives an excellent base for paneling, wallpaper or textured paint.

Mid-height partitions separate this kitchen area from the rest of the living space.

HOW TO TAKE OUT A WALL

The following instructions are for non-load-bearing walls only. Before you remove any wall, disconnect electrical wiring and drain plumbing pipes in the wall. There is always a possibility of a shock, of a fire, or of water damage to the home. Even if you have shut off the circuit to the plugs in the wall you are removing, there is a possibility still that there is a live wire in the wall cavity. Shut off power at your circuit box. There also could be a plumbing pipe in the wall even if there are no plumbing fixtures immediately adjacent to it. Determine the path of your plumbing risers from your basement. Drive a long, thin nail through the subflooring from the basement to give you a guide marker if you are not sure which wall they pass through.

If you are not completely familiar with the wiring and plumbing in your home, shut the electricity and water completely off when you begin removing the wall surface. If you need light or power tools, leave one circuit on in a completely different area of the house and run a heavy-duty extension cord to your working area for a lamp or your tools. Once the wall surface has been removed, all electrical conduit and plumbing lines will be visible.

How to Remove a Masonry Wall
Check in the attic to be sure that the wall does not extend into an upper story. If the mortar is old, it may crumble. This makes it easy to remove bricks intact. Then you can clean the excess mortar from the bricks. Remove a brick or block on the top row, using a hammer and masonry chisel. This first brick or block will be the hardest to take out. For the rest of the work there will be more room to chip out the mortar. Remove the rest of the units in that row and work across the succeeding courses until you have disassembled the whole wall.

Safety precautions. Because this is dusty work, wear a breathing mask. Cover or remove all furniture in the room. *Always* wear goggles to protect your eyes; even experienced workers have lost an eye performing such a job.

Never try to remove a first-floor brick wall if a section of the wall continuing on the second floor is to remain. Although you can provide temporary or permanent support for such a wall, the cost will be prohibitive. It is more reasonable to design around the situation. If you remove a portion of a brick wall for a door or passageway, install a steel lintel in the wall by mortaring it above the opening before you begin to completely remove the brick.

How to Remove Frame Walls
A stud-framed wall usually will be much easier to remove than a masonry wall. The surface material is first taken off, and then the wood framing disassembled.

Removing a wallboard panel. Gently pry off the base molding. Use a pry bar and hammer for this, but take it easy as you pry. When the molding has been removed, pull out the nails and store the molding out of your way.

With a hammer, break out the gypsumboard panel back to the studs to which the sides of the panel have been nailed. If you go very slowly, you can remove the entire damaged panel by removing chunks of the panel and pulling the nails as you go. Do it in small pieces rather than jerking off the whole panel at once.

When you come to the panel joints, cut the gypsumboard tape that spans the joints along the sides and at the ceiling line. Do this with the razor knife.

With the panel removed, you should have a neat, clean hole in the wall with the studs exposed and gypsumboard panels overlapping the side studs by about half the width. Repeat for each panel.

Paneled walls. If the walls are paneled, work carefully and try to remove the panels intact. To remove the paneling, pry a little at a time along one edge. Do not try to pry one nail up completely before moving to the next. Work on each nail a little at a time until you have freed an edge. Then work on the next set of nails. You may need a long crowbar to reach the middle portion of a wide panel.

Removing the wall framing. The stud wall can easily be disassembled

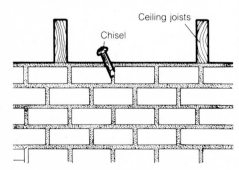

When removing a masonry wall, start working at the top of the wall. Chip out mortar between bricks with a cold chisel and a mallet.

Removing a load-bearing wall is beyond the scope of most homeowners. Support for ceiling joists is required when this type of wall is taken out, or when more than one wall stud is cut.

and taken down once the surface material is removed. Use a nail claw to lift out large nails without severely damaging the framing lumber. Sharpen the claws of the hammer from time to time with a file to keep an edge that will slip under the nail head.

Remove the framing one piece at a time, beginning with the studs. Pull the toe nails out at the top and bottom and "wiggle" the stud out from the remaining framing. Do not hit the stud hard; this could cause damage. If the stud does not come out easily, tap it lightly with a hammer, alternately at the top and bottom. Do not strike the stud in the middle. Continue until all the studs are removed.

Work carefully, because when the studs are out, the top plates might fall down. To prevent this, leave a stud at each end to support the top plate, which should not have been nailed to the ceiling joists. Pull any nails out of the top plates and remove it. Then take out the two end studs. Finally, remove the nails or pins holding the bottom plate down and lift it out of place.

Creating a Mid-height Wall

If you want to remove the top half of a wall, first mark and cut the surface material. Cut through the studs with a reciprocating saw or crosscut saw. Cap studs with a 2x4 (or whatever lumber is needed) to serve as a nailing surface

for wallboard. Disconnect the studs where they meet the top plate.

How to Cut a Doorway

If you are removing only a portion of a wall in order to create a door, measure and mark the area to be removed. Always allow for the widths of the framing members. Gently pry off the baseboard. Remove the wall surface so that each side aligns with the middle of a stud.

Removing gypsumboard. Cut along marked lines with a utility knife and straightedge. Then remove the inside framing.

Removing plaster. Determine the thickness of the plaster and set a circular saw equipped with a masonry blade at that depth to cut through the plaster. You may also use a hammer and chisel.

Work carefully to avoid cracking the areas that are not to be removed. Once the plaster has been removed, pry out the lath with a hammer.

Plan your door size carefully so that it fits within studs. If your studs are every 16 inches, then a multiple of 16 inches would always have to be the horizontal dimension of the new door. Otherwise, when you cut the rough opening, you will probably end up with a section where the lath and plaster have no support. In this case, install a stud to provide the necessary support.

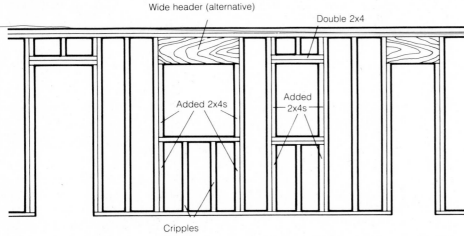

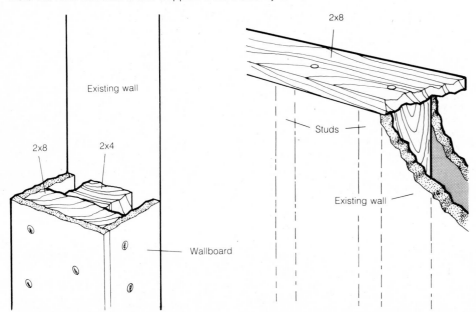

Shown are two typical framing methods for a window and a doorway. Cripples are added when more than one wall stud is cut. Cripples restore stability to the wall.

A wallboard surface can be added to the top of the mid-height wall to match the remainder of the wall. Use gypsumboard nails.

A wooden sill can be installed directly on top of the studs when part of a wall has been cut away. Jack studs support ends of the sill.

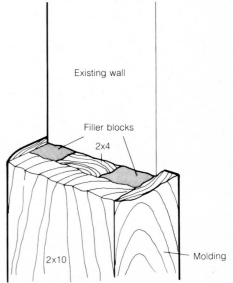

A finished hardwood sill, with curved moldings to cover adjoining edges, is placed over a 2x4 and filler blocks.

BUILDING A PARTITION WALL

The construction of an interior wall will substantially change any room. The prospect of "building a wall" may seem to be a very difficult task but, in reality, a wall that is an interior partition is not difficult to construct.

STEP 1: FINDING THE BEST LOCATION

If you have a solid floor with a good finish, you may build your new wall directly on the existing floor. Decide where the wall is to be located after consideration of the size of your original room, traffic flow, and anticipated use of the newly divided area.

The wall should sit directly over a joist if located parallel to the joists, or you will have to install nailers between joists for secure nailing of the bottom plate. Check the location of studs in the walls into which the new partition will run. If possible, locate the new partition so that it will fit halfway between studs. This will mean less opening and patching of existing walls.

STEP 2: SNAPPING GUIDELINES

Snap two chalklines 3½ inches apart at the proposed location. The 3½ inch width is the same as the actual width of the 2x4 to be used as the base plate of the wall.

Check to see that the dimensions of the two spaces on either side of the wall are what you expected. Arrange furniture or chalk furniture plans on the floor and walk around to appreciate the space. If you feel one side is cramped, adjust the chalklines; once in place, the wall will be permanent and you will have no such choice.

STEP 3: CONNECTING TO WALL FRAMING

Open the walls into which the new partition will run. If the junction is very close to a stud, open the wall up to the studs on either side of that stud. If the new partition meets the old wall halfway between the studs, open the wall to the centerlines of the studs on either side.

STEP 4: FASTENING TO FLOOR

If the new wall sits directly over a joist running parallel to the new partition, or if the new partition runs perpendicular

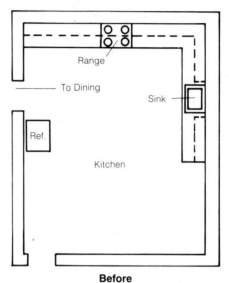

Before

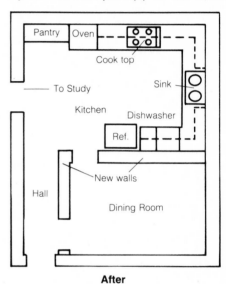

After

A spacious but poorly utilized kitchen can be remodeled for efficiency. A new dining room can be created in part of the space because of the better kitchen design.

to the joists, you will not have to add floor supports for nailing. However, if the new partition sits between joists, you will have to add 2x4 blocking between the joists of the basement ceiling to provide a secure nailing surface for the bottom plate. Nail blocking through the sides of the joists into the ends of the 2x4 sections. Position nailer blocking snugly against the subflooring, working from the basement.

STEP 5: INSTALLING BOTTOM PLATES AND WALL "Ts"

Lay 2x4 bottom plate(s) on the floor.

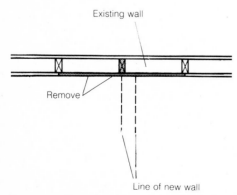

Remove wallboard or plaster to the center of the studs on either side of the intersection of the new wall and the old wall.

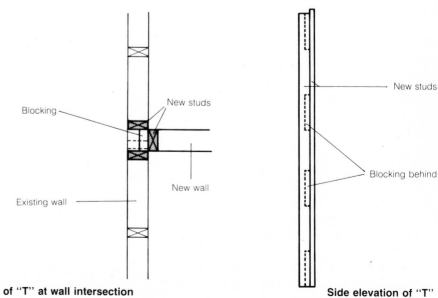

Plan of "T" at wall intersection   **Side elevation of "T"**

Remove stud that will interfere with installation of T intersection. Blocking holds spacing of the T section that fits into the old wall and provides nailer for first stud in the new wall.

Remeasure and check locations before nailing to floor and joists (or blocking) with 12d common nails.

STEP 6: INSTALLING WALL "Ts"

The new wall is joined to the existing walls with "Ts". Construct the Ts from 2x4s. Two of the boards in the Ts will fit between the bottom and top plates of the existing wall as if they were regular studs. These are fastened with nails to short sections of 2x4 blocking. This blocking is also the nailing surface for a third board that serves as the end stud of the new wall. It is nailed flush with the blocking, and is outside the old wall. This part of the T will sit on the new bottom plate and reach from the new wall bottom plate to the top plate. Cut the board 1½ inches short of the distance from the bottom plate to the ceiling to allow for the installation of the top plate. Construct a T for each end of the new wall. Toenail into existing top and bottom plates and into the new bottom plate.

STEP 7: ADDING TOP PLATES AND STUDS

If the length of the top plate is short enough so that a single 2x4 will reach from one side of the room to the other,

slip the top plate over the Ts and toenail it into place. Locate studs at 16 inches on center by measuring 16 inches from the face on a T and marking the bottom plate in 16-inch increments; place an "X" where each stud will go. Toenail the studs over the X marks. If the top plate is in position, toenail the studs to the top plate. If the top plate is made up of two sections, install a stud at the end of the first top plate section. Then place another stud next to it to support the end of the second section of the top plate.

If you have had to provide special blocking for the bottom plate, you also

will have to open the ceiling to provide blocking for nailing the top plate. This will require patching (this can be done when repairing the walls). You will have to cut out the ceiling to expose all of the two joists between which you install blocking. The ceiling opening should reach to the centerlines of the joists. This assumes a two-story house. If you have a one-story house, blocking may be added from above, working in the attic for access to the ceiling joists.

Install the upper wallboard sections first. Rub colored chalk on the junction boxes of any outlets or switches you

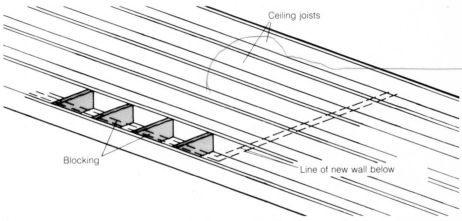

A new partition run parallel with ceiling joists will require nailer blocks. Install these blocks between the joists at 16 inches on center for secure and lasting construction.

Studs are on 16 inch centers. Mark bottom plate and 16 inch increments. Place new studs next to the mark to maintain spacing.

Doorway, enlarged by reframing, opens on space made by removing partition between rooms.

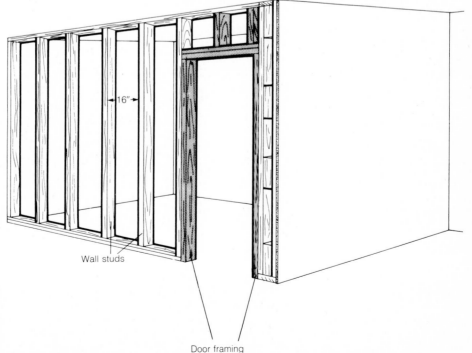

Stud spacing is 16 inches on center maximum. Proper framing of the door may require additional studs placed inside the 16 inch spacing. Jack studs support doubled header.

Project continued on next page

have installed and hold the wallboard against the boxes. This will mark the position on the sheet. Cut out with a keyhole saw.

If there is a gap of an inch or so at the floor/wall joint, cover it with baseboard. Use a board to lever the sheet of lower wallboard against the upper and nail it into place.

STEP 8: FRAMING A DOOR

Decide on the size and type of door you want. Purchase of a prehung door will simplify the process; the unit will

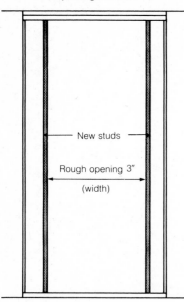

Opening for door

New studs

Rough opening 3"
(width)

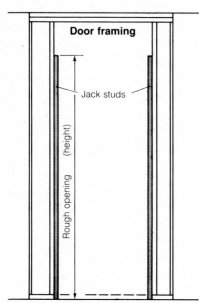

Door framing

Jack studs

Rough opening
(height)

Remove bottom plate

Studs for dooring framing are located so that there are 3 inches more space than the final rough opening to allow for jack studs.

come with installation instructions and precise measurements for the rough opening. Before you begin wall framing, mark the rough opening width for the door on the bottom plate. Place a stud on either side of the opening so that the space between the studs is 3½ inches greater than the rough opening of the door. This leaves room for studs and shims. Cut out the bottom plate between these studs.

STEP 9: INSTALLING JACK AND CRIPPLE STUDS

These are 2x4s that are nailed to the previously installed studs. The jack studs are as long as the rough opening is high. Cut two 2x4s for a doubled header to fit across the jack studs. Complete the framing by installing cripple studs between the top plate and the headers, as shown. If you substitute an extra-wide header for the double 2x4s, you will not need cripple studs.

STEP 10: COVERING THE WALL

If you are planning to add any electrical outlets or switches, do the electrical work at this time. When the framing and any other work is complete, cover the wall with plasterboard. Begin by patching any holes made for the installation of the Ts and blocking. Cut the wallboard to fit and nail it in place with as narrow seams as possible. Set the nails just below the surface of the wallboard, dimpling the surface with the hammer. The seams and dimples will be filled later.

For the expanse of the wall, install the wallboard (½ or ⅝ inch thick) horizontally. This places the long seam at a comfortable working level and will make finishing easier. Completely cov-

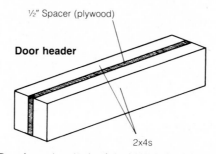

½" Spacer (plywood)

Door header

2x4s

Door frame header is of doubled 2x4s with a ½ inch plywood spacer to match the full width of the 2x4 jack studs.

er the wall, including the doorway. Mark the doorway onto the wallboard. Cut out an opening for the door flush with the studs you installed on each side of the doorway by drilling a hole near the center of the door area and, using a keyhole or sabre saw, cutting over to the studs. Cut out the opening.

Finishing the Wallboard

Apply a thin coat of joint compound on all the seams and over all the nail-heads. Then, using a "finishing" knife (similar to a putty knife), apply a smooth layer of seaming tape. When this is dry, apply a second coat, about 6 to 8 inches wide. Let this dry and sand smooth. Apply another coat that is 12 to 14 inches wide. When this has dried, wipe with a damp sponge to smooth. Sand if necessary.

To finish the corner joints between the old and new walls, you will have to apply a thin coat of joint compound, fold a length of tape in half vertically and install down the corner. Apply second and third coats of joint compound as directed above.

STEP 11: FINISHING THE INSTALLATION

Hang the door in the opening as directed by the manufacturer. This usually requires removing the door itself from the hinges and slipping the interior frame into the rough opening. Level and plumb the frame with shims as needed and attach to the wood framing. Rehang the door on the hinges and install facing materials as provided or as directed. You may have to purchase molding and mitre-cut it to fit. Install baseboards and attach switch and outlet face plates.

If you are planning to wallpaper, you may wish to do this before attaching the moldings and baseboards. However, measure and cut moldings to fit before papering or painting to avoid marking or scarring the wall when measuring and fitting the pieces.

If you plan to paint the walls, give the wall a base coat before adding the baseboard and door facing. If you are painting the molding, drill pilot holes for the nails and paint with primer before installing.

ARCH OVER A COUNTER

The arch over the countertop in our example is a functional as well as decorative unit. It is shown over a standard base cabinet which may have cooking units mounted on top, if you wish. When low over the cooking units, as this arch is, it helps trap cooking vapors which are sucked out by the exhaust fan mounted in the soffit. Also, lights may be mounted in the soffit, as indicated in the section illustration.

One note of caution: when building arches or cabinets over cooking units or where there is danger of fire, be sure to check with the building department about allowable materials and material distances from heat sources.

CONSTRUCTION DETAILS
The arched cooking area shown in our example is enclosed between two stud wall "wing walls" and backs up against a partition wall. This example could be freestanding, if such an arrangement works for you.

The base cabinets shown are standard cabinets as discussed in Chapter 3. The 1-foot soffit is also standard. Below the 1-foot soffit, another soffit is built as shown in the section illustration to enclose the exhaust fan(s) and lighting. The front face of the lower soffit extends downward to become the arch.

When surfacing an arch over an oven or range top, heat-resistant materials such as brick are preferred. Use of thinner, split brick will cut down on weight.

Project continued on next page

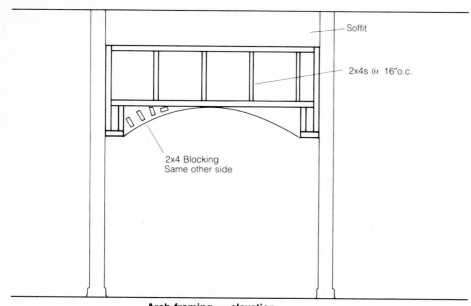

Arch framing — elevation

The arch over this countertop is simply stud wall construction dropped down from the soffit above.

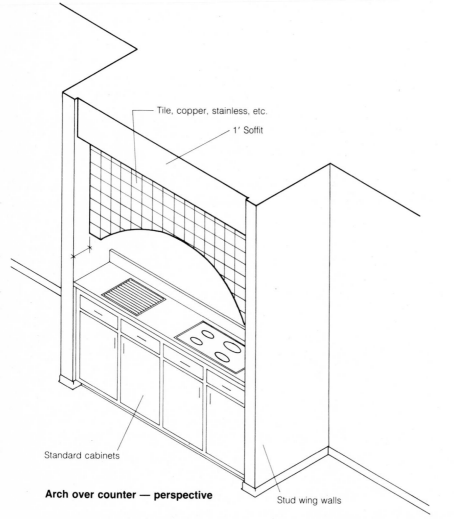

Arch over counter — perspective

The arch and wing walls are designed to enclose space over a standard base cabinet. This design can fit against a partition wall or be free-standing.

CONSTRUCTION SEQUENCE

Step 1: Building the Surround

First, build the wing walls using ordinary stud wall construction procedure. The walls may be finished with materials that match your wall finishes. Again, take note of fire code requirements for materials close to heat sources. Frame in the upper and lower soffits and install the exhaust fan and lighting within the soffit framing.

Step 2: Building the Arch

The arch framing illustration shows the blocking within the curved portion of the arch. The arch is formed by a sheet of ½-inch plywood on each side fo the arched portion of the soffit. The arch is a chord, 10 inches high at the top. The framing is shown approximately 10½ inches high to allow for the underside material on the arch — tile, metal, whatever the material used for finishing. Also, the blocking within the arch (2x4 scraps) is recessed approximately ½ inch to allow you to bend a strip of plywood to the underside of the arch.

Step 3: Finishing the Arch

The arch can be covered with any of several surface finishes. If wallboarded, textured paint for a stucco look is often chosen. Other popular materials are tile or brick (or simulated brick).

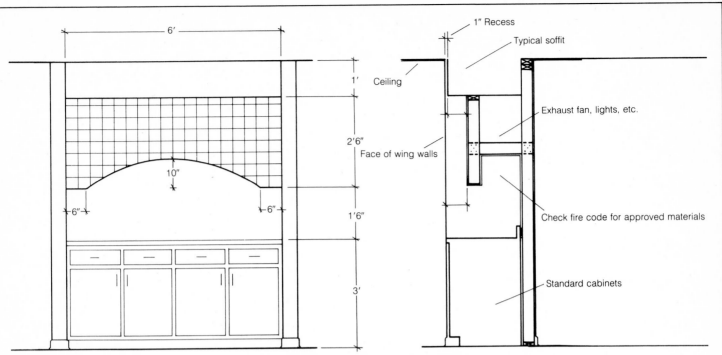

Arch over counter — front view and section

The arch is covered with plywood, which is good backing for most finish surfaces. For rigidity, nail the plywood to 2x4 scrap blocking within the arch.

An arch need not be restricted to over-countertop locations. Free-standing framing against the wall can be covered with wallboard and then, as shown, faced with Z-Brick.

CREATING A PASS-THROUGH

HEIGHT SUGGESTIONS

The height of a pass-through can be whatever is convenient and comfortable for you. Because openings of this type usually are used as a serving counter through to the dining room, or an eating bar with stools, the counter can be as much as 39 or 40 inches above the floor.

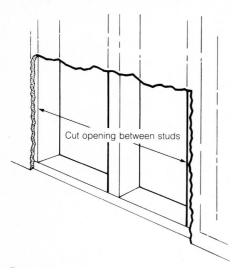

To create a pass-through, start by cutting away the wallboard or plaster between studs slightly wider than the opening you desire.

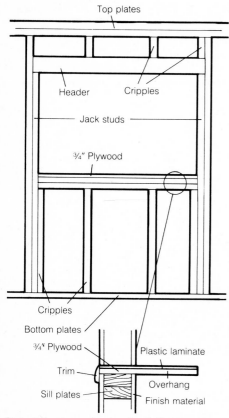

Pass-through opening framing is like that of window. Long jack studs support header and cripples hold ends of counter supports.

CUTTING THE OPENING

Remove the lath and plaster or gypsum wallboard according to the instructions (above) under "How to Remove a Wall". You will need to take out the wall surface from floor to ceiling. Plan the opening as a multiple of stud width; 32 or 48 inches for example, is quite serviceable. Because you only are cutting one or two studs for an opening of this size, and assuming you will be working on an interior non-load-bearing wall, you need not worry about support problems.

Allowing for the thickness of the sill plate and the header, cut the stud (for a 30-inch opening) that is centered in the opening.

FRAMING THE OPENING

You will need a double 2x4 at the top of the opening and a double 2x4 at the bottom. Sides also will be framed by 2x4s nailed to the studs. The side pieces must be cut shorter by the thickness of the horizontal top and bottom framing members.

Cut 2x4s to equal the height of the opening from the floor, less the thickness of the header, and nail these 2x4s to the side studs and to the floor plate. Install a double header across the top of the opening by nailing into the tops of the newly added side 2x4s from above and into the bottom of the cut stud, from below.

Mark the desired height of bottom of the opening. Measure to the bottom of the opening from the floor. Cut 2x4s to that length, less the thickness of the sill plate. Cut and nail these short 2x4s into the already doubled side studs. Nail the opening's sill plate, from above, to the new 2x4s and to the cut stud.

ADDING THE COUNTER

You can cover a plywood counter with

This opening, which serves as a pass-through, also allows natural light from the adjacent room to enter the kitchen to make the room brighter.

laminate or wood veneer (with protective coats to prevent damage) or you can build a frame with plywood and tile.

Attach the plywood counter before you laminate, countersinking the wood screws.

Laminating the Counter
The procedures for laminating are the same as those offered in Chapter 2 under "Creating an Angled Countertop." As indicated there, the laminate strips are applied first to the edges. The edge is then trimmed or filed flush. Laminate is next adhered to the top, covering the joint at the edge of the counter. A contact adhesive with a water base is suggested.

Building a Tiled Counter
Again, follow tiling instructions in Chapter 2, under "How to Tile a Countertop". The basic materials include field tile, trim tile (for edges), grout, and mastic. Because a tiled counter is heavy, it is supported by a frame built of 2x2s or 2x4s. To this is nailed a ¾ inch Exterior plywood, to which the tile surface is added.

FINISHING THE WALL AND TRIMMING THE OPENING
Fill in the areas above and below the opening with wallboard. Finish with tape and spackling compound. Final finishing depends on your decorating wishes. The opening may be wallboarded and then painted, or finished with a wood molding as a frame with mitered corners. You could even rim it with ceramic tile.

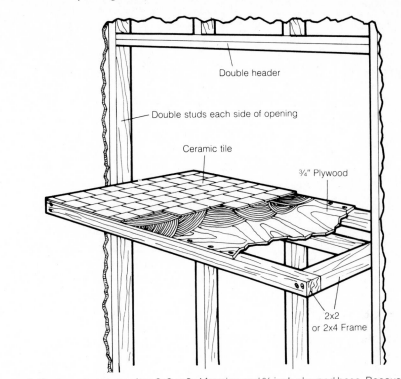

A ceramic tiled countertop requires 2x2 or 2x4 framing and ¾ inch plywood base. Because ceramic tile is heavy, pass-through must be well mounted.

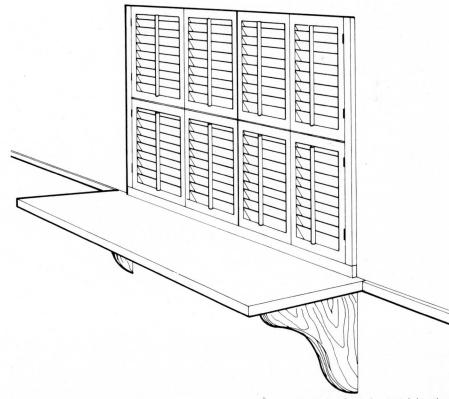

Counter of pass-through fits into or around framing. Wood brackets provide extra support to the countertop framing.

If you wish to provide privacy or mask the view of the kitchen while doing formal entertaining, install shutters in the pass-through. Foam-core solid doors are a better choice if you want an acoustical baffle. Choose style appropriate to your decor and needs.

10
LIGHTING, RANGE HOODS, VENTILATION

Windows for Air Circulation

With the increasing emphasis on caulking and weatherstripping in order to prevent heat loss or gain, many kitchens with only nonmovable (closed) windows need some other means of providing air circulation. Substitution of a unit that can be opened is one answer. Awning windows come on sliding hinges so they can be pushed out and give better and more accessible air passage than is possible with other windows.

Window location is important in developing cross-ventilation. Avoid placement near a stove; drafts will blow out pilot lights on gas ranges, or you could receive a burn while reaching across the range to open or close a window. Window fans can be used to stimulate air circulation. The fresh air will be pulled in and the stale air will be vented away.

Advantages of Decorative Ceiling Fans

Fans hung from the ceiling can be decorative showpieces that contribute to air movement in the kitchen. The fan circulates the air and thus cuts down on the amount of heating or cooling needed. The fans always should fasten to a stud, not just the ceiling surface.

How does the fan help? We have all been in air-conditioned buildings or homes where the temperature was at the recommended level yet we perspired and felt hot. However, if the air were moving, even slightly, we would feel more comfortable. Since a ceiling fan uses relatively little power, the fan can save a relatively large amount of energy that otherwise would be used for the air conditioner.

Likewise, during the winter, there are times when we are comfortable while we are sitting, but are uncomfortably warm when we work near the ceiling. The ceiling fan corrects this situation by circulating the warm air that has risen up near the ceiling down to where we are "living." As a result, the furnace need not run as long, thus saving energy used for heating.

Ceiling fans are available in many different designs and sizes, with variable speed controls and even with built-in lights. The fans are quite often mounted in place of the ceiling light, so that an integral light becomes more of a necessity than a luxury. The fans are particularly useful in homes with high ceilings.

A range hood draws off cooking steam, heat and grease and substantially lowers the heat in a kitchen during meal preparation.

Once thought of as an out-of-date fixture, the ceiling fan improves heating and cooling efficiency. Some models combine fan and ceiling lights. (For installation instructions, see page 148.)

A simple ceiling fan model is activated by a pull chain rather than a wall switch.

ADDING RECESSED LIGHTING

Recessed lighting is most often used to provide task lighting in a kitchen. It focuses illumination upon a localized area and, therefore, is desirable above a countertop or a cutting block.

Because recessed fixtures aim light downward and do not take advantage of reflected light from a ceiling, they are rarely used for general lighting. However, if this is desirable, several recessed fixtures can be installed, spaced evenly throughout the room. You will have to work around the joists in the ceiling.

TASK LIGHTING SUGGESTION

One option for use in a recessed fixture is a reflector bulb. This has a coating designed to throw light in a desired direction, which is a desirable feature over a work area. Because all of the light coming from a reflector bulb is aimed exactly where you want it, you can install bulbs of lower wattage and still have the same intensity as nonreflectors of higher wattage.

RECESSED SOFFIT INSTALLATIONS

An excellent means of locating task lighting in a kitchen is to recess it into the underside of a soffit. The opening for the fixture can be provided for at the time the soffit is built, with supports spaced as needed, or the opening can be cut into the soffit material later.

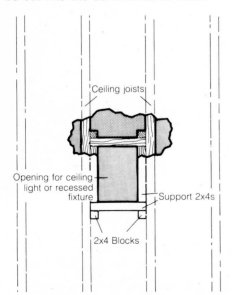

Opening for a ceiling light or recessed fixture must be boxed with 2x4s attached to ceiling joists to provide support for the fixture.

SAFETY AND SPACING REQUIREMENTS

Heat builds up around a recessed fixture; therefore, for safety reasons, the National Electrical Code has set out specific regulations about the placement of these fixtures. Other than at points of support (such as a joist), the sides of the fixture must be at least ½ inch from all combustible materials. All insulation must be kept at least 3 inches away from the fixture. Otherwise, the insulation will hold the heat given off by the light. Finally, you must allow for a constant flow of air around the fixture enclosure.

SUPPORTING THE HOUSING IN THE CEILING

To install a recessed fixture, you must first create the ceiling opening so it falls between the joists in your ceiling. Then fish cable over to the opening. Use the fishing methods discussed under "Installing a Ceiling Fan" (above).

A ceiling fixture usually comes complete with a metal housing. This must be nailed to supports between the joists of your ceiling. If you have access to the attic area, nail two 2x4 supports between the joists to support the fixture. Space them so the fixture housing will fit snugly between the 2x4s.

If the ceiling joists are enclosed, you will have to cut open the ceiling and work from inside the room in order to add the support.

Step 1: Fitting the Supports

Cut two 2x4s that will fit snugly between the joists. Working from below,

Installed recessed fixtures are unobtrusive but provide excellent area lighting.

tape the 2x4s into position. Mark along the joist at the edge of each end of the 2x4 supports. Remove the 2x4s from the ceiling opening.

Step 2: Installing Ceiling Cleats

Cut four 4-inch blocks from a 2x4. Drive two 8d nails about half-way through each of these cleats. Then place a cleat next to one of the marks on a joist. Remember that the supports will be nailed to the cleats, so leave the needed space. Pound the nails on the cleat the rest of the way through the block and into the joists. Do this at each of the marks.

Step 3: Installing the Supports

Reposition the supports between the joists. Tap them into position against the cleats. Then toenail the supports to the cleats.

Step 4: Wiring the Unit

Bring the electrical cable to the ceiling opening. Connect the wires to the fixture: black wire to black, white to white, and ground to ground. Always use caps as well as electrician's tape.

Step 5: Finishing the Installation

Nail or screw the fixture to the supports. Patch and finish the surrounding wallboard.

The recessed lighting above this sink was installed by the homeowner. The units are placed to provide light to each sink bowl.

INSTALLING A DECORATIVE CEILING FAN

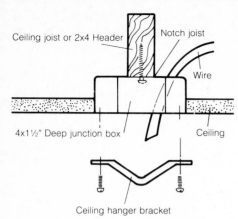

Level ceiling flush mounting

Ideally, the junction box for a ceiling fan is attached with wood screws to a ceiling joist after the ceiling surface is cut out.

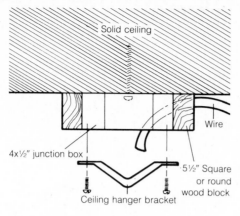

Level ceiling surface mounting (no attic space)

You may also frame around a junction box that must be mounted on the surface of the ceiling. The box attaches to the joist.

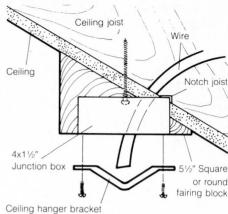

Slanted ceiling surface mounting

Because the fan should hang level, a junction box on a slanted ceiling must be mounted with blocking and a notched joist.

WIRING RUNS PARALLEL TO JOISTS

Installation Choices

Ceiling fans may be flush-mounted, surface-mounted or installed with a swag kit. The ceiling junction box to which the fan is hung should be fastened securely to a ceiling joist or to a 2x4 that is supported perpendicularly between the joists. Do not mount the fan to a junction box that is supported only by plasterboard. If the fan is mounted to an existing ceiling light fixture that is operated by a wall switch, the fan is simply mounted to the junction box with the hardware provided with the fan. If it is a variable-speed fan, a new switch is installed in place of the old one. If there is no switch-controlled ceiling fixture, it may be necessary to run an electric cable from the ceiling box to a wall box.

The alternative is to use a swag kit. Here, the electrical wire is run through a chain that is routed across the ceiling and down to a wall receptacle. Operation of the fan is controlled by a switch on the fan housing.

Installation Procedures

Tools and materials. For this job you will need an 18-inch drill bit, usually called an electrician's bit, 2 fish-tapes, and a saw.

Step one: cutting the opening. Locate the ceiling joists in the desired area of the bathroom where the fan will be placed. Mark the area to be cut out, using the template that is provided with

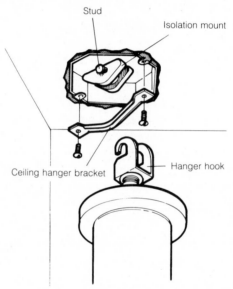

An isolation mount installed in the junction box absorbs motor vibration and limits the sound transfer to the framing.

the fan. If no template is given, make one using the fan housing as a guide. Whether you cut the opening so it is centered between joists or adjacent to a joist will depend on the mounting method used with the fan. Follow the directions provided.

Step two: running the cable. You will have to run an additional electric cable to the fan, unless you are replacing a ceiling light with a fan-and-light combination. If the fan operates independently of the light, you will need a separate switch. If the unit is equipped with a heater, you may need a separate circuit to the main service panel.

Stringing cable through attic. If you are running a cable from an attic, it is a

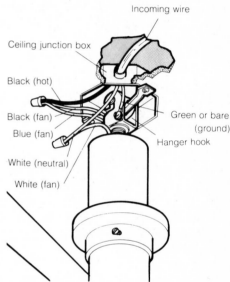

Wiring is hooked up between incoming power and the fan as shown. If your fan does not have a light, you will not have the blue wire.

relatively simple matter to run the cable along the side of a ceiling joist, or under the attic flooring to the point in the ceiling in the room where the fan is to be placed. A cable also will need to run through a plate and into the wall for the switch.

Stringing cable through basement. Running the cable from or through the basement involves cutting through a sill plate into the wall and up to the ceiling.

Stringing cable in 2-story houses. Two-story homes present the biggest challenge, as the cable must be fished through the wall and the ceiling, whether you start from the basement or the attic. In most two-story homes you will have to fish wire through a wall and ceiling that are closed in with plaster or plasterboard.

Step three: cutting openings. A few inches down from the ceiling, cut a hole into the wall in which the switch will be located for the ceiling fan. Drill diagonally up through the hole and through the top plate into the ceiling cavity. Directly in line line with this, cut the opening for the switch. Cut the opening for the ceiling fan.

Step four: fishing the cable. Insert a fishtape up through the hole in the ceiling and a second one through the upper-wall hole. It may take some work to get the two tapes to interlock so you can pull the fishtape in the wall through and out the ceiling hole. Tape the new cable to the fishtape and pull it through until it extends from both openings.

Now pull the cable from the wall hole near the ceiling down to the switch opening, using a fishtape.

When fishing lines through wall and ceilings, keep the openings aligned if at all possible.

This ceiling fan attaches to the joist and an extension runs down through the tin ceiling. An escutcheon plate covers the opening, which is cut through the patterned ceiling tile.

RUNNING WIRING PERPENDICULAR TO THE JOISTS

First, cut the hole for the fan. Then make the opening for the wall switch. Cut another opening in the wall directly above the switch and immediately below the ceiling. Mark a line from this latter opening to the hole in the ceiling. Locate each of the ceiling joists on this line and cut out the plaster and notch the joists for the cable. Carefully feed the wire above the ceiling through each notch. A length of coat hanger wire, and an assistant, will make the job easier.

At the corner of the wall and ceiling, notch the top plate and feed the wire down into the wall. Pull the wire taut and use a staple at each joist location. Patch the holes with patching plaster or plasterboard.

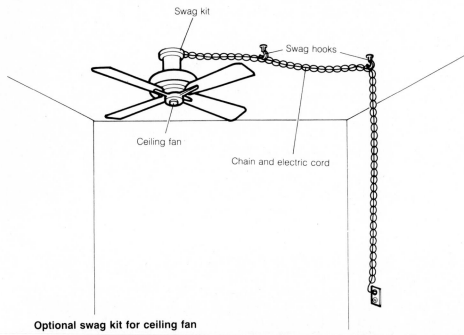

Swag kit

Swag hooks

Ceiling fan

Chain and electric cord

Optional swag kit for ceiling fan

If you do not wish to run power cable to the ceiling fan location, many manufacturers offer swag kits that allow you to mount the fan on the ceilng but run the cord to an outlet.

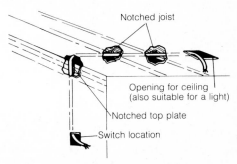

Notched joist

Opening for ceiling (also suitable for a light)

Notched top plate

Switch location

To control a ceiling fan from a wall switch, run cable from the switch to the ceiling opening. For cable perpendicular to joists, notch joists and cover cable with protective plates.

ADDING A RANGE HOOD

When installing a range hood in your kitchen, plan so that the front edge of the hood does not impair the cook's view of the rear burners. If the depth of the hood is under 18 inches, the bottom edge should stand no less than 56 inches above the floor. If the hood's depth is 18 inches or over, the bottom edge should stand no less than 60 inches above the floor.

HOOD STYLES

Hoods come in two styles, ducted and ductless. After passing the air through a filter to remove grease and odors, a ductless hood pushes the air back into the room. The filter must be changed quite often, and the hood does not remove heat or moisture.

A ducted hood removes the heated air from the room. Plan as short and straight a path as possible for the ducting, in order to ease its installation and to get the best performance from the hood. Always vent ductwork to the outside of your home. Never vent into an attic or unused house space; the resulting grease buildup creates both fire and health hazards.

INSTALLING A RANGE HOOD
Step 1: Removing an Old Hood

A range hood is fairly large and heavy, so work with a helper. Before removing the existing hood, turn off the power to the circuit that feeds the hood. The wiring is usually housed in a junction box behind a metal pan covering. Loosen the terminal screws and remove the wires. Separate the cable wires and completely wrap each wire end with electrical tape.

Step 2: Choosing the Ductwork

Ductwork comes in pieces of several sizes and shapes to accommodate a variety of pathways. Either wall or roof caps finish off the outside openings. To prevent fire hazards, purchase metal rather than plastic ducting.

You can purchase either standard sheet metal duct or flexible metal duct. Flexible duct is quite easily dented or crushed, more so than conventional ducting. On the other hand, it is light and goes around corners without requiring elbows or other adapters.

Since flexible ducting is available only in round shape, you must install a rectangular-to-round converter to connect the hood to the duct.

Step 3: Connecting Up to the Old Ductwork

If the duct opening in the new hood is in the same position as (or similar to) the duct opening already in existence, your task is simple. If the two do not match, try to use two pieces of elbow ducting to angle the channel over to the old vent. Then patch the old cabinet opening. If this procedure is not feasible, abandon the old duct and install an entirely new run.

Sometimes new ducting is the best course, especially if the old duct is too grease-laden for safe use. To deal with the old duct, you must

(1) remove the old ductwork and

If your cooktop is in a counter open to another room, a range hood is a necessity. The fan will pull cooking odors and grease up and away from the open counter and the adjacent room.

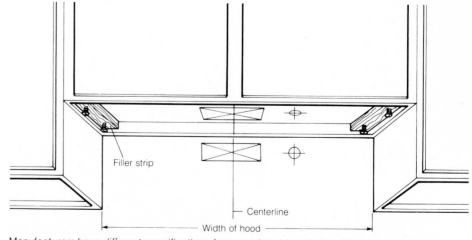

Filler strip

Centerline

Width of hood

Manufacturers have different specifications for range hood installation. Most duct openings run up through the cabinet or out through the wall. Use filler strips to level.

(2) patch the holes that remain, or screw down the damper in the exterior wall and caulk it closed securely; then fill the duct with insulation and repair only the cabinet or wall opening.

Step 4: Laying Out the Duct Path
A duct's pathway depends upon your home's construction and hood's location. If the stove sits against an exterior wall, the shortest path is straight out through the back of the hood. Be sure that the damper in the hood's duct and the one in the wall cap cannot interfere with each other. If they do, remove the hood damper.

Another satisfactory path utilizes a short vertical pipe from the top of the hood and then angles out through the wall. In most homes, this duct path travels up through the cabinet or soffit above the hood, rather than through the insulation between the kitchen wall and the exterior shell.

If the hood is on an interior wall, you must avoid extremely lengthy and twisted paths. Go straight up through the wall space to the roof, if possible. If you cannot, pass the ducting through the soffit to an outside wall.

Step 5: Inserting the Duct
Although the primary purpose of a duct is to provide a passage for exhaust fumes and residue, it can also provide a passage for the flames of a grease fire. To be certain that any fire is enclosed in the metal ducting, as you connect sections together, tape the joints very securely with duct tape.

Cutting an Opening. First, cut the opening in the exterior of the house with a sabre saw, a keyhole saw, or a reciprocating saw. This opening should be slightly larger than the ducting. (If local codes require, install casing strips around a wall opening in a wood house.)

Inserting the Ducts. To install a straight path, tape one section to the next, one at a time, and lower the duct from above. If your path has a center angle, insert the section from the outside. Then push the vertical section to meet it. If you do not have access to the junction of the sections, cut a small access hole and tape the junction as securely as all other joints.

Step 6: Capping and Sealing the Duct
If the duct comes through an exterior wall, trim the duct even with the siding and install a wall cap according to instructions. Fasten the wall cap to the duct to the wall and caulk the opening well.

If the duct comes through the roof, it should extend at least $\frac{3}{4}$ inch above the high side of the roof. Using plastic roof cement, completely seal the opening between the duct and the roof. Use a lot of sealant, to prevent later water seepage. Then insert the high-side edge of the roof cap under the shingles and apply plastic roof cement all around the cap.

Step 7: Making the Final Hookup
The power must be off to make this connection. Fish cable to the hood. Fasten the cable to the hood with the connecter locknut. Use wire nuts to splice the black cable wire to the black hood wire. Do the same with all white wires. Finally, using the green ground screw, attach the cable ground wire to the grounding bracket built into the hood. Comply with all local codes (regulations may vary). Replace the wiring box cover and screws. Be careful not to pinch any of the wires.

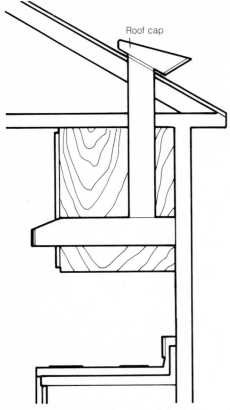

A straight vertical duct is most efficient. The roof cap prevents rain or wind entry.

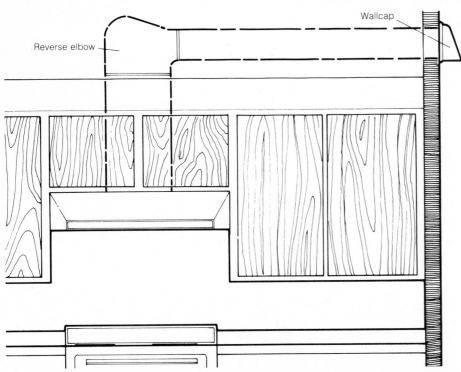

When you have no alternative, use a horizontal run of duct. You must install a reverse elbow to change duct direction. A wall cap protects the ducts from the elements.

ADDING A SUSPENDED LUMINOUS CEILING

The best size fluorescent for use in a luminous ceiling is a 4-foot length of 40-watt rapid-start lamp. (Rapid starters also come in other lengths.) In order to determine the number of lamps you need, sketch out the dimensions of the ceiling. Plan for the lamps to lie in parallel lines that are between 18 and 24 inches apart. (The narrower space gives a more even light, but it is also more expensive.) On both ends, allow about 8 inches between the end of the line of lights and the walls. Now figure the length of the lines in feet, and divide by four. If necessary, supplement the 4-foot lamps with shorter ones to obtain the coverage you need.

HOW THE SYSTEM WORKS
Components

The fluorescent fixture. There are three parts to a fluorescent fixture. The body, called the channel, houses the wiring of the system and the ballast, which creates a momentary increase of voltage needed to light the fluorescent lamp. At both ends of the channel there are electrical knockouts. Along the bottom you will find several screwholes. At each end of the channel, protruding at right angles to it, is a metal strip, called a lamp holder. The two hold the fluorescent lamp. The second section is a protective lid for the channel. Openings are provided, through which the lamp holders fit. Once on, the lid fastens to the channel, over the wiring and ballast, with one or two screws at each end. Finally, there is the fluorescent lamp itself, which snaps into the receptacle at each end of the fixture. During most of the installation of the luminous ceiling (or of any fluorescent fixture) you will work only with the channel.

Power source. A luminous ceiling relies upon a central, switch-controlled junction box in the ceiling. If you do not have one, you must install one. Remember to shut off the circuit that feeds the fixture before you begin work. If a box is already in place you need only remove the old fixture. Fasten a box extender to the junction box in the ceiling. (The extender will look just like the box in the ceiling, except it will have no back.) The extender will

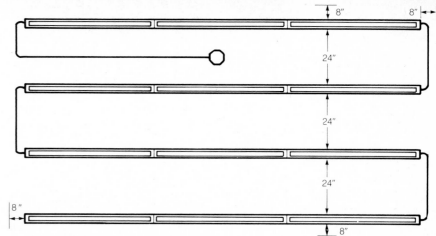

A luminous ceiling is created by installing fluorescent fixtures spaced 24 inches apart over the entire ceiling. Suspended diffuser panels spread light evenly in the room.

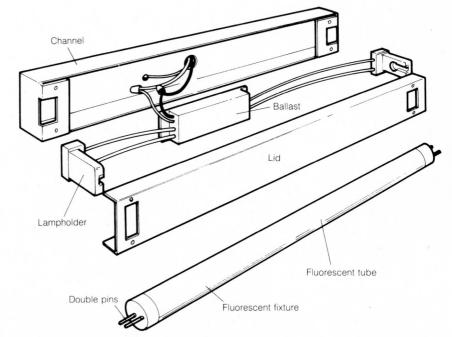

An individual fluorescent fixture consists of a channel through which wiring is run, the ballast that prevents lamp hum, the hood and the double-pin fluorescent tube.

house the cable for the lines of lights. The lines themselves will be connected to each other with jumpers and then to the junction box. For a good, reflective surface, paint the ceiling with two coats of flat white ceiling paint.

Installation Procedures

Step one: installing the channels.

To fasten the channels to the ceiling, you will need a screwdriver, screw anchors (to ensure the stability of the installation), and channel connectors to hold adjoining channels together. Then starting at either end, hold the channel against any of the lines on the ceiling. Draw in the positions of the screw holes.

Before you secure the channels in place, remove the knockout holes at the ends of the individual channels that will butt against each other. Fasten the channels to the ceiling, butting the ends together as you go. Use a ½ inch conduit connector, which comes in two parts, a screw and a lock nut, to secure the butted ends of the two channels. Run the screw through the knockout holes of two adjoining channels; fasten with the lock nut.

Step two: assembling tools and materials for wiring.

To connect the channels to each other you will need single conductor wires (black, white, and green) equal to at least one and one-quarter times the total planned length of your lines. You also will need wire nuts, electrician's tape, a wire cutter, a wire stripper, and two-part cable connectors to secure the cable to the junction box.

Finally, you will need cable. Be sure you purchase the same kind of cable already in the circuit you are tapping. To determine the amount of cable you need, multiply the number of lines of lights you have by the distance between each line. Then start at one end of an outermost line of lights. Measure the path that a cable will have to take from that corner in order to connect with the ceiling junction box. Add this to the above total; divide by 12 to convert from inches to feet. To allow for connections and for the fact that the cable will never lie completely flat and straight, plan on using one and one-half of the total feet.

Step three: connecting the wires.

To wire the adjoining fixtures in a line of lights together, you will need to use jumper wires. Begin with the first fixture in an outermost row. Measure the distance between its black wire and the black wire in the next fixture. Cut a jumper equal to this length and splice the black wire of channel one and the jumper wire together with a wire nut. Do the same with the white wire and a white jumper. Take the two jumper wires and pass them through the channel connector between channel one and channel two.

Cut jumpers to connect the black and the white wires of the second channel to the third. Then splice together the black jumper from channel one, the black jumper from channel two and the black wire of channel two. Do the same with the white wires. Then pass the channel two jumpers through the channel connector to channel three. Continue this process until the entire line of lights is connected. Do the same for all the lines.

When you have wired all lights in a line, you can connect the lines to each other and then to the junction box. Move to the end of an outermost line. Remove the knockout at the end of the last channel. Then remove the knockout at the end of the last channel in the next line. (The two knockouts will be directly across from each other.) Cut 30 to 32 inches of cable. Strip 2 inches of sheathing from both ends of the cable, exposing the black, white, and green wires inside. Then strip about an inch of insulation from those wires. Using a 2-part cable connector, fasten one end of the cable through the knockout in the outermost line. Splice black to black, and white to white. With a metal screw, fasten the green ground wire to the channel. Now move to the next line and fasten the other end of the cable to the knockout you prepared earlier. The first and second row are now connected to each other at one end.

Move the opposite end of the second line. It must be connected to the third line, in the same manner as above. Once completed, connect the third and fourth. Continue until all the lines are connected. The result will look like a continuous zig-zag pattern.

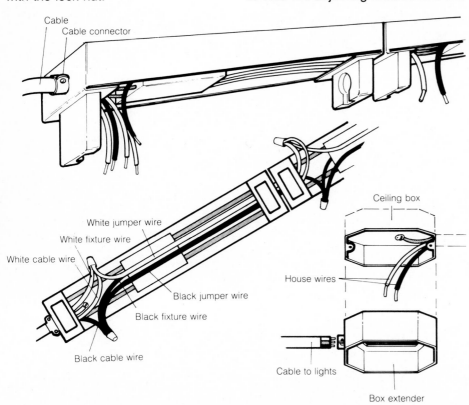

Cable
Cable connector
White jumper wire
White fixture wire
White cable wire
Black jumper wire
Black fixture wire
Black cable wire
Ceiling box
House wires
Cable to lights
Box extender

The wiring for the luminous ceiling runs from the junction box through a cable to the first fixture. The fixtures are wired together, one to another, and then to the power cable.

Project continued on next page

Step four: connections to the junction box. When the lines are all connected, you are ready to connect the final line of lights to the junction box. Strip 2 inches of casing from one end of the remaining cable. Now run the cable from the channel to the junction box, attaching it to the ceiling as you go, using cable staples. (Be careful so that you do not pierce the cable sheathing.) Strip about 8 inches of sheathing from the cable end and then an inch of insulation from the wires. Connect the cable through the opening in the extender box, using a two-part cable connector. Splice the black fixture wire and the black circuit wire. Do the same with the white wires. Fasten the two green ground wires to the base of the junction box.

Attach the protective lids to the channels. Insert the fluorescent lamps into the lamp sockets, turn on the circuit, and test to make sure that everything works properly. Then turn off the circuit.

Step five: installing the panels. Each panel will be suspended in a metal grid. It should be installed from 10 to 12 inches away from the lights, and the distance between it and the floor should be no less than 7½ feet. The grid includes these components: an L-shaped metal framing, which fastens to the wall; main L-shaped runners, which hang from the ceiling by means of eye screws and hanger wires; and T-bars, which span the main runners.

Decide on the height of the luminous ceiling and draw a corresponding line on the walls all the way round the room. Using a carpenter's level, check that the line is completely level. Then nail the edge framing along the line.

The manufacturer's instructions will tell you how far from the edge framing the first main runner should be (usually 2 to 4 feet). Measure out, and draw a line along the ceiling, parallel to the wall. Measure every so often to be sure that the line is straight. Install the eye screws every two feet along the ceiling line. If your ceiling is of wallboard, you should first install screw anchors and then insert the eye screws. If the ceiling is plaster, you will have to drill holes first, using a bit size slightly smaller

than the eye screws. You can then install the eye screws directly into the ceiling.

Now cut the hanger wires; their lengths should be twice the distance from the ceiling to the runner. Pass a fourth of the hanger wire through the screw eye; fold the end back against the wire itself; twist the end around the wire. Now lift the runner into position — have a helper for this. Pass the free end of the hanger wire through the opening provided in the main runner. Check the runner's height to be sure that it is the same as the distance between the ceiling and the edge frame. Hook the wire so it will support the runner. (Your helper probably will have to

hold the runner for a while, until you have hooked several wires.) Go on to the next screw eye and repeat.

Once you have completed the hangers for a runner, check to be sure the runner is level. Make any necessary adjustments. Then bend the hooks closed and twist the ends firmly around the wires. Place all the runners in the same manner. The distance between them will be determined by the size of the plastic panels you are using.

Once the main runners are in, install the T-bars. These will fit into special slots built into the main runner. The size of the plastic panel determines the distance between the T-bars.

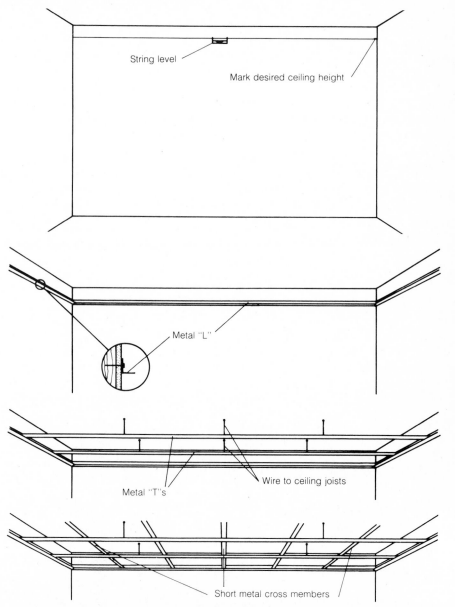

The level of the ceiling is marked on the wall and Ls, Ts and cross members installed as shown.

11
ADDING NOISE PROTECTION

NOISE LEVELS IN THE KITCHEN

During the hours of meal preparation, it is usual for several appliances to be used simultaneously: water may be running; a radio or television set may be turned on; the refrigerator may be going through an automatic cycle; a blender or mixer may be in use; a microwave may be pressed into service; a vent fan often is running, and the disposal can be found grinding a batch of waste. With all this activity, the noise level in the kitchen can reach a point where it will cause actual physical discomfort in the kitchen.

In addition, much of this kitchen noise may penetrate to other areas of the home and create a further nuisance. Kitchen noise that reaches formal dining areas is particularly annoying when you are entertaining.

How Noise Affects Us

As noise levels increase, body reactions become more drastic. The first system to be affected is the digestive tract. Noise at a relatively low level begins to speed peristalsis, and increase the flow of saliva and gastric juices. On a long-term basis, this can contribute to the development of ulcers. As noise increases, blood pressure changes, blood vessels constrict, eyes dilate, and adrenalin levels go up. A person subjected to high noise levels becomes extremely tense and begins to make more and more frequent errors.

NOISE CONTROL

There are two basic categories of kitchen noise contributors: one is the noise generated naturally by the appliances themselves; the other is the passage of noise by plumbing pipes, plumbing and electrical fixtures, through structural framing, walls and ceilings.

Reducing Noise From Appliances

You can control some of the noise in the kitchen through your choice of appliances. Before making a final choice when purchasing a new type of appliance or replacing an old appliance, ask to see and hear each potential choice in operation. If the features, costs and reliability of the models are nearly the same, choose the appliance that is the quietest.

When codes allow it, use a long section of flexible cable to attach permanently installed electrical appliances, such as a vent fan, disposal, or dishwasher, to the power source.

To cut down the amount of noise transmitted from appliances that tend to vibrate from motor activity, connect them to drain pipes or ductwork with flexible, vibration absorbing material such as rubber tubing or automobile radiator hose.

Leveling the Appliances

Any appliance will generate more than normal noise if it is operated when it is not level. Check the kitchen floor for level and adjust the position of the refrigerator so it

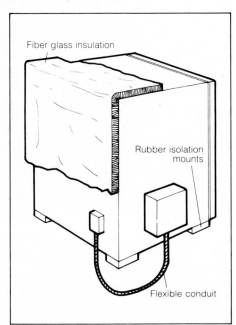

The natural vibration of a dishwasher creates a lot of sound. Fiberglass insulation provides a cushioning blanket.

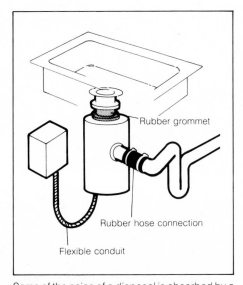

Some of the noise of a disposal is absorbed by a rubber or plastic drain connection and flexible electrical conduit to the power source.

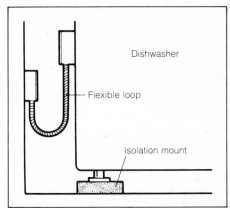

Cushion a dishwasher by installing isolation mounts to prevent transmission of sound to the floor. Flexible conduit is also helpful.

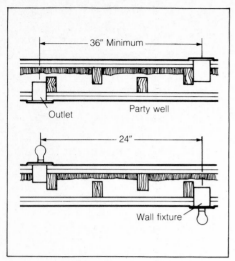

Because junction boxes are cut into the wall, they allow sound transmission. Spacing boxes 36 inches apart will help baffle sound.

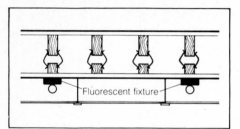

Spring clips hold base frame for fluorescent lights to joists. The clips absorb vibrations to prevent transmission to framing.

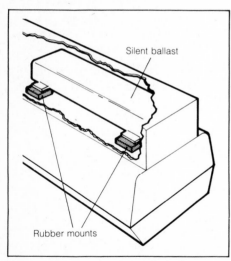

Use the proper ballast and install it in fluorescent fixtures with rubber mounts to absorb any hum that may develop in fixtures.

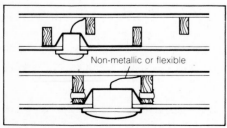

Flexible conduit will not eliminate sound transfer if you link joists. Do not connect above clips or across staggered joists.

is level. Small appliances should also be level. If your countertops are not level, mixers, blenders, can openers and coffee pots will operate at a higher than intended noise level. In addition, the out-of-level position will create strain and wear on the appliance. This, of course, will shorten the life of the appliance.

The life and sound level of a dishwasher will be significantly improved by maintaining an exact level position. If you support the appliance in a level position by using solid rubber blocks as shims, this will absorb vibration and lower sound transmission. An insulation blanket placed across the top and down the sides of the dishwasher will also absorb vibration and sound. Use a flexible electrical cable to connect the appliance to the power source and add a rubber tubing connection to the drain. Pad the water supply pipe as it passes through the wall to make the whole unit noticeably quieter.

Preventing Noise Transmission

Insulating the walls. One of the first things to consider is the installation of sound insulating walls. Application of an extra layer of material on a wall will help, but a staggered stud wall that allows weaving of insulation material through the studs will give a great deal of sound protection.

Placing switches and outlets. Avoid placing any switches or outlets back-to-back. Position junction boxes on opposite sides of the same wall so that there is 36 inches of lateral distance between them.

Fastening ceiling fixtures. Attach ceiling fixtures so that fasteners are set into furring strips attached to the ceiling

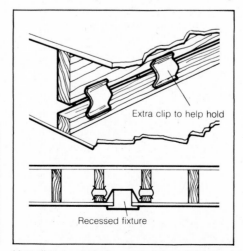

Use clips to separate support from joists and keep all connections below the joists to prevent sound transfer to the framing.

joists with spring clips. The clips will absorb any noise that may develop in the fixture.

Ceiling tips. Consider installing an acoustical ceiling in your kitchen. The steps are the same as those for the suspended ceiling discussed in Chapter 10.

Plumbing noise: problems and solutions. Use rubber gaskets around sinks and all pipes as they pass through walls. If you have a powder room adjacent to a kitchen, use rubber gaskets with the hanger bolts that lock the toilet to the floor. Be sure that air chambers are installed at each faucet so water hammer does not develop when you turn off the running water.

How to add an air chamber. Air chambers are simply pipe columns fitted vertically in the line behind faucets. Most often, the air chambers are hidden in walls, and so are not a recognized part of plumbing. The function of the air chamber is to provide a cushion of air that absorbs the energy of the suddenly stopped water.

If your plumbing does need an air chamber, you can install one by cutting the supply lines under a sink or vanity and installing a Tee. A short nipple and reducing coupling (bell) is turned into the Tee, and then a length of pipe larger than the line is screwed into the coupling and a cap is turned onto the top of it.

The air chamber must be vertical, and the pipe should be larger than the supply line it cushions. For example, if the supply line is ⅜ or ½ inch, the air cushion should be 1 or 1½ inches respectively. The larger the line, the more air it will contain.

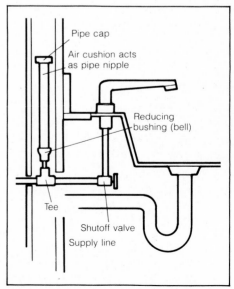

Water hammer noise is annoying and destructive to pipes. A straight pipe air chamber will absorb the change in pressure.

Using an alternate type of air chamber. An alternate kind of air cushion is a coil of copper tubing. The coil acts something like a spring, and the spring action combined with the air provides a very effective damping action to reduce or eliminate water hammer.

Restoring air to an existing air chamber. The air chamber is a length of pipe about 18 to 24 inches in height which has been filled with air. Over a period of time the air can be absorbed by the water, and thus lose its effectiveness. If this is the case, shut off the main water valve and drain the entire system through a faucet or valve in a low part of the system, such as in the basement. Once the system has drained entirely, you turn on the water again and the whole system will fill with water, except for the air chambers. These dead-end pipes will once again contain air and will offer an air cushion to prevent water hammer.

Fastening loose pipes. There is another condition that will cause water hammer: pipes that are not properly fastened to walls or other surfaces. The inertia of

While most air cushions are inside a wall, they can be installed under a sink or a vanity if the supply lines are accessible. In most cases this air cushion would have to be shorter than if it were inside the wall. The largest pipe size practical should be installed. For a homeowner-plumber, that would mean a 1½ inch pipe. An air cushion just 12 inches high would be quite effective for a ⅜ inch line, and probably could be fitted under most sinks.

moving water is quite high, and when the water is shut off this inertia can move pipes, even if there is an air chamber in that line. This goes back to the principle that for every action there is an opposite and equal reaction. When the water compresses air in the air chamber, it will reverse its motion after a fraction of a second. If there are loose pipes, they will jump as the energy of the stopped water passes back along the line.

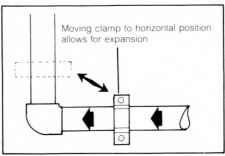

Attach support clamps so plumbing pipe can move slightly when expanding or contracting.

If your plumbing has air chambers but there still is a hammering at some faucets, even the outside hose connections, check that line for spots where it is slack or loose. It may just be that some pipe clamps have loosened over the years. A larger nail might be the answer, or a wood screw that will hold more securely than a nail.

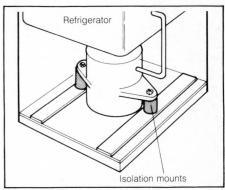

Isolation mounts on refrigerator absorb most motor noise.

APPLIANCE NOISE LEVELS

30-45 db	50-75 db	80-85 db	90-100 db
Threshold of awareness	Interference with conversation Low grade physical response	Threshold of annoyance	Causes noticeable physical response
Refrigerator	Coffee grinder Pots & pans Faucet/running water Dishwasher 12" portable fan	Disposal Electric mixer Knife sharpener Electric can opener Range hood vent fan	Wall exhaust fan Sink drain Simultaneous use of range hood vent fan and disposer or dishwasher

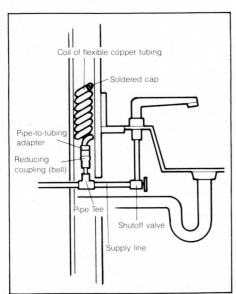

A better air chamber has a coil that allows more absorption of the water pressure in the same vertical space.

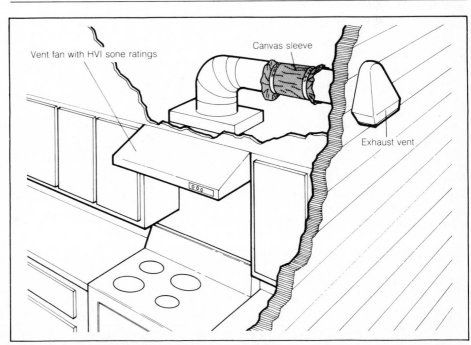

Range hood fans are often loud because they are powerful. Sound is transmitted to the house as the duct passes through framing. Use canvas to baffle and mute the sound.

INDEX

CREDITS

We wish to extend our thanks to the individuals, associations and manufacturers who graciously provided information and photographs for this book. Specific credit for individual photos is given below.

Allmilmo Corporation c/o Hayes-Williams Incorporated, 261 Madison Ave. New York, New York 10016 45, 68, 113, 126 lower right, 131

American Hearth & Home Company Box 278-A/Main St. Mountainville, RR#2, Lebanon, NJ 08833 80 lower right

American Olean Tile 1000 Cannon Avenue, Lansdale, Pennsylvania 19446 7, 10, 11 lower, 15 lower left, 71 upper right, 113, 127

American Plywood Association Box 1119A, Tacoma, Washington 98401 57

American Standard Inc., 1 Centennial Products, P.O. Box 6820, Piscataway, NJ 08854 13 lower

James W. Brett, Architectural Photography, 1070 Orange Grove, Tucson, Arizona 85704 7, 32

Craig Buchanan, Photographer, 490 2nd Street, San Francisco, California 94107 21, 70 upper, 118

Bull Field Volkmann Stockwell, Architecture & Planning 350 Pacific Avenue San Francisco, California 94111 24 upper

Casablanca Fan Company, Consumer Products Division, 182 South Raymond, Pasadena, California 91109 146 lower left

Ceramic Tile Institute 700 North Virgil, Los Angeles, California 90029 7, 15 upper right, 17 upper, 66 upper

Childcrest Distributing Inc. 6045 North 55th Street, Milwaukee, Wisconsin 53218 22 upper left

James F. Clapper, Designer, James Furniture 2805 West Breezewood Lane, Neenah, Wisconsin 54956 114-116

Corning Glass Works, Inc. Corning, New York 14830 41

Country Floors 300 East 61st Street, New York, New York 10021 8

D'Image Associates, Inc., Four North St., Waldwick, NJ 07463 27

Emerson Environmental Products, Division of Emerson Electric Co. 8400 Pershall Road, Hazelwood, Missouri 63042 146 lower right

Feincraft Design Center, 5 Washington St., Morristown, NJ 07960 71 upper left

GAF Floor Products 140 West 51st Street, New York, New York 10020 79 upper

General Tire and Rubber Co. 1 General St., Akron, Ohio 44329 71 lower, 75 lower right

Lori and Donald Glickman, Designers, 2831 North Shepard, Milwaukee, Wisconsin 53211 50

Harmann Studio Inc. 11 N. 3rd Street, Sturgeon Bay, Wisconsin 54235 73

Alan Horowitz 4845 North Newhall, Milwaukee, Wisconsin 54917 147 lower left

Herb Hughes 3033 Willow Lane, Montgomery, Alabama 36109 101, 136, 139

In-Sink-Erator, Division of Emerson Electric, 4700 21st Street, Racine, Wisconsin 53406 132

International Tile and Supply 1288 La Brea Avenue, Los Angeles, California 90019 7, 19 upper, 30, 67 lower

KitchenAid, Division of Hobart Manufacturing. Troy, Ohio 45373 Information on pages 127-129 adapted with permission.

The Kohler Company Kohler, Wisconsin 53044 136, 152

KraftMaid Cabinetry, Inc., 16052 Industrial Parkway, Middlefield, OH 44062 25, 49 lower left, upper right, 70 lower left, 76 lower, 126 lower left

Carl Landgren 1640 North Jackson, Milwaukee, Wisconsin 53202 70 lower right

Lord & Burnham Irvington, New York 10533 110

Mary McLaughlin, Managing Editor, *Working Mother* magazine 23 right

Gerhard C. F. Miller Sturgeon Bay, Wisconsin 54235 73

Richard V. Nunn, Media Mark Productions Falls Church Inn, 6633 Arlington Blvd., Falls Church, Virginia 22045 42, 128

Pacesetter Homes, Inc. 12705 Scarborough Court, New Berlin, Wisconsin 53151 120, 135 lower left

Thomas D. Parsons, designer, Hans Hansen Importers, Racine, Wisconsin 53405 23 left

Pella/Rolscreen Company, 102 Main St., Pella, IA 50219 29, 77 upper right, information and art on bay windows 101-103 and greenhouses 94-99 adapted by permission

Tom Philbin 14 Lakeside Drive, Centerport, New York 11721 43, 59 lower left, 109

Pittsburgh Corning Corp., PC GlassBlock®, 800 Presque Isle Drive, Pittsburgh, PA 15239 75

Poggenpohl USA Corp. P.O. Box 10-F, Teaneck, New Jersey 07666 49 lower right, 69 upper

Rutt Custom Kitchens, P.O. Box 129, 1564 Main St., Goodville, PA 17528 11 upper, 26, 69

S & S Construction 8383 Wilshire Boulevard #700, Beverly Hills, California 90211 142

Cookie Samuels, Mahwah, NJ 07430 cover, 14 lower left, 16, 18 lower left, 20, 27, 28, 31, 65

Schlott Realtors, 1550 Route 23 North, Wayne, NJ 07470 18 lower left, 28, 65

Everett Short, Photographer, 95 Christopher Street, New York, New York 10014 23 right, 72, 75 upper left, 135 center

Summitville Tiles Inc., P.O. Box 73, Summitville, OH 43962 13 upper right, 19 lower

The Hammer & Nail Inc., Robert Lidsky, RSPI, 232 Madison Ave., Wyckoff, NJ 07481 26, 74

Tile Council of America c/o Lis King Box 503, Mahwah, New Jersey 07430 6, 66 lower, 75 lower left, 78, 79 lower, 113, 126 lower center

David Ulrich, Ulrich Inc. 100 Chestnut Street, Ridgewood, New Jersey 07450 6, 9, 12, 13 upper left, 14 upper left, and right, 15 lower right, upper left, 16, 18 center, right, 24 lower, 76 upper, 77 upper left, lower, 80 upper left and right, lower left, 144, 146 upper right

Velux-America Inc. P.O. Box 3208, Greenwood, SC 29648 100

Z-Brick, Division of VMC Corporation, 13929 Northeast 190th Street, Woodinville, Washington 90872 141

Special thanks to:

Mr. and Mrs. Allan Birnbaum, cover, 16

Mr. and Mrs. John Goomas, 27

Mr. and Mrs. David Hoyle, 20 upper

Mr. and Mrs. Vern Jarosak, 65

Mr. and Mrs. Albert F. Lilley, 14 lower left

Mr. and Mrs. Blair Richardson, 20 lower

Mrs. Joy Schepisi, 31

Mr. Kevin Schmidt, 18 lower left

Mr. and Mrs. Alan Weingarten, 28

Metric Conversion Charts

LUMBER

Sizes: Metric cross-sections are so close to their nearest Imperial sizes, as noted below, that for most purposes they may be considered equivalents.
Lengths: Metric lengths are based on a 300mm module which is slightly shorter in length than an Imperial foot. It will therefore be important to check your requirements accurately to the nearest inch and consult the table below to find the metric length required.
Areas: The metric area is a square metre. Use the following conversion factors when converting from Imperial data: 100 sq. feet = 9.290 sq. metres.

METRIC SIZES SHOWN BESIDE NEAREST IMPERIAL EQUIVALENT

mm	Inches	mm	Inches
16 x 75	⅝ x 3	44 x 150	1¾ x 6
16 x 100	⅝ x 4	44 x 175	1¾ x 7
16 x 125	⅝ x 5	44 x 200	1¾ x 8
16 x 150	⅝ x 6	44 x 225	1¾ x 9
19 x 75	¾ x 3	44 x 250	1¾ x 10
19 x 100	¾ x 4	44 x 300	1¾ x 12
19 x 125	¾ x 5	50 x 75	2 x 3
19 x 150	¾ x 6	50 x 100	2 x 4
22 x 75	⅞ x 3	50 x 125	2 x 5
22 x 100	⅞ x 4	50 x 150	2 x 6
22 x 125	⅞ x 5	50 x 175	2 x 7
22 x 150	⅞ x 6	50 x 200	2 x 8
25 x 75	1 x 3	50 x 225	2 x 9
25 x 100	1 x 4	50 x 250	2 x 10
25 x 125	1 x 5	50 x 300	2 x 12
25 x 150	1 x 6	63 x 100	2½ x 4
25 x 175	1 x 7	63 x 125	2½ x 5
25 x 200	1 x 8	63 x 150	2½ x 6
25 x 225	1 x 9	63 x 175	2½ x 7
25 x 250	1 x 10	63 x 200	2½ x 8
25 x 300	1 x 12	63 x 225	2½ x 9
32 x 75	1¼ x 3	75 x 100	3 x 4
32 x 100	1¼ x 4	75 x 125	3 x 5
32 x 125	1¼ x 5	75 x 150	3 x 6
32 x 150	1¼ x 6	75 x 175	3 x 7
32 x 175	1¼ x 7	75 x 200	3 x 8
32 x 200	1¼ x 8	75 x 225	3 x 9
32 x 225	1¼ x 9	75 x 250	3 x 10
32 x 250	1¼ x 10	75 x 300	3 x 12
32 x 300	1¼ x 12	100 x 100	4 x 4
38 x 75	1½ x 3	100 x 150	4 x 6
38 x 100	1½ x 4	100 x 200	4 x 8
38 x 125	1½ x 5	100 x 250	4 x 10
38 x 150	1½ x 6	100 x 300	4 x 12
38 x 175	1½ x 7	150 x 150	6 x 6
38 x 200	1½ x 8	150 x 200	6 x 8
38 x 225	1½ x 9	150 x 300	6 x 12
44 x 75	1¾ x 3	200 x 200	8 x 8
44 x 100	1¾ x 4	250 x 250	10 x 10
44 x 125	1¾ x 5	300 x 300	12 x 12

METRIC LENGTHS

Lengths Metres	Equiv. Ft. & Inches
1.8m	5′ 10⅞″
2.1m	6′ 10⅝″
2.4m	7′ 10½″
2.7m	8′ 10¼″
3.0m	9′ 10⅛″
3.3m	10′ 9⅞″
3.6m	11′ 9¾″
3.9m	12′ 9½″
4.2m	13′ 9⅜″
4.5m	14′ 9⅓″
4.8m	15′ 9″
5.1m	16′ 8¾″
5.4m	17′ 8⅝″
5.7m	18′ 8⅜″
6.0m	19′ 8¼″
6.3m	20′ 8″
6.6m	21′ 7⅞″
6.9m	22′ 7⅝″
7.2m	23′ 7½″
7.5m	24′ 7¼″
7.8m	25′ 7⅛″

All the dimensions are based on 1 inch = 25 mm.

NOMINAL SIZE	ACTUAL SIZE
(This is what you order.)	(This is what you get.)
Inches	Inches
1 x 1	¾ x ¾
1 x 2	¾ x 1½
1 x 3	¾ x 2½
1 x 4	¾ x 3½
1 x 6	¾ x 5½
1 x 8	¾ x 7¼
1 x 10	¾ x 9¼
1 x 12	¾ x 11¼
2 x 2	1¾ x 1¾
2 x 3	1½ x 2½
2 x 4	1½ x 3½
2 x 6	1½ x 5½
2 x 8	1½ x 7¼
2 x 10	1½ x 9¼
2 x 12	1½ x 11¼

NAILS

NUMBER PER POUND OR KILO

Size	Weight Unit	Common	Casing	Box	Finishing
2d	Pound	876	1010	1010	1351
	Kilo	1927	2222	2222	2972
3d	Pound	586	635	635	807
	Kilo	1289	1397	1397	1775
4d	Pound	316	473	473	548
	Kilo	695	1041	1041	1206
5d	Pound	271	406	406	500
	Kilo	596	893	893	1100
6d	Pound	181	236	236	309
	Kilo	398	591	519	680
7d	Pound	161	210	210	238
	Kilo	354	462	462	524
8d	Pound	106	145	145	189
	Kilo	233	319	319	416
9d	Pound	96	132	132	172
	Kilo	211	290	290	398
10d	Pound	69	94	94	121
	Kilo	152	207	207	266
12d	Pound	64	88	88	113
	Kilo	141	194	194	249
16d	Pound	49	71	71	90
	Kilo	108	156	156	198
20d	Pound	31	52	52	62
	Kilo	68	114	114	136
30d	Pound	24	46	46	
	Kilo	53	101	101	
40d	Pound	18	35	35	
	Kilo	37	77	77	
50d	Pound	14			
	Kilo	31			
60d	Pound	11			
	Kilo	24			

LENGTH AND DIAMETER IN INCHES AND CENTIMETERS

Size	Length Inches	Length Centimeters	Diameter Inches	Diameter Centimeters*
2d	1	2.5	.068	.17
3d	1/2	3.2	.102	.26
4d	1/4	3.8	.102	.26
5d	1/6	4.4	.102	.26
6d	2	5.1	.115	.29
7d	2/2	5.7	.115	.29
8d	2/4	6.4	.131	.33
9d	2/6	7.0	.131	.33
10d	3	7.6	.148	.38
12d	3/2	8.3	.148	.38
16d	3/4	8.9	.148	.38
20d	4	10.2	.203	.51
30d	4/4	11.4	.220	.58
40d	5	12.7	.238	.60
50d	5/4	14.0	.257	.66
60d	6	15.2	.277	.70

*Exact conversion

WOOD SCREWS

SCREW GAUGE NO.	NOMINAL DIAMETER Inch	NOMINAL DIAMETER mm	LENGTH Inch	LENGTH mm
0	0.060	1.52	3/16	4.8
1	0.070	1.78	1/4	6.4
2	0.082	2.08	5/16	7.9
3	0.094	2.39	3/8	9.5
4	0.0108	2.74	7/16	11.1
5	0.122	3.10	1/2	12.7
6	0.136	3.45	5/8	15.9
7	0.150	3.81	3/4	19.1
8	0.164	4.17	7/8	22.2
9	0.178	4.52	1	25.4
10	0.192	4.88	1¼	31.8
12	0.220	5.59	1½	38.1
14	0.248	6.30	1¾	44.5
16	0.276	7.01	2	50.8
18	0.304	7.72	2¼	57.2
20	0.332	8.43	2½	63.5
24	0.388	9.86	2¾	69.9
28	0.444	11.28	3	76.2
32	0.5	12.7	3¼	82.6
			3½	88.9
			4	101.6
			4½	114.3
			5	127.0
			6	152.4

Dimensions taken from BS1210; metric conversions are approximate.

BRICKS AND BLOCKS

Bricks

Standard metric brick measures 215 mm x 65 mm x 112.5. Metric brick can be used with older, standard brick by increasing the mortaring in the joints. The sizes are substantially the same, the metric brick being slightly smaller (3.6 mm less in length, 1.8 mm in width, and 1.2 mm in depth).

Concrete Block

Standard sizes

390 x 90 mm
390 x 190 mm
440 x 190 mm
440 x 215 mm
440 x 290 mm

Repair block for replacement of block in old installations is available in these sizes:
448 x 219 (including mortar joints)
397 x 194 (including mortar joints)

PIPE FITTINGS

Only fittings for use with copper pipe are affected by metrication: metric compression fittings are interchangeable with Imperial in some sizes, but require adaptors in others.

INTERCHANGEABLE SIZES mm	INTERCHANGEABLE SIZES Inches	SIZES REQUIRING ADAPTORS mm	SIZES REQUIRING ADAPTORS Inches
12	⅜	22	¾
15	½	35	1¼
28	1	42	1½
54	2		

Metric capillary (soldered) fittings are not directly interchangeable with imperial sizes but adaptors are available. Pipe fittings which use screwed threads to make the joint remain unchanged. The British Standard Pipe (BSP) thread form has now been accepted internationally and its dimensions will not physically change. These screwed fittings are commonly used for joining iron or steel pipes, for connections on taps, basin and bath waste outlets and on boilers, radiators, pumps etc. Fittings for use with lead pipe are joined by soldering and for this purpose the metric and inch sizes are interchangeable.

(Information courtesy Metrication Board, Millbank Tower, Millbank, London SW1P 4QU)